Ds and Fs

WON'T DO

*A Bible-based discussion of four Ds
(Distraction, Doubt, Discouragement,
and Depression) and three Fs
(Frustration, Failure, and Fear).*

ROSEMARIE DOWNER, PH. D.

Ds and Fs Won't Do

by

Rosemarie Downer

Copyright © 2023

ISBN: 979-8-9875327-0-6

Independently Published

First Edition

DEDICATION

Life has a way of throwing unforeseen curb balls at us. The journey through life is full of potholes and sharp turns. These unexpected incidences can make us doubt God, distract us, make us feel like a failure, frustrate us, and even make us fearful. This book is dedicated to all those who are challenged by life's issues and who, at times, feel overwhelmed by them. Know that these things come to try you. If you endure, they will only make you stronger. I pray that this book will enlighten you and further equip you to live like the "more than conqueror" that God has already pronounced you to be.

FOREWORD

We live in a world where information is just a click of a button away. Information on almost any subject can be instantly accessed by simply asking Google or Serie. Yet, I cannot help but wonder why, with all the available information, people are still challenged in how to live meaningful lives. Why is hopelessness and frustration still increasing, and why are people still discouraged and depressed over life's circumstances in a world with so much information?

In *Ds and Fs Won't Do*, Dr. Downer challenges us to think differently about the human condition and about the real cause behind the problems we face. The book takes you as if it were on a journey from the fundamental cause of our human dilemmas through a path to total freedom. Here, you will be exposed to new language about overcoming and new ways of thinking about how people can thrive and become their best.

The structure of the book arises systematically from the key idea that we are more than our negative experiences, that we are more than conquerors, and that failure is not the end. Drawing on timeless instructions and principles from Scripture, Dr. Downer meticulously paints a compelling picture of deliverance and hope for those struggling under the weight of Satan's deceptions and lies. She not only provides the reader with profound insight into the enemy's schemes, but she also provides practical tools for the journey toward healing and deliverance.

A special merit of this book is its careful and systematic development of each major theme and the scope and quality of its content. It is an engaging and inspirational read, one that will leave you challenged, intrigued, refreshed, and hopeful. I am thankful that Dr. Downer has chosen to address some of the deep concerns that many within and without the church have been living with for many years.

Reading this book has been for me an insightful and rewarding exercise. I recommend this book as a must read, not only for those seeking to overcome debilitating experiences, but for anyone desirous of living a meaningful and hopeful life of faith.

—Clarence Duff, Ph.D.
Senior Pastor, Church of God
Sabbath-Keeping Ministries,
Brampton, Ontario, Canada

TABLE OF CONTENTS

Depression is a last-ditch effort of the devil to take us under. It is his way of snuffing out our life and strength. Whether medically diagnosed or not, or whether clinically depressed or not, you must understand that this is a drastic effort of the devil to kill us.

Depression is mental darkness. If depression is darkness, then the inverse must be light, and light can only be found in Jesus Christ. The ultimate cure for this debilitating, life-sucking grip of the enemy is the light that only Jesus can shed in the dark places of one's life.

Depression is crippling. It looks like a giant to many, but even giants can come down. The God you serve is bigger than depression. Remember, He has a name that is above every other name. Therefore, His name is above the thing named depression. Know your God.

What does frustration look like? In my mind, I see little nuisances that should not bother us but instead cause us much irritation. These nuisances come unexpectedly and catch us off guard, rendering us frustrated.

It is not the big things that frustrate us. It is the seemingly insignificant things picking at us that make us frustrated. Because these things appear to be small, we fail to realize the cumulative impact they have on us. This is a subtle attack from the enemy.

It is true that there is nothing new under the sun, but it is not true that we all experience the same things. However, there is one thing that we all at some point in life will experience and that is failure. Failure is a common denominator of life.

The devil wants us to believe that when we fail at something, we have failed at life. Do not believe it; it's a lie! Failure is not final. In fact, failure can open doors to a fresh start in life if we recognize this fact.

The papa in any household is the head and from him comes all the offspring. In the devil's household, fear is the papa, and from him comes many offspring.

Thich Nhat Hanh says, "Fear keeps us focused on the past or worried about the future." Being focused on the past and worried about the future will only keep you stuck. With such a mindset, you cannot move forward. But no one wants to be in the same place over time. Therefore, you must overcome fear.

Distraction, doubt, discouragement, depression, frustration, failure, fear or whatever the challenge may be, how do we overcome them? What is the one thing that can remedy these things?

LIFE IS A LONG ADVENTURE

We are all uniquely designed by God. We all have a unique personality, and we are all here to fulfill our distinctive God-given purposes. Therefore, our lives will all take different directions, and our experiences will be exclusively ours. But though we are all different, there are things that are common to all of us.

Life is a long adventure of lessons learned by overcoming obstacles in life, and it is the obstacles that are common to us all. Some of the obstacles that we all face are distraction, doubt, discouragement, depression, frustration, failure, and fear. As humans that are endeavoring to develop and thrive, we will pursue goals and seek out new experiences, thus setting the stage for these obstacles to occur.

Although the seven obstacles—distraction, doubt, discouragement, depression, frustration, failure, and fear—are common denominators in our lives, many people do not handle them very well. Many do not know the source of these obstacles or know how to address their root cause. Also, many do not use the knowledge or the skills they possess to address these obstacles. Additionally, many do not apply the Word of God to counteract these obstacles.

1

This book, *Ds and Fs Won't Do,* will refresh your thinking so that you will come to convincingly know that you cannot settle for or stop at any of these obstacles. I will take you through a timely discourse that exposes the nature and source of each obstacle, show you how we can turn these obstacles into opportunities, and explain how you can use the Word of God to overcome them.

Perhaps you've made some mistakes that are haunting you, maybe you are distracted and cannot focus on your goals, or maybe you are discouraged because all your efforts seem to have failed. This book you now hold in your hands will give you the tools you need to get past the D or F that is slowing you down or blocking you.

Greater is in you. Greater things are ahead of you. This is the beginning of a new phase of your life. Let's get started!

THE INDISCRIMINATE ADVERSARY

Persecution or those forces that rage open warfare against us are not the only things with which we should be concerned. It is quite easy to be on guard when the danger is obvious. We can muster the courage for the fight when the enemy of our souls shows up like the enemy. But there is greater need for alertness and awareness of the enemy when he creeps up surreptitiously or when he entices us with false peace and pleasures.

If you have enlisted in the army of God, you must realize that you have an enemy, and this enemy is not selective. As soon as it becomes apparent to him that you are not with him, his sole agenda is to steal from you, kill you and what you have, and destroy you and what you have. John 10:10 (NIV) tells us that *"The thief's purpose is to steal and kill and destroy."* This enemy, the devil, is a thief. He is a liar and he is a murderer. His goal is to rob you of your destiny. He may go about doing this in any number of ways, some of which seem harmless, but do not be deceived. Despite how he comes at you, regardless of how harmless or simple the attack is, his goal is to deny you the promise of eternal life with your Heavenly Father.

WHO IS OUR ADVERSARY?

Our adversary has several names. Two of the most common names by which he is addressed are Satan and the devil. According to Encyclopedia.com, the word devil literally means "slanderer." Satan is a slanderer because he seeks to smear or discredit God and humanity. In the Garden of Eden, he sought to slander God's character by contradicting what God told Eve. In modern biblical translations, the devil is known to be the adversary of God and of God's people. Other words we can use for adversary are enemy, foe, opponent, opposition, and rival. Satan, the devil, is our adversary.

Let me be clear: Satan is not a red-horned bull or villain. Like God, we cannot see him, but we can see his works. Because we cannot see him, some people question his reality, but he is as real as you and I are real. He is not a theory. He is not a character in a scary story or movie. His existence is based on reality, not fantasy.

God created angels and assigned unique roles and characteristics to them. A main role that angels fulfill is to worship God. God chose to create angels to dwell in heaven, and Satan, named Lucifer while in heaven, was one of them. So, Satan was once an angel who resided in heaven. In Ezekiel 28:12–15, the prophet Ezekiel referred to Lucifer as the seal of perfection, full of wisdom and perfect in beauty. He added that Lucifer was adorned with every precious stone, his settings and mountings were made of gold, he was anointed as a guardian cherub, he was on the holy mount of God, and he was blameless in his ways. Lucifer clearly had a high rank in God's presence, but at some point, he turned against God in pride. Verses 15–17 of Ezekiel 28 (NIV) say:

> *You were blameless in your ways from the day you were created till wickedness was found in you. Through your widespread trade you were filled with violence, and you sinned. So, I drove you in disgrace from the mount of God, and I expelled you, guardian cherub, from among the fiery stones. Your heart became proud on account of your beauty, and you corrupted your wisdom because of your splendor. So, I threw you to the earth; I made a spectacle of you before kings.*

So, although God had other beings in His Kingdom, He was still the king of that Kingdom. There would be only one will in heaven and it was God's. Satan, then Lucifer, was a shining star in heaven. We can safely say that he was one of God's favorite angels. For a period of time, all the angels' wills were perfectly aligned with God's, but Lucifer began to notice that he had clout. He was uniquely created, and he was good at what he did. He also noticed that God was getting all the worship and honor from him and from the other angels, and he began to think more highly of himself than he ought.

We'll soon see that he was also popular among the other angels. He had influence. He had favor with God and his fellow angels. Consequently, he became proud and thought he should be like God. He rebelled against God, and thus introduced a will other than God's into God's order. Pride caused Lucifer to focus too much on his wonderful attributes and jealousy made him want the worship that was given to God. This resulted in him raising himself up against his Creator and declaring that he would be a god.

Lucifer is described by Ezekiel as a perfect being. He was uniquely adorned, and he was completely blameless from the day he was created until the day he fell prey to pride. Lucifer's location on the "holy mountain of God" indicates his involvement in the government of God. Reference to him walking "in the midst of the stones of fire" communicates a nearness to God in a place just beneath God's glory at the footstool of God (Ezekiel 1:27). Also, according to Ezekiel 10:1–14, Lucifer is among the "covering cherub," the angels with the closest access to God and who guard His holiness.[1]

Pride caused Lucifer to covet the throne of God. He thought he should be sitting on the throne and not God. He thought he was good enough to be worshipped like God was being worshipped. From then to this very moment, God hates pride and refuses to share His glory with another, so He evicted Lucifer from His Kingdom. Isaiah 42:8 (NIV) says, "I am the Lord; that is my name! I will not yield my glory to another or my praise to idols." God's words do not change. He refused to give His glory or praise to idols then, and He still refuses to do so today.

God is and will always be the one and only King in His Kingdom, so He threw Lucifer from heaven into the earth. That resulted in Lucifer being expunged as a profane thing from the mountain of God, from heaven. Satan was quite influential while in heaven, and as much as I do not want to, I must admit that he is still very influential today. If that was not so, there would be no need to write a book such as this one. There would be no need to fast and pray like we do. There would be no need for the many sermons that have been and still being preached, the many Bible lessons that are being taught, or the many prayer meetings and conferences that have been and are being held.

Scripture tells us that Lucifer, along with one third of the angelic host, was defeated by the Archangel Michael and was cast down from Heaven to the earth where he became known as Satan. Satan went from Lucifer, Light Bearer, to Satan the Adversary, the devil, the Accuser of the brethren. While God had created countless millions of angels, only four of them are named in Scripture. They are:

1. Gabriel, whose name means "God is Mighty."
2. Michael, whose name means "Like God."
3. Raphael, whose name means "God Heals."
4. And Lucifer, whose name means "Light Bearer."[2]

All of them were created good! But after Lucifer became proud, he suffered a degrading name change. Note that Satan did not take this gross demotion handed down to him by God lightly. First, he attempted to divide the Kingdom of God. Anything that is divided is inherently weak, so he thought he could weaken the impact, the supremacy, and unparalleled image of the Kingdom of God by causing division.

I often say this is the origin of church splits. The first church split occurred in heaven. Lucifer came from heaven to earth with the same divisive spirit that was manifested in him while in heaven, and that curse lays heavily upon the church today. As a result, today we frequently see churches splitting because people feel they are not recognized enough for what they can do, or they feel they should be equal to the pastor. This is pride. This is the expression of a direct deposit of the Luciferic spirit on anyone acting in this manner.

Second, notice that Lucifer did not leave heaven by himself. He took one-third of the angelic host with him. There is no specific Bible reference that says a third of the angels fell from heaven with him, but when put together, certain passages—for example Revelation 9 and 12—suggest that that is what happened. Revelation chapter 12:1–5 (NIV) says, "A great sign appeared in heaven: a woman clothed with the sun, with the moon under her feet and a crown of twelve stars on her head. She was pregnant and cried out in pain as she was about to give birth. Then another sign appeared in heaven: an enormous red dragon with seven heads and ten horns and seven crowns on its heads. Its tail swept a third of the stars out of the sky and flung them to the earth. The dragon stood in front of the woman who was about to give birth, so that it might devour her child the moment he was born. She gave birth to a son, a male child, who 'will rule all the nations with an iron scepter.' And her child was snatched up to God and to his throne."

In Revelation 12:9, John identifies the dragon that was hurled down to the earth as "that ancient serpent called the devil, or Satan, who leads the whole world astray." However, "his angels were cast out with him." The dragon was not thrown to earth alone. In fact, this is how Satan carries out his destructive works today. The fallen angels are his demons who carry out his bidding. We associate the angels, now demons, that were ejected from heaven with Satan with the "third of the stars" that the dragon's tail swept from heaven to earth in Revelation 12:4.

If the "stars" of Revelation 12:4 are indeed a symbolic reference to Satan's "angels" in verse 9, then what we have is a reference to the fall of a portion of the heavenly hosts of angels who followed Satan in his rebellion. Two thirds of the angels remained loyal to God and are called the "holy angels" in Scripture (Mark 8:38); one third of the original angels joined Satan and are called "unclean spirits" or "demons" today (Mark 9:25).

The one-third angels that left heaven with Lucifer had directly experienced the glory of God. They were not told about His majesty, nor did they have to read about God. They did not experience His glory vicariously. Instead, they dwelled around the throne of God both day and night, worshiping Him. They incessantly sang, "Holy, holy, holy." This tells me that they had the privilege of seeing God in all His splendor. They saw the multiple aspects of His glory, and that is why they were always amazed by His glory sufficiently to keep singing, "Holy, holy, holy." But Lucifer was influential enough—or they were weak enough—to turn them against the One they were created to worship, the One whose splendor and glory they themselves beheld. Lucifer must have had considerable influence to divert to him the devotion of angels who had directly experienced the majesty and glory of God, especially since no matter how great Satan was, he could not measure up to the God of creation.

Satan influenced the one-third angels to doubt the sovereignty of God. How many times have we experienced a great move of God in our lives and soon thereafter faced a challenge that Satan uses to try and plant doubt in our minds? How many times have we had a need for God's provision, but instead of using our past victories through Christ to strengthen our faith, we allow Satan to plant seeds of doubt in our minds? Faith and doubt do not complement each other. Faith in God is what we need. We are told in Scripture that without faith it is impossible to please God (Hebrews 11:6). So, when we allow Satan to make us doubt God, it is not pleasing to Him.

Lucifer was deceived by himself. Just like all the other angels, God created him, and therefore by definition, is certainly not God and can never be God. Lucifer is a created being, and for that reason, he is subject to God like every other created being in heaven and earth. Unknown to Lucifer, he has no more rights or power than God allows.

THE IMPACT OF THE FALL

Revelation 12:7–9 (NIV) says, "Then war broke out in heaven. Michael and his angels fought against the dragon, and the dragon and his angels fought back. But he was not strong enough, and they lost their place in heaven. The great dragon was hurled down—that ancient serpent called the devil, or Satan, who leads the whole world astray. He was hurled to the earth, and his angels with him." Verse 12b of the same chapter says, "But woe to the earth and the sea, because the devil has gone down to you! He is filled with fury, because he knows that his time is short." Ezekiel 28:16–17 gives the account of Satan's fall. God cast Lucifer "as a profane thing out of the mountain of God, God cast him to the ground and made him a spectacle before kings."

"But woe to the earth and the sea, because the devil has gone down to you! He is filled with fury, because he knows that his time is short" (Revelation 12:12). This is enough to tell me that the direct effects of Lucifer's eviction from heaven are significantly bad. "Woe" connotes anguish, grief, affliction, distress, sadness, despair, wretchedness, and misery. Because of the presence of Satan in the earth, the earth is full of these things. "Therefore, just as sin entered the world through one man, and death through sin, and in this way death came to all people, because all sinned" (Romans 5:12, NIV).

The effects of Satan's descent to earth are numerous and far reaching. The result is sin, and sin has affected every aspect of our lives. It has affected our lives here on earth, and if we are not prudent, it will impact our eternal destiny.

Sin separates us from God. Lucifer, now Satan, no longer has fellowship with God. Lucifer sinned and that puts him at enmity with God. This is not Satan's desire; it's a consequence, and he wants the very same for us. Therefore, Satan's goal is to persuade us to sin so that we too will be separated from God. This is his full-time job. He has made it his priority to fully equip his imps, the one-third angels that were evicted from heaven with him, to master the craft of tempting us to sin. They come at us relentlessly with temptations, and the more we yield to their temptations to sin, the more sin becomes customary. Ultimately, our conscience dies to sin, and we fall into a lifestyle of sin. That is what Satan exists to achieve, and he is ruthless.

The first evidence of Satan's attempt to accomplish his mission is in the Garden of Eden where he tempted Eve to eat of the tree that God had forbidden Adam and Eve to eat from. Before this act of disobedience, Adam and Eve had perfect communion and fellowship with God. It was this act of disobedience that broke their fellowship with God. Sin comes with guilt and shame, so naturally, they were ashamed before the God with Whom they once had sweet fellowship, and because of shame, they hid from Him (Genesis 3:8–10).

What occurred with Adam and Eve is not a one-time incident. Man has been hiding from God ever since. Today, when we fall into sin, the first thing we do is stop attending church, stop praying, stop reading our Bible, and stop fellowshipping with the saints. Ofttimes, the absence of these disciplines—such as regular Bible-reading, a personal prayer life, and fellowship with the saints—precede yielding to sin. Often, we gradually decline in these essentials until we eventually fall fully into the act.

Satan is a strategist. Normally, it's not an abrupt action that gets us into sin. Satan is patient; he gradually wears us down until we yield to his temptations. Note that he does not always lure us to obviously wrong deeds. He sometimes uses seemingly harmless and innocent things to distract us from the essentials of our walk with God, which over time weakens our ability to resist him and thus causes us to sin. In fact, I believe he tempts us with seemingly innocuous things more often than with blatant sin. But either way, abruptly or gradually, sin separates us from God. Sin breaches our fellowship with our Father.

Neither Adam nor Eve took responsibility for their behavior and the act of evading responsibility for one's own action still exists among man today. It is often easier for us to blame someone else for our errors than for us to take responsibility. When God asked Adam, "Who told you that you were naked? Have you eaten from the tree that I commanded you not to eat from?" (Genesis 3:11, NIV), Adam said, "The woman you put here with me—she gave me some fruit from the tree, and I ate it." (Verse 12). "Then the Lord God said to the woman, 'What is this you have done?' The woman said, 'The serpent deceived me, and I ate'" (Verse 13).

Have you ever tried to minister to a fellow brother or sister who you know was slipping in their walk with the Lord, and every time you try to bring their behavior to their attention, they placed blame on someone else? It's the pastor…he isn't caring enough. There's no love in the church. The church members are hypocrites. Someone at the church hurt them. People at the church don't really care about them. The excuses can go on and on. It is never their fault. This is deception at the hands of Satan, and in the face of deception, restoration is unlikely. Adam and Eve did the same thing. Adam blamed the woman and the woman blamed Satan. Today, we blame everyone and everything but ourselves. We are influenced by the devil when we blame everyone and everything else and make excuses.

As a result of Satan's fall, God pronounced the sentence of death on man. Because of sin, death is an inevitable reality. None of us is exempt. "For the wages of sin is death, but the gift of God is eternal life in Christ Jesus our Lord" (Romans 6:23, NIV), and "all have sinned and fall short of the glory of God" (Romans 3:23, NIV). Furthermore, we were shaped in iniquity, and our mothers conceived us in sin (Psalm 51:5). The death sentence becomes even more grave because we not only die physically, but if we die without Christ, we experience eternal death.

Failure to acknowledge the purpose for which we were created is another consequence of the fall of Lucifer. As a result of the many lies that Satan tells us, many of us go through an identity crisis. Many of us live our lives not knowing the truth about who we are, why we are here, and whose we are.

The main purpose of humanity on earth is to bring glory to God. We were made for His pleasure (Revelation 4:11). We were made to do His good works (Ephesians 2:10), which will in turn express His glory on the earth. God is constantly looking for available vessels who He can work through to manifest His glory here on earth. Satan does not want us to know and embrace this fact. He wants us to live with the deception that we are not good enough.

Jesus left the earth with a completed mission but an incomplete ministry. He was sent to earth by His Father to pay the ransom for our sins by His death, burial, and resurrection, and He did just that. But His ministry to mankind is not complete and it can only be done through us.

Satan wants us to believe that God cannot use us, and sadly, he has been far too successful at influencing many in the body of Christ to believe this lie. It is sin that gave Satan the authority to influence us in such a manner. We are Christ's mouth, His eyes, His ears, His hands, and His feet, but many of us never embrace this glorious privilege and, as a result, never fulfill the call of God on our lives.

Only through Christ can the broken fellowship between God and man be restored, because in Christ we are made as righteous and sinless in God's eyes as Adam and Eve were before they sinned. "God made him who had no sin to be sin for us, so that in him we might become the righteousness of God" (2 Corinthians 5:21, NIV), so the means by which we can be fully restored to God is available to all.

THE UNRESOLVED ISSUE

Satan has a huge unresolved issue with God our Father. He is not the least bit pleased with being evicted from heaven. He hates not having access to the benefits of heaven, and if he cannot have them, he does not want anyone else to have them. I think it's fair to say he is obsessed with making sure we do not enjoy the blessings of God here on earth or in the eternal Kingdom to come. In opposition to Jesus, who now lives forever to make intercession for us (Hebrews 7:25), Satan lives solely to get us to reject the way of life and redemption and to accept the way of death and destruction.

He is angry that God is getting the worship that he so desperately wanted while in heaven and still wants. He knows that his end is eternal damnation. But while that is a massive impending doom, Satan knows that he cannot touch God. Therefore, his next best option is to attack the followers of

God: you and me. So, until the day of his doom, his aim is to have a significant negative impact on us by harassing us in our everyday lives.

God sent His only Son into the world to restore man back to fellowship with Him. Christ died and rose from the dead to redeem us back to His Father, making it possible for us to be channels through which God can flow to complete the work that Jesus left for us to do. Satan does not want us to be available for God's use, and God wants us to be available for His use, so there is an ongoing war taking place over our souls.

As followers of Christ, we dare not be ignorant of Satan's strategies "in order that Satan might not outwit us. For we are not unaware of his schemes" (2 Corinthians 2:11, NIV). We must be vigilant and sober because this war between Satan and God is a matter of life and death, the Kingdom of God and hell. We cannot be light-hearted or flippant about our walk with the Lord.

Snakes move about stealthily—they slither. They move smoothly with a twisting or oscillating motion. They move so smoothly that you often cannot sense them coming. Their presence is often discovered after they've struck. Satan moves like a snake, so he has a way of sneaking his way into our lives without us knowing. He is not only deadly when he strikes, but often he is so well camouflaged that we do not see him coming and sometimes don't even recognize him when he is at work.

Satan knows that his ultimate punishment is eternal torment. But he also knows that he can influence us to follow him, just like he did with Adam and Eve and the one-third angels in heaven. The degree to which evil is present in the world today is evidence that Satan has a bigger goal than one-third. It is clear that he and his imps are working overtime to gain followers. The war is on.

God our Father is the head of His Kingdom, and by reason of allegiance, all those who are members of the Kingdom of God become involved with this unresolved issue by default. Just like God, this puts us in an adversarial position with Satan. Therefore, all that's required for Satan to hate us is a devoted life to God.

Chapter One: Seven Main Takeaways

1. The effects of Satan's descent to earth are numerous and far reaching. The result is sin, and sin has affected every aspect of our lives.

2. Satan no longer has fellowship with God. Lucifer sinned and that puts him at enmity with God. This is not Satan's desire; it is a consequence, and he wants the very same for us.

3. As a result of the many lies that Satan tells us, many of us go through an identity crisis. Many of us live our lives not knowing the truth about who we are, why we are here, and whose we are.

4. The main purpose of humanity on earth is to bring glory to God.

5. Satan wants us to live with the deception that we are not good enough.

6. As followers of Christ, we dare not be ignorant of Satan's strategies and devices.

7. Satan moves like a snake, so he has a way of sneaking his way into our lives without us knowing.

CHAPTER TWO

WHAT HAS YOUR ATTENTION?

You can't do big things if you're
distracted by small things.
— Anonymous

The mind is an interesting and very important part of the body. According to Wikipedia, the mind comprises a set of cognitive faculties that enable consciousness, perception, thinking, judgement, and memory. Because we are conscious, we know the day of the week, we know what month of the year we are in, and we are aware of where we are when our eyes first open in the mornings. Due to being conscious, we can hear and recognize the birds chirp in the mornings, and we can make decisions, complete our daily tasks, and respond appropriately with happiness, sadness, and even anger to varying stimuli.

Our mind also causes us to perceive things; it focuses our attention. The thing upon which our mind is set has our attention. This faculty of the mind—the ability to perceive, focus on, and recognize things—causes us to see, hear, and become aware of things and understand, or interpret them.

Perception is our mental impression of our experiences and encounters.

Thinking is an extremely important faculty of the mind. Our mind allows us to use our thoughts or rational judgment intelligently to process information, which then leads us to make judgements, form opinions, and come to conclusions. The outcome is based on our perception and understanding of the stimuli we process through our senses.

Thinking allows us to make sense of, interpret, represent, and act upon what we experience. Thinking also helps us make predictions about what to expect. Thoughts are the results of thinking and are the formulation and arrangement of ideas that are pondered in the thinking process. Thoughts are the result or product of either spontaneous, deliberate, or timely acts of thinking. Our thoughts inspire many of our actions and interactions and they determine whether we are focused or distracted.

THE MIND AND DISTRACTIONS

One is distracted when something or someone directs their attention from a thing or person to another. Distraction takes our mind off what we are supposed to be doing. But one cannot be distracted if they do not have a focus, target, or goal. Your mind or attention must be set on something for it to be distracted.

We live in a highly engaging but sorely distracting world, and thus are bombarded daily with numerous distractions. Faced with information overload and our frantic schedules, our minds often go in varying directions and, more frequently, away from and not on the focal thing we should be doing.

Our increasingly information-saturated world with the frequent pop-up windows, smartphones with texts, chat, email, and social media, and the now unhealthy expectation of around the clock availability and immediate responses increase the chances of being distracted exponentially. The combination of these scenarios imposes a distracted mind upon all of us.

When our minds are distracted, we go off course and we pay attention to things that do not move us closer to our goal or to the completion of the task at hand. A distracted mind renders us powerless in effectively handling interruptions. An incoming text from a friend to talk about plans for the weekend is a distraction while writing an email to a client. But because our mind is not trained to focus on the task at hand, we could easily be redirected to answering the text and within minutes find ourselves browsing the internet, reading our email, or checking our social media accounts when we should be working. Without doubt, technological innovations have enhanced our lives in many ways, but they are also the source of relentless disturbances and brain overload.

While technology is very instrumental in distracting us, it is not the only thing that draws our attention away from the main thing we should be doing. What we consider very casual daily activities can also distract us. For example, suppose you have the goal of retrieving something from the freezer and setting it out to cook later for dinner, but on your way to the kitchen, you stop to fold laundry and that one diversion takes you on a path from one task to another, none of which lead you to the freezer. The laundry was always there, so why choose to fold them when you should be heading to the freezer? What happened? The laundry is a piece of information, a stimulus that is irrelevant to your goal but is strong enough to divert you from your goal. Could it be then that to reduce distractions, we must ensure our goal or our task at hand is mentally more important than the information or stimulus that is not relevant to our goal?

It is essential that we mentally prioritize our goals because distractions seek the attention of our minds. Therefore, if we establish in our minds that the goal is the main concern and we maintain that stance, the distractions will less likely override the goal. Perhaps the ability to establish solid goals with a plan to achieve the goal, and steadfastness in the plan is the remedy for distraction. Adam Gazzaley and Larry D. Rosen assert that "Our ability to establish high-level goals is arguably the pinnacle of human brain evolution."[3] So, can we agree that the ammunition needed to fight against distraction lies in the brain?

THE POWER OF DISTRACTION

Consider a scenario as simple as a fussy or crying baby. Often, if you shake a rattle or wave a toy in the face of the baby, it distracts the baby and will cause the baby to calm down, at least for the moment. The toy or rattle will redirect the baby's attention. You are a parent with young children, but you are in school trying to complete your master's degree. You are attempting to study for your comprehensive exams, but the children are noisy. Every time you try to focus, you find yourself listening to the chatter and laughter of the children. You are distracted by the children. The noises made by the children are redirecting your attention from your studies to the children.

Distraction can take place in a moment, in a short period of time, or it can be ongoing. For example, you had a disagreement with a coworker. At the time of the verbal exchange, you said all you wanted to say, or so you thought. The discourse ended respectfully and in everyone's mind the disagreement was resolved, but you cannot stop thinking about this one thing you should have said. Maybe if you had said that one thing, everyone in the office would know not to ever treat you in a like manner. So, this thought keeps surfacing in your mind—when you're at home, when you're driving, and especially when you're at work—you cannot seem to silence it. You are distracted, and this is an ongoing distraction.

Distraction is a common experience for all of us, but some of us are more easily distracted than others. We often place blame for being distracted on the chaotic and overly stimulated environment in which we live, but we all live in the same environment. We are all bombarded with text messages, emails, phone calls, and the thousands of other notifications, social events, church events, family events, appointments, and business interests demanding our attention. So why are some people more distracted than others?

While I agree that we live in an environment that is overloaded with stimuli, the real problem is not our environment. I propose two reasons for being habitually distracted: a wandering mind and poor organization and planning. Research done by psychologists Matthew Killingsworth and Daniel Gilbert report that the human mind is wired for a state of continuous distraction. In a study conducted with 2,250 adults, they concluded that we spend approximately forty-seven percent of every waking hour "mind wandering," which is also called "stimulus-independent thought."[4] Mind wandering is a natural behavior, and therefore, it takes place without any effort on our part. Often, we are unaware that our minds are wandering.

What has your attention while you are waiting in that little room with the door closed for the doctor to come in? What are you thinking while you're waiting for the host of a virtual meeting to give you access to the meeting? Often, without trying, your mind wanders to things that are not related to the immediate environment—anything but the task at hand. This is the default mode of the brain and is therefore common to all of us.

Mind wandering is harmless in many situations and can be helpful at times. For example, while going through your morning routine, it may be helpful to think about the tasks that await you at work versus thinking about the mundane tasks of getting ready for work that require little to no mental effort. Similarly, mentally planning what you will do after jogging may be more beneficial than thinking about the act of jogging itself. But although mind wandering can be beneficial, they are distracting at times and distractions can be costly.

Distraction can cause poor planning and lack of organization, but poor planning and poor organization can increase the likelihood of being distracted. It becomes significantly easier to be distracted when you have no plan to keep you focused on the goal, leading to poor organization.

For example, trying to do too many things at once is already overwhelming and being overwhelmed could contribute to you not having a plan for you to proceed. If you are trying to execute one thing, let alone several things, but do not have a plan, you will likely be confused about how to accomplish the task or tasks. Simply because you do not have a plan, your attention will be drawn to anything that looks like a viable approach to completing the tasks. In that case, you are distracted.

In a worse situation, you have a task to complete, but you not only do not have a plan which then leads to you being distracted, but you are also distracted from the onset and that precludes you from having a plan. In this case, you have the task, but it has not yet resonated as a goal. Your mind is elsewhere. You are grossly distracted, so instead of focusing on the task, you are preoccupied with other things. There is no plan and no organization, making it very unlikely you will successfully complete the task.

We mistakenly underestimate the power of distraction and because of this misconception, we fail to do what is necessary to guard against it. Because of this, distraction plagues humankind and causes much damage and setbacks in our lives. Consequently, any area of our lives can be impacted by distraction if we do not guard against it intentionally. To the degree that the adversary uses distraction, he seems to know that we underestimate its impact, and being the subtle opportunist that he is, distraction is one of the most widely used strategies against us. It is a remarkably efficient tool that is used by our adversary.

Distraction occurs in all areas of our lives—our personal lives, in our professional lives, and in matters concerning our walk with the Lord. But while this is a widely used strategy of the enemy, we cannot always blame Satan for distraction. Often, we are distracted because we are undisciplined and unorganized and that gives Satan much with which to work, so it starts with us.

In Ephesians 4:25–27, the Apostle Paul warns the brethren to put off lying and anger because these things give Satan a foothold. I am proposing that our lack of awareness of the seriousness of distraction also gives Satan a foothold in our lives. The word "foothold" literally means "place," and was often used in a military context in reference to an invading army securing a place behind enemy lines from which a deeper attack could be launched.[5] By underestimating distraction, we give Satan an open door for his advancement against us.

Before advancing, Satan observes our actions and listens to our words to find a place where he can get a foothold. And yes, he starts with a foothold, but if not addressed, he will advance to creating a stronghold. Once Satan gets a foothold, he uses lies and deceits to build a fortress of deception: a stronghold. This then keeps us from experiencing the presence of God and the abundant life that Christ offers (John 10:10b).

By using distraction, Satan's goal is to make us feel like we're living in the abundant life that is promised to us when in fact we are not. This is deception, and it is his primary mission to deceive us. This is spiritual warfare, but "The weapons we fight with are not the weapons of the world. On the contrary, they have divine power to demolish strongholds" (2 Corinthians 10:4, NIV).

Distractions can keep us from being successful in any and all areas of our lives. We can be distracted from our exercise routine and resort to being sedentary versus being active and fit. We can be distracted from doing our daily chores and become lazy and unproductive. Students can be distracted from their studies and become academic underachievers. We can have good intentions to pray at a specific time each day, but without fail, something will sneak its way in every time to distract us. Taken separately, incidents of distraction appear as if they have no effect, but sustained and habitual distraction will, without doubt, lead to disaster.

CHAPTER TWO: SEVEN MAIN TAKEAWAYS

1. We live in a highly engaging but sorely distracting world and thus are bombarded daily with numerous distractions.

2. It is essential that we mentally prioritize our goals because distractions seek the attention of our minds.

3. Distraction can cause poor planning and lack of organization, but poor planning and poor organization can increase the likelihood of being distracted.

4. We mistakenly underestimate the power of distraction, and because of this misconception, we fail to do what is necessary to guard against it.

5. Often, we are distracted because we are undisciplined and unorganized and that gives Satan much with which to work, so it starts with us.

6. Our lack of awareness of the seriousness of distraction also gives Satan a foothold in our lives.

7. Taken separately, incidents of distraction appear as if they have no effect, but sustained and habitual distraction will, without doubt, lead to disaster.

FOCUS IS A MUST

*If we really want to get focused, or if we really want to
manage the distractions of life more skillfully, we must learn
to manage more effectively one of our most precious
resources, our attention.*

To focus is to center one's attention on an interest or an activity. One must focus in order to accomplish a goal, complete an activity, or maintain an interest. This applies to spiritual and nonspiritual matters alike.

The high-performing seventeen-year-old girl, a senior in high school who is preparing for college, can become distracted when she becomes friends with a nineteen-year-old boy in her neighborhood. She is now choosing to spend time with her new friend rather than studying and is even questioning whether she wants to go away to college. She is distracted.

Mom picked up her son from day care and is walking with the child to the car. It takes mom longer than needed to take that short walk from the building to the car because four-year-old Matthew stops to look at and pick up every rock he sees, and if he's not picking up a rock, he is pulling away from her to kick whatever debris he sees in his path. Matthew is distracted.

An adult woman is on her way to a baby shower, but she needs to pick up a few more items for the event. Her plan is to make a quick stop at the store to purchase a few specific items. She even has a list of the items she is planning to purchase. But while walking through the aisles, she sees several signages—buy one get one free, thirty percent off, fifty percent off—for items not on her list and are not really needed. She stops and looks at the discounted items. In fact, she spends quite a bit of time deliberating whether she should purchase these items. Eventually, she places them in her cart. She is in the store significantly longer than planned, she spent more money than she intended, and she got to the baby shower later than planned. All these things happened because she became distracted.

You just came from a conference that was invigorating and spiritually enriching. One of the speakers challenged the attendees to revive their prayer and personal devotion life. It was a powerful sermon, and you were convicted. While at the conference, you recalled the days when you were quite disciplined in praying and reading your Bible every morning. You recalled when you fasted regularly and even did deep Bible studies on your own. Having heard the sermon, you decided to make some changes. Your plan is to go back to reading your Bible daily and praying each morning to start your day. You are excited and cannot wait to get started.

Based on your schedule, you set the time and place for your morning devotions. You started implementing it the very week you returned home from the conference, and you stayed on schedule for almost two weeks. Toward the end of the second week and into the third week, you missed a few days because other things during that time demanded your attention and you responded to them. You engaged in whatever they were that demanded your attention then moved on with the rest of the day. You did not pray, and you did not read your Bible. You are distracted.

This pattern continues until you find yourself back to where you were when you attended the conference—a weak, near nonexistent prayer and Word life. The things that demanded your attention and lured you from your goal are insignificant things that could be done after prayer. For example, before prayer you went to use the restroom. You took your phone with you and while in the restroom, you checked to see what text messages came in while you were sleeping. You respond to the text messages and then you check your email. By the time you look up from your phone, you surmise that you don't have enough time to pray and be at work on time. So, you forego praying, got ready for work, and left the house. You are distracted.

Another example: you were doing laundry the night before but did not finish. So, on your way to your prayer spot, you stop to transfer a load of laundry from the washing machine to the dryer. But there's also a load of laundry in the dryer that needs to be folded. You fold the laundry you took from the dryer, then you put it and the laundry you folded the night before away. After doing so, you prepare to leave for work without thinking to pray. You are distracted.

The impact of distraction can be serious, as seen with the seventeen-year-old high school student and the threat to one's prayer life. Being distracted could cost her admission to college, which could in turn impact her future. Prayer is an absolute necessity to a believer's walk with God. Prayerlessness renders the believer powerless, and without prayer, we will not have the fortitude to resist the temptations of the devil. Prayer connects us to God. Prayer opens our heart and spirit to God's correcting voice. Jesus prayed and so must we. Anything other than a continual attitude of prayer and communion with God is sin. Anything that interrupts our connection to God is wrong. This can be very costly to a believer.

The devil knows what prayer does in the life of a believer, and he knows the damage it does to him. Therefore, he works supremely hard to distract us from praying. How many times have you been in prayer and a crowd of things that are not related to your prayer keep coming to your mind—the email you need to send, the phone call you need to return, the items you need to pick up at the store, the errands you need to run that day, the project you started at work the day before but didn't complete?

Even if Satan cannot stop us from praying, he continues to try while we are praying. His attempts at distracting us are relentless. To overcome him, we too must be relentless in resisting him. We must be vigilant, because "Your enemy the devil prowls around like a roaring lion looking for someone to devour." (1 Peter 5:8, NIV).

Like the scenario given above, sometimes you don't even make it into prayer. How many times have you set a goal to pray at a certain time every day, but without fail whenever that time comes, you find yourself doing something you had not planned on doing at that time? Usually, the lure is to do this or that and then pray. And that voice in your head consoles you by telling you, it won't take long, you need to get it done anyway, so there is no harm in quickly doing it and then go into prayer. It could be something as simple as putting out the trash, getting something from your car, hanging up a piece of garment in the closet, emptying the dishwasher, making a quick call, or sending a text. After all, the person has called you several times and you weren't able to talk, so it's fitting that you return their call now that you have the time to do so.

In your mind, none of these activities will take long. The plan is to get it done and then go into prayer. But that is the art and power of distraction. When distracted, you are pulled away from the goal and "pulled away" does not mean for a moment. "Pulled away" means moving from the objective to something else. This is why, in the scenarios above and any others like them, most of us end up not praying at all. We divert from the plan and instead hang up that single piece of garment in the closet and from there we see shoes that need to be put in place, other pieces of garments that need to be put away, then we make the bed, and on and on we go, doing everything but pray. We have been distracted.

WORDS OF WARNING AGAINST DISTRACTION

The Word of God warns us against distraction because our Heavenly Father knows how costly this can be. Let us look at a few of these Scriptures.

> **Proverbs 4:25–27** (NIV, emphasis added) — *Let your eyes look straight ahead; <u>fix your gaze directly before you</u>. Give careful thought to the paths for your feet and be steadfast in all your ways. <u>Do not turn to the right or the left</u>; keep your foot from evil.*

In these three verses, Solomon is giving his son Rehoboam some advice that may be the hardest to follow. He instructs his son to do six things. In verse 25, Rehoboam is instructed to look straight before him and fix his eyes on what's ahead of him. In verse 26, he is told to think about the path he takes and let his ways be established. Finally, in verse 27, Rehoboam is charged to stay the course; he must not look to the right or the left, and in the same verse, he is told to abstain from doing evil. In summary, Solomon advised his son to focus and not be distracted.

Solomon was telling his son to choose intentionally the things on which he fixed his eyes. He must choose with much care the things to which he gives his attention, and when he identifies those things or that thing, he must look right at it, nothing else. Despite the many options that are available or the many other things that he could be doing, he must choose and remain dedicated to his choice. By doing so, he will be focused and not be distracted.

It takes focus to find the right path in life, and it takes focus to stay on the right path in life. The Word of God was written for our admonition and for our learning, so here we are admonished to fix our eyes and focus our attention on what is directly before us. We must focus on our goals and carefully think about how we will accomplish them. How we will accomplish our goals is the path we take. Once we determine the path we will take, we must follow through and we must do so persistently. Our paths include our choices, the things to which we give our time and attention. We must always think about the choices we make and where they may lead us. We must think about the decisions we make and where they could take us. To make sure that we are not distracted from the right path, we must constantly give serious thought to the path we are on and make the necessary changes without delay.

The line that separates right from wrong is incredibly thin. The line that stands between obedience and disobedience is also quite thin and is sometimes blurry. It only takes one thing to distract us or to get off the right path and onto the wrong path, and that thing need not be major. It could be a simple insignificant thing that veers us off course. If a huge tractor trailer is coming down a highway, even though it is very big in size, a small object such as a bird or a larger object such as a car can cause it to veer off the highway. Our lives are no different. We can get distracted by large or small objects and incidents.

Only when we carefully think about the path our feet take will our *"ways be established."* With the tendencies of the flesh in a world of wickedness and the host of things that are vying for our attention, heading in the right direction does not happen by accident nor does it happen easily. We must be intentional about avoiding distractions. Solomon wanted his son to establish his way and to solidify his direction. To do this, Rehoboam would have to constantly and sincerely evaluate the path he was on, and we must do the same.

> **1 Corinthians 7:35** (NIV, emphasis added) — *I am saying this for your own good, not to restrict you, but that you may live in a right way in <u>undivided devotion</u> to the Lord.*

The Apostle Paul is admonishing his audience to live a life that is wholly devoted to the Lord. He is not teaching against marriage, but he is pointing out to the church of Corinth that being single positions one to have an undivided devotion to God and the ministry. He added that this undivided devotion is for their temporal and spiritual advantage as it would enable them to better meet and contend with persecution for the sake of the Gospel. He also points out that by remaining unmarried, they might be freer from the cares and encumbrances of life and more at liberty to serve the Lord.

Paul did not think, and neither was he proposing, that marriage was unlawful, that the single life was a more chaste way to live, or that one must remain single. He gave his advice, laid out the advantages and disadvantages of both conditions, and left the decision to his audience. But in essence, he is saying that being married presents more distraction from spiritual matters than being single. He is implying that a life of singlehood is free from distractions such as family, children, and spousal relationships that a life of marriage, family, and parenting introduces. He is saying that being single will likely eliminate distractions from these things and make room for one to wait upon the Lord and serve Him wholeheartedly, which, in Paul's opinion, was choosing the good part with Mary while others, like Martha, were troubled, divided, and distracted by other things.

Be it marriage or singlehood, in the absence of distraction, we are devoted to the cause, we are focused, and being focused is not a restriction, it is for our own good.

> **Luke 21:34** (NIV) — *Be careful, or your hearts will be weighed down with carousing, drunkenness and the anxieties of life, and that day will close on you suddenly like a trap.*

It's interesting that partying, drunkenness, and being overtaken with the cares of life are mentioned together in the same warning. One would think that if a person sees it fitting to party to the point of becoming drunk, they must be living a carefree life. So, it is quite odd to warn about all three together. But whether that is the case or not, the warning I want to bring to your attention is this: we must not be distracted by the cares of life.

The warning given in Luke 21:34 might be issued as such because the distraction could start with excessive eating and drinking, and these behaviors can oppress, and place demands on the stomach and the body that make the senses and the mind dull and unfit to handle the cares of life. So, because the mind, due to drunkenness, is unfit to manage the cares of life, the incumbent is overtaken or distracted by them. Being overtaken with the cares of life will then distract from spiritual and religious exercises such as reading, meditation, and prayer.

Being weighed down by cares of this life—school, work, family, relationships, self-care, church, recreation, ministry, housing, what you shall eat or drink, or wherewith you shall be clothed—are as damaging to the soul as overindulgence is to the body. Clearly, we can be inebriated with wine and be overtaken by self-indulgence, and we can be overwhelmed with life. We can be distracted by both, and both scenarios are detrimental.

DISTRACTION FROM WHAT?

To meet the criteria for distraction, one must be redirected from their main focus. Often, this main focus is better than the thing to which the person is redirected. This is why the prefix to the word is "dis," which according to dictionary.com means, "apart, asunder, away, utterly," or having a privative, negative, or reversing force. "Traction" means a quality or feature that evokes interest, liking, or desire. Therefore, when one is distracted, they are pulled away from or taken apart from the thing of interest or preference. Note the word "utterly." This means that when we are distracted, we are removed entirely from our goal. The intent of distraction is to block us from accomplishing the goal. The aim is to remove us from the path to the goal entirely.

Martha Was Distracted

> **Luke 10:38–42** (NKJV, emphasis added) — *Now it happened as they went that He entered a certain village; and a certain woman named Martha welcomed Him into her house. And she had a sister called Mary, who also sat at Jesus' feet and heard His word. But Martha was <u>distracted</u> with much serving, and she approached Him and said, "Lord, do You not care that my sister has left me to serve alone? Therefore, tell her to help me." And Jesus answered and said to her, "Martha, Martha, you are worried and troubled about many things. But one thing is needed, and <u>Mary has chosen that good part</u>, which will not be taken away from her."*

I believe Martha started out with the right focus and all the right intentions, but she got distracted. Instead of focusing on the better part—Jesus Himself—she became concerned with preparing a meal for Jesus. Same thing with us today. Sometimes, we are distracted by ministry activities to the degree that we miss the value in Jesus Himself.

Martha was so entrenched in what she was doing that she could not see why her sister Mary was not helping her. In her eyes, Mary was wasting time by sitting at Jesus' feet. Instead, she thought Mary should be in the kitchen with her preparing a meal for Jesus. So, Martha became angry because her sister was not helping but was sitting at the feet of Jesus, listening to His teaching. And not only was Martha angry with her sister, but she was also greatly upset with her Lord: "Lord, don't you care that my sister has left me to do the work by myself? Tell her to help me!" (Luke 10:40, NIV). These are strong words: "Don't you care, Jesus?"

But Martha got this response from the Lord: "'Martha, Martha,' the Lord answered, 'you are worried and upset about many things, but few things are needed—or indeed only one. Mary has chosen what is better, and it will not be taken away from her'" (Luke 10:41–42, NIV). Martha thought she was doing the best thing for Jesus, but Jesus told Martha that she was wrong, and that Mary had made the better choice. The mere fact that Jesus said her name twice should tell us that Jesus places more value on us spending time with Him than on us making sure everything for the ministry is well planned.

Preparing a meal is indeed a lovely and kind thing to do to show hospitality to Jesus, but it was a distraction from something even better. It wasn't that Mary did not understand what needed to be done. The problem was that Martha thought urgent and good things like serving Jesus a meal was most important. It was indeed urgent and good but not most important.

Ofttimes, we think we are doing the right thing at the right time, but we are not. Martha thought she was, but Jesus made it clear to her that she had not chosen the better part. She might have chosen the good part but not the better part. To avoid distraction from the better part, we must be able to detect the things that have the potential to derail us, and we must aim for the important and better at all costs.

PETER WAS DISTRACTED BY HIS SURROUNDINGS

> **Matthew 14:25–31** (NIV) — *Shortly before dawn Jesus went out to them, walking on the lake. When the disciples saw him walking on the lake, they were terrified. "It's a ghost," they said, and cried out in fear. But Jesus immediately said to them: "Take courage! It is I. Don't be afraid." "Lord, if it's you," Peter replied, "tell me to come to you on the water." "Come," he said. Then Peter got down out of the boat, walked on the water and came toward Jesus. But when he saw the wind, he was afraid and, beginning to sink, cried out, "Lord, save me!" Immediately Jesus reached out his hand and caught him. "You of little faith," he said, "why did you doubt?"*

Two things happened to Peter in this scenario: he was distracted, and he doubted. I will discuss doubt in the next two chapters. Peter stepped out of the boat with one goal in mind and that was to walk on water to get to Jesus. He was distracted from his goal when he focused his attention on his surroundings.

It is important to note that Peter stepped out of the boat into deep waters, boisterous winds, and high waves, and that he did in fact walk on water toward Jesus until he took his eyes off Jesus, his goal. So, Peter did have some success before he started sinking. Peter was successful because he responded to the one word that Jesus said to him, "Come." Peter believed the word spoken to him by Jesus, so he began his walk on the water by faith in the word of the Lord. Yes, the water was deep, the wind was strong, and the waves were high, but Peter still stepped out on the word of the Lord. Given these conditions, it is fair to say that Peter was strongly convinced and was determined to walk to Jesus. But even with such a strong conviction, he was distracted.

In most cases in our lives, we know without any uncertainty what we should do. We know without doubt that the source of the directive to do a certain thing is authentic and we believe the source. Therefore, we set out to achieve the thing, but the activities of our surroundings are a distraction. Like Peter, many of us start out with success toward whatever that thing is but soon thereafter are distracted by life, family, tragedies, losses, and even gains.

When Jesus reached out His hand and caught Peter, He said, "You of little faith. Why did you doubt?" This tells me that when we are given a dictate from the Source, our Lord, life circumstances will occur, storms will irrupt, and we may find ourselves in unchartered territories—no man on earth had ever walked on water. But to thwart distraction, we must have faith and we must not doubt.

Peter did not see the actual wind, but he saw the damaging effects of the wind, and then he started to worry. For him to see the effects of the wind, he had to take his eyes off Jesus, his goal. What he saw made him afraid, and that is when he started to sink. He was distracted.

How many times have we started out with focus and strong, steady strides toward a purpose, but things start happening around us that catch our attention and cause us to doubt? To avoid distraction, we must focus on our goals. To accomplish our goals, we must be all in, and we must choose and remain steadfast. There is no other alternative. This must be the case in pursuit of all endeavors—our life goals and our walk with the Lord.

THERE IS NO MIDDLE GROUND

Walking with the Lord is a life of absolutes; there are no gray areas and no middle ground. We must decide to wholly follow the Lord or not. Anything outside of the mindset to wholly follow the Lord places us on Satan's side. However, the problem with most of us is that we allow Satan to convince us that living life on the edge, near the outskirts of God's will, is acceptable, but that is a lie. It is either we are all in or not.

Joshua told the children of Israel, "But if serving the Lord seems undesirable to you, then choose for yourselves this day whom you will serve, whether the gods your ancestors served beyond the Euphrates, or the gods of the Amorites, in whose land you are living. But as for me and my household, we will serve the Lord" (Joshua 24:15, NIV). Jesus teaches in Matthew 6:24 (NIV) that "No man can serve two masters. Either you will hate the one and love the other, or you will be devoted to the one and despise the other. You cannot serve both God and money." We must choose.

For Satan, mostly God and some of him is acceptable, but for God, it must be all God and nothing else. Jesus taught in Matthew 6:24 that "no man can serve two masters," and Satan knows this very well. He also, being the deceiver that he is, knows that if he introduces extreme acts of disobedience to God, most of us would recognize them and not yield to his temptations. So instead, he tempts us to mitigate and dilute our devotion to God, and sadly, he is successful at keeping many of us living on the peripheral of God's will. Too often, he keeps us in the middle ground between his will and God's will for our lives, and he is quite satisfied with this because he knows that for God it is all or nothing. There is no middle ground when it comes to following Christ, which means, if we are not fully devoted to Christ, Satan has now gotten what he wants.

We are at high risk of being overrun by the enemy of our souls when we do not know how he operates. To keep us walking the middle line, he often uses seemingly harmless, even good things to distract us from what's best for us. These distractions when considered independently are not sinful, but their cumulative impact is nothing less than sinful.

According to 1 John 3:4, sin is the transgression of God's law. Therefore, ambitious life goals—for example, relationships, education, and career—do not transgress God's law, but the value we place on them can put these things above God, making them idols in our lives. These good things, if not kept in perspective, can distance us from God.

We are in transgression of God's law when we place our life goals above God. By doing so, we give Satan the opportunity to change our course into doing things that take us further from God. When we make these goals our idols, we give Satan room to introduce things that support our goals but threaten our relationship with God, but to the naked eye, it seems harmless. This is why it is not wise to measure spirituality or our relationship with God with material blessings. The material blessings that we enjoy and will likely say God has blessed us with could be costing us a meaningful relationship with Him. In many cases, while these things take us farther from God, they take us closer to our goals, and this makes it more difficult to see what the enemy is doing.

It is these harmful things, the things Satan packages in such a manner to make them appear harmless or even beneficial, that place us in the middle ground. Being in the middle ground—a place that is unacceptable to God, because for Him, there is no such thing—unknown to us, we lower our threshold for sin. Sin becomes more tolerant. We make excuses for sin more quickly than before. We minimize the seriousness of sin. This is why we find even our very brethren in Christ telling us at times not to be so serious. "It doesn't take all that," they say. "You're too intense. You're too serious; lighten up." Satan has deceived these loved ones into making excuses for the very things that separate them from God. There is no middle ground, so the two alternatives are to wholly follow the Lord or to follow Satan.

Most people continue attending church while all these harmful but seemingly good things are introduced into their lives. Satan knows that attending church is not what will save us, so he does not mind if we keep going to church. In fact, attending church while being influenced by him works in his favor because churchiness often meets the standard of the middle-ground believer. Such believers do not see their shortcomings, because church attendance meets their standard. They are churchy but carnal and don't seem to know it. This gives the adversary plenty to work with against them. These believers will likely say they love the Lord, but their lives say they love the world. No one can love the Lord and love the world. If we love the world, the love of the Father is not in us (1 John 2:15).

It was members of the church who Jesus called lukewarm in Revelation 3:16. A lukewarm state is neither hot nor cold. In fact, it is downright insipid. The brethren of the church in Laodicea were in the middle, but Jesus was very clear that being in the middle is detestable to Him. He said He would spit (spew) them out of His mouth.

A highly sensitive spirit and a soft heart toward God are absolute essentials for total devotion to Him. With high sensitivity to the Holy Spirit, you will be aware when He is telling you what to do and directing you where to go. When Satan introduces that seemingly harmless thing, the Holy Spirit will tell you not to yield. If you are sensitive to Him, you will hear and if you have a soft heart toward God, you will obey.

Satan knows that undivided devotion to the Lord is an absolute in our walk with the Lord. So, he is masterfully tricky, subtle, and sneaky when he seeks to distract us. Regrettably, this strategy to use seemingly harmless things in very imperceptible ways to persuade many in the body of Christ to fall short of absolute surrender and settle for a churchy lifestyle instead is shamefully successful. Therefore, many are simply churchgoers, and many of these churchgoers are even active in the ministry while being distracted. They are distracted with things that are detrimental to their spiritual wellbeing but seem inoffensive.

To make sure his strategies are established and executed without any glitches and to ensure that his imps are fully trained, Satan convened a gathering with his staff to properly train and inform them about how to best distract the followers of Jesus Christ.

Satan Called a Convention

An Inspirational Christian Story about Losing Focus on Jesus[6] — Author Unknown

Satan called a worldwide convention of demons. In his opening address he said, "We can't keep Christians from going to church. We can't keep them from reading their Bibles and knowing the truth. We can't even keep them from forming an intimate relationship with their Savior. Once they gain that connection with Jesus, our power over them is broken. So let them go to their churches; let them have their covered dish dinners, but steal their time, so they don't have time to develop a relationship with Jesus Christ. This is what I want you to do," said the evil one: "Distract them from gaining hold of their Savior and maintaining that vital connection throughout their day!"

"How shall we do this?" his demons shouted. "Keep them busy in the nonessentials of life and invent innumerable schemes to occupy their minds," he answered. "Tempt them to spend, spend, spend, and borrow, borrow, borrow. Persuade the wives to go to work for long hours and the husbands to work 6 to 7 days each week, 10 to 12 hours a day, so they can afford their empty lifestyles. Keep them from spending time with their children. As their families fragment, soon their homes will offer no escape from the pressures of work!"

"Over-stimulate their minds so that they cannot hear that still, small voice. Entice them to play the radio or cassette player [mp3 and YouTube] whenever they drive. Keep the TV, the DVD player, and their CDs going constantly in their homes. Keep them on the IPAD, the laptop, the cell phones and on social media, and see to it that every store and restaurant in the world plays non-biblical music constantly (minor change added). This will jam their minds and break that union with Christ. Fill their coffee tables with magazines and newspapers. Pound their minds with the news 24 hours a day. Invade their driving moments with billboards.

Flood their mailboxes with junk mail, mail order catalogs, sweepstakes, and every kind of newsletter and promotional offering free products, services, and false hopes."

"Give them Santa Claus to distract them from teaching their children the real meaning of Christmas. Give them an Easter bunny so they won't talk about his resurrection and power over sin and death. Even in their recreation, let them be excessive. Have them return from their recreation exhausted. Keep them too busy to go out in nature and reflect on God's creation. Send them to amusement parks, sporting events, plays, concerts, and movies instead. Keep them busy, busy, busy!"

"And when they meet for spiritual fellowship, involve them in gossip and small talk so that they leave with troubled consciences. Crowd their lives with so many good causes they have no time to seek power from Jesus. Soon they will be working in their own strength, sacrificing their health and family for the good of the cause. It will work! It will work!"

It was quite a plan! The demons went eagerly to their assignments causing Christians everywhere to get busier and more rushed, going here and there, having little time for their God or their families and friends. Having no time to tell others about the power of Jesus to change lives. I guess the question is, has the devil been successful at his scheme? You be the judge!

CHAPTER THREE: SEVEN MAIN TAKEAWAYS

1. The Devil knows what prayer does in the life of a believer, and he knows the damage it does to him. Therefore, he works supremely hard to distract us from praying.

2. It takes focus to find the right path in life, and it takes focus to stay on the right path in life.

3. Distractions can inhibit us from succeeding in life, and to succeed in life, we must set goals and focus on them.

4. With the tendencies of the flesh in a world of wickedness and the host of things that are vying for our attention, heading in the right direction does not happen by accident. We must be intentional about avoiding distractions.

5. To avoid distraction from the better part, we must be able to detect the things that have the potential to derail us, and we must aim for the important and better at all costs.

6. Walking with the Lord is a life of absolutes; there are no gray areas and no middle ground. We must decide to wholly follow the Lord or not.

7. We are at high risk of being overrun by the enemy of our souls when we do not know how he operates.

DOUBT BY CLOUDED VISION

*In the absence of faith, we are completely blind, but with
doubt, we have a clouded vision.*

Thee is quite a bit of talk in Christendom about doubt,
and the jury is still out on whether a believer who
should be walking by faith in Jesus Christ can be
doubtful at the same time. Thus, the remaining questions are:
Can one have faith and doubt at the same time? and is there a
difference between doubt and unbelief? This leaves us with
three words to deliberate: doubt, faith, and unbelief.

I will first address faith as it is the word with which most
of us are familiar, followed by unbelief, and lastly by doubt.

FAITH

According to Wikibooks, Hebrew Roots, in Greek, the root
word from which we get faith is the noun *pistis*, and for believe,
the verb is *pistueo*. Faith means belief, firm persuasion,
assurance, and firm conviction. Faith is confidence in what we
hope for and the assurance that the Lord is working, even
though we cannot see it.[7]

Hebrews 11:1 (NIV) says, "Now faith is confidence in what we hope for and assurance about what we do not see." Said differently, faith is the assurance that the things revealed and promised in the Word of God are true, even though we have not yet experienced them or seen them with our natural eyes. Faith gives the believer conviction, which is the certainty and confidence that what he expects will come to pass. Faith is proof or evidence of what is hoped for. Faith is the currency that "purchases" what's hoped for; it is the force or power that brings into reality the thing that is hoped for. In other words, faith is so real that the believer possesses, in the spiritual realm, that which they hope for before they see it.

Without faith we cannot withdraw anything from heaven. Without faith we cannot please God (Hebrews 11:6). Faith is the power that connects the believer, who is in the natural, to the spiritual realm. Faith links the believer with God and makes Him—His character, His nature, His Word, His promises, His name—become a reality to us.

UNBELIEF

Unbelief is the opposite of faith. Unbelief connotes blindness and faith connotes sightedness. One cannot be blind and have sight at the same time. Therefore, I propose that one cannot have faith and unbelief at the same time. The King James Version Dictionary defines unbelief as incredulity, skepticism, distrust of God's promises and faithfulness, and weak faith. Based on this last definition—weak faith—is the Word of God saying one can actually have faith, even if it is weak faith, and also do not believe? Are faith and unbelief mutually exclusive?

In Mark 9, we see a father with a son who was possessed by a demon. The father took his son to Jesus' disciples to be

50

healed, but they could not heal the boy. The father then brought the boy to Jesus.

> **Mark 9:21−24** (NIV) — *Jesus asked the boy's father, "How long has he been like this?" "From childhood," he answered. "It has often thrown him into fire or water to kill him. But if you can do anything, take pity on us and help us." "'If you can'?" said Jesus. "Everything is possible for one who believes." Immediately the boy's father exclaimed, "I do believe; help me overcome my unbelief!" (Emphasis added)*

The words "if you can" caught Jesus' attention. Jesus responded to the father by repeating these words to him in the form of a question and added that "Everything is possible for one who believes." Because the father said the words "if you can," it appears as if Jesus surmised that the man did not believe. But, if the father did not believe, why would he take the boy to Jesus in the first place? By taking the boy to Jesus to be healed, is he not demonstrating some degree of belief, be it small? If there is any degree of belief, is that not faith? So, what did Jesus mean when he said, "Everything is possible for one who believes"? Is He saying the father did not believe because he said, "If you can"?

Earlier, I mentioned that the KJV Dictionary defines unbelief as weak faith. That definition is based on Scriptures such as Mark 9:24 and Matthew 6:20. Jesus is not saying the father was in a state of unbelief; He was pointing out that his faith was weak. The father brought the boy to Jesus, so he must have had faith, but the fact that he places the word "if" before his statement told Jesus that his faith was weak. So, unbelief in this passage does not mean no faith, it does not mean utter unbelief or no belief; it means little or weak belief. Faith is there, but it is weak.

After Jesus healed the boy, "the disciples came to Jesus in private and asked, 'Why couldn't we drive it out?' He replied, 'Because you have so <u>little faith</u>. Truly I tell you, if you have faith as small as a mustard seed, you can say to this mountain, "Move from here to there," and it will move. Nothing will be impossible for you'" (Matthew 17:19–21, NIV, emphasis added).

The KJV of Matthew 17:19–21 (Emphasis added) uses the word unbelief while the NIV uses little faith:

> *Then came the disciples to Jesus apart, and said, Why could not we cast him out? And Jesus said unto them, Because of your <u>unbelief</u>: for verily I say unto you, If ye have faith as a grain of mustard seed, ye shall say unto this mountain, Remove hence to yonder place; and it shall remove; and nothing shall be impossible unto you.*

The Greek word that is used in these passages of Scripture is *oligopistian*, translated "little faith." Oligopistos occurs only six times in the New Testament: Matthew 6:30, 8:26, 14:31, 16:8, 17:20, and Luke 12:28. They always mean "of little faith/trust or of little faith, trusting too little."[8]

In Scripture, a poor person is called penniless, even if their small fortune is not technically zero pennies. That could very well be the reason the word unbelief is used even though the person has some faith, though little.

In John 3:35–51, Jesus is conversing with the crowd of over five thousand that He has miraculously fed. They saw the miracle that He had done, so they have followed Him across the sea, and now, as He tells them who He is, they are insisting that He perform more signs before they can believe Him. This is unbelief. The prefix "un" means "not." Therefore, these people were not believing who Jesus said He was.

"Why doesn't the crowd believe?" They saw Jesus perform the miracle of feeding over five thousand people with five loaves and two fishes, and they saw Him heal the sick. They spent time with Him and have most likely heard Him teach at least once. But in verse 29, when Jesus called on them to believe in Him, they recoiled, and demanded another sign instead. "What sign do you do, that we may see and believe you?" they asked. The implication of this question is that they do not believe Him.

Due to unbelief, the Israelites could not enter the Promised Land. They saw the mighty works of God with their own eyes for many years. They saw Him do great miracles while they were in Egypt, on their way out of Egypt, and while they were traveling through the wilderness, yet they were stricken by unbelief.

The Israelites were in their homes listening to the Egyptians' shrieking wails as the Egyptians watched their firstborn die before their eyes. None of the firstborn of the Israelites died, but all firstborn of the Egyptians died, yet the Israelites could not believe God.

After 430 years of slavery in Egypt, Pharaoh finally gave the Israelites, God's people, their freedom. Approximately 600,000 men plus their families were on their way out of Egypt with Moses as their leader. But after their departure, Pharaoh sent his army after the Israelites. Behind the Israelites was Pharaoh's army—all the horses and chariots of Pharaoh, his horsemen and his army—and before them was the Red Sea. There was no way to escape except the way they had come in, and the Egyptian army had blocked that path.

Moses cried out to the Lord in Exodus 14:15–18 (NIV):

Then the Lord said to Moses, "Why are you crying out to me? Tell the Israelites to move on. Raise your staff and stretch out your hand over the sea to divide the water so that the Israelites can go through the sea on dry ground. I will harden the hearts of the Egyptians so that they will go in after them. And I will gain glory through Pharaoh and all his army, through his chariots and his horsemen. The Egyptians will know that I am the Lord when I gain glory through Pharaoh, his chariots and his horsemen."

The Lord miraculously allowed the children of Israel to pass through the Red Sea on dry ground to safety. As Pharaoh's army pursued the Israelites through the dried-out sea, God closed back the parted waters and drowned the entire army of Egyptians. This is not a story the Israelites heard of or read about. No one told this tale to them. They experienced it themselves, yet they were an unbelieving nation.

Because of their unbelief, they were unwilling to rely on God and follow the plan He had for them. They wanted to do things their way, which caused them to wander through the wilderness for forty years. During that time, they provoked and blatantly disobeyed God, and as a result, did not enter the land God promised their forefathers. The land of Canaan was the Father's plan and desire for His people, but their unbelief kept them out. Unbelief is a sin, and like it did for the Israelites, it will cost us our blessing. It will forfeit the promises our Heavenly Father has made to us.

Hebrews 3:15–19 (NIV, emphasis added) — *As has just been said: "Today, if you hear his voice, do not* *harden your hearts as you did in the rebellion." Who were they who heard and rebelled? Were they not all those Moses led out of Egypt? And with whom was he angry for forty years? Was it not with <u>those who sinned</u>, whose bodies perished in the wilderness? And to whom did God swear that they would never enter his rest if not to those who disobeyed? So we see that they were not able to enter, because of their <u>unbelief</u>.*

The Israelites saw the miraculous works of God again and again, but they still failed to trust in God. We are not very different from the Israelites. Many of us complain, become afraid, and are stricken with anxiety when faced with life's challenges even though God has moved mightily on our behalf on prior occasions. That is unbelief.

We stand strong in Christ by faith (2 Corinthians 1:24), but unbelief separates us from Christ (John 3:18–19). We must believe the Word of God to stand strong. The opposite of faith is unbelief.

DOUBT

Oxford Languages defines doubt as a feeling of uncertainty or lack of conviction, to consider something questionable or unlikely, to hesitate to believe, to distrust, to be apprehensive about, or to be undecided in opinion or belief.

To doubt, we must have a reference point on which to focus the doubt. Therefore, we can only doubt what we hear, see, know, or even believe. Doubt is not the absence of faith; doubt is the questioning of faith. Faith says, "God can," but doubt says, "Will He?" Doubt questions what is. Doubt casts a shadow on what is, rendering it obscured. We might question our ability to tread water for ten minutes. There might be questions concerning our public speaking skills. And we may be uncertain about the future of our country, job, or relationships. This is doubt.

We all experience bouts of doubt; it is a normal part of our lives, but we should keep it under control, it should not control us. If not controlled, doubt will cripple us and steal from us. Doubts about our physical security while walking through a city might prevent us from experiencing what the city has to offer. If controlled, doubt could drive us to new heights. For example, my concern about my public speaking skills may make me join a Toastmasters club. It could cause me to focus on being a better public speaker, learning as much as I can about it.

What about doubt concerning our faith and relationship with God? James likened a doubting person to an unstable and chaotic wave of the sea:

> **James 1:6–8** (NIV) — *But when you ask, you must believe and not doubt, because the one who doubts is like a wave of the sea, blown and tossed by the wind. That person should not expect to receive anything from the Lord. Such a person is double-minded and unstable in all they do.*

Doubting is double-mindedness, and that is what James is referring to here. He is warning against doublemindedness. We are doubleminded when we know the Word of God, but instead of holding on to His Word by faith, we make a calculated effort to undermine His Word and then justify our behavior. Said succinctly, James is talking to the believer who knows the Word of God, but for whatever reason, choses to question the Word. These believers are called doubleminded because they know the Word of God but are torn by inner conflicts, making it impossible to lean confidently on God and His gracious promises.

Unlike doubt, faith is "a settled trust and confidence in God based on His character and promises as revealed in Scripture" (English Standard Version Study Bible). Doubt mitigates our faith. Jesus addressed this issue with the faither of the sick son. The man had some faith—enough to bring the boy to Jesus—but doubt made him question Jesus' ability to heal the boy. So, like the father of the sick child, when we ask God for something but do not fully trust that He can and will answer our request according to His timing and sovereignty, we are unstable in our thinking, we are doubting Him.

There are a few examples of doubters in the Scriptures that can help us better understand doubt and reveal to us that doubt must be dealt with and restrained in our lives.

Examples of Doubters

The following examples of doubters will show that the believer is not alone in doubting.

Asaph

Asaph was a Levite who David had appointed to be a musician in the service of the Lord (1 Chronicles 16:4−7). Several of the Psalms are attributed to Asaph, including Psalm 73. This psalm starts with Asaph asserting that his feet had almost slipped because he envied the wicked and their prosperity.

Doubt had crept into Asaph's mind concerning the benefits of serving God. He might have questioned why God had not honored his pursuits for blessings, yet those who did not serve God seemed to be better off than he was.

Asaph was struck with doubt, but he did not let that doubt fester and cause him to fall. Yes, he almost fell, but he did not fall. Psalm 73:2–3 (NIV) says: But as for me, my feet had almost slipped; I had nearly lost my foothold. For I envied the arrogant when I saw the prosperity of the wicked.

Upon seeing and acknowledging the condition of his heart, Asaph went into the temple (Psalm 73:16–17) and brought his troubled thoughts before God. And, when he did, he came to understand the destiny of the wicked. He learned in his time before the Lord that their prosperity was only temporary and that it was destined to end with destruction.

This experience drew Asaph closer to God. His doubt led him to the brink, but he took it to God and God helped him see that He was sufficient for him. Asaph received a deeper understanding of the ways of God, and he was strengthened by that insight. Because of how Asaph handled the situation, doubt was not spiritually harmful to him, instead it helped him grow in faith.

THOMAS

Not until Thomas saw the risen Lord did he believe that Jesus had risen from the dead. Thomas was one of the twelve who had followed Jesus for three years. He was not with the other disciples when Jesus first appeared to them after His resurrection, so he found it hard to believe that Jesus was alive. After all, he had seen Jesus die. For him, the thought that Jesus was now alive was too much to believe.

Thomas said, "Unless I see the nail marks in his hands and put my finger where the nails were, and put my hand into his side, I will not believe" (John 20:25, NIV). Like Thomas, our senses will limit us in matters concerning the Kingdom. Doubt demands evidence. Faith, on the other hand, needs no visible evidence, it is the essence of what we want from God; it is "the evidence of things not [yet] seen" (Hebrews 11:1, emphasis added). Faith does not require natural proof or data.

Thomas wanted proof, so Jesus said to him, "Put your finger here; see my hands. Reach out your hand and put it into my side. Stop doubting and believe" (John 20:27, NIV). Jesus did not chasten Thomas for his doubt, but instead, Jesus challenged Thomas to believe.

GIDEON

God saw greatness in Gideon, but Gideon did not see the same thing in himself. Gideon thought so little of himself that he even doubted that God could use him. Is that you or do you know anyone like that?

> **Judges 6:12, 14–15,** (NIV, emphasis added) — *When the angel of the Lord appeared to Gideon, he said, "The Lord is with you, <u>mighty warrior</u>." The Lord turned to him and said, "Go in <u>the strength you have</u> and save Israel out of Midian's hand. Am I not sending you?" "Pardon me, my lord," Gideon replied, "but how can I save Israel? <u>My clan is the weakest in Manasseh, and I am the least in my family</u>."*

Amazing! The God Who created Gideon, the God Who knows everything about him told Gideon that he was strong and that he was a mighty warrior, but his response was loaded with excuses: his clan was the weakest, and not only that, but he was also the least in his family. Gideon had low self-esteem. He thought very little of himself and what God said to him was not changing his self-concept.

Gideon had so much doubt that even after being told by the God Who created him that he was indeed a mighty warrior, he wanted a sign from God to show him that it was so (Judges 6:17). Again, we see here that doubt demands evidence, and sometimes doubt can be so overwhelming that we demand an abundance of evidence.

Gideon asked for a sign, and he got it, but was that enough? How much doubt was Gideon really battling?

> **Judges 6:21** (NIV) —*Then the angel of the Lord touched the meat and the unleavened bread with the tip of the staff that was in his hand. Fire flared from the rock, consuming the meat and the bread. And the angel of the Lord disappeared.*

In Judges 6:14, the angel of the Lord said to Gideon, "Go in the strength you have and save Israel out of Midian's hand. Am I not sending you?" but look at what happened in verses 36 to 38 (NIV, emphasis added):

> *Gideon said to God, "If you will save Israel by my hand as you have promised—look, I will place a wool fleece on the threshing floor. If there is dew only on the fleece and all the ground is dry, then I will know that you will save Israel by my hand, as you said." And that is what happened. Gideon rose early the next day; he squeezed the fleece and wrung out the dew—a bowlful of water.*

It is clear to Gideon that the messenger is an angel of God, so he knows the authenticity and the authority of the word he is receiving, but he finds it difficult to accept. This is exactly what doubt is. We know or are aware of the thing, but we question the truth of the thing. He starts out with "if," which connotes uncertainty, then he proposes to seek more evidence for only then could he know that God would indeed save Israel by his hand. God gave him his quest. The next morning, Gideon could squeeze out a bowl full of water from the fleece. But wait, was that enough to settle Gideon's doubt? No.

> **Judges 6:39–40** (NIV) — *Then Gideon said to God, "Do not be angry with me. Let me make just one more request. Allow me one more test with the fleece, but this time make the fleece dry and let the ground be covered with dew." That night God did so. Only the fleece was dry; all the ground was covered with dew.*

Gideon offered to test God yet another time, and God passed the test. Gideon saw a problem, but he couldn't see the solution. Gideon doubted how God could use one man to turn the tide against Israel's oppressors. He thought, maybe, but surely not him. Gideon was in deep doubt. He tested God twice, even after God proved to him the first time that it was Him.

Doubt demands evidence, but even with evidence, we often do not believe. We know the truth that we have received or experienced, but doubt blurs our vision, and casts obscurities on the truth.

Doubt Versus Unbelief

It is important to understand the difference between doubt and unbelief. Faith says, "He can." Doubt says, "Will He?" But unbelief says, "He can't." To doubt is to question what you know, unbelief is a determined refusal to believe. One must have something to doubt, and doubt usually focus on or question what the person knows, has been told, or has experienced. Doubt is a struggle faced by the believer, but unbelief is a condition, a state of mind of the unbeliever. Doubts come and go, but unbelief is a conclusion someone reaches—a deliberate decision to not believe. Doubt and faith can coexist in someone's life, but unbelief cannot coexist with faith. Unbelief is like complete blindness and doubt is like blurred vision.

Doubt is like temptation and unbelief is like sin. Just as sin can creep in during moments of temptation, if not addressed, doubt can mushroom into unbelief. Therefore, it is essential that we deal with our doubts before the Lord. Asaph did just that, and in the end, his doubt was a source of spiritual growth and enlightenment, not his detriment.

Consider Job and his wife. They both experienced the same disasters. In one day, they lost everything, their business, wealth, property, and their seven children, but they both responded in completely different ways. Job wrestled with God. He questioned God and potentially doubted Him because he could not understand the ways of God in that moment. But his wife closed the door on God and on anything to do with Him: "Curse God and die" she said. Job might have doubted, but his wife suffered the fate of unbelief. Their response to suffering was most revealing about their relationship with God, and our response to trying times will be most revealing about our relationship with our Father.

CHAPTER FOUR: SEVEN MAIN TAKEAWAYS

1. Unbelief is the opposite of faith. Unbelief connotes blindness and faith connotes sightedness. One cannot be blind and have sight at the same time.

2. We stand strong in Christ by faith, but unbelief separates us from Christ.

3. Doubt is not the absence of faith; doubt is the questioning of faith.

4. Faith says, "He can." Doubt says, "Will He?" But unbelief says, "He can't."

5. Doubt is a struggle faced by the believer, but unbelief is a condition, a state of mind of the unbeliever.

6. Doubts come and go, but unbelief is a conclusion someone reaches.

7. Doubt is like temptation and unbelief is like sin. Just as sin can creep in during moments of temptation, if not addressed, doubt can develop into unbelief.

WHY DOUBT?

Your faith can move mountains and your
doubt can create them.
—Anonymous

According to Christian philosopher and author Os Guiness, "To doubt is to waver between the two, to believe and disbelieve at once and so be "in two minds."[9] Doubting does not make you an unbeliever, neither does doubting mean you have no faith. The father who brought his son to Jesus to be healed "exclaimed, 'I do believe; help me overcome my unbelief!'" (Mark 9:24, NIV). And as explained in the preceding chapter, unbelief here does not mean no belief; it means weak faith. So, the father was telling Jesus that he did have faith in Him, but he was also grappling with doubt. Thus, a believer could experience doubt while still very much being a believer. In fact, Scripture is full of examples of believers experiencing and wrestling with doubt while being believers.

Doubt can be spiritually fatal, but it can also spur a person on to spiritual growth. Whether viewed as fatal or advantageous, the concept of doubt is not welcomed in most Christian circles, and I don't think it should be either. We should not make room for doubt. We should consciously resist it at all costs. God is faithful and true, and there is no variance in Him. He said so in His Word, and He proves it to us over and over. He loves us endlessly and unconditionally. His thoughts toward us are always good, and so why should we doubt this good Father?

We are not perfect, and our loving Father knows that. So yes, despite the faithfulness of our loving Father, we will doubt sometimes, but we should not accommodate it. We should not welcome it or make it a natural part of our faith-walk. I am in no way suggesting that we condemn those who struggle with doubt, but I am proposing that we set our standard to the level of unwavering faith in Jesus, not doubt.

WHY DO WE DOUBT?

Some wrongfully assume that people doubt because of some sort of intellectual deficiency. Maybe they just don't have enough facts. Maybe they just didn't get all the details. Or maybe they just aren't highly intelligent. But doubt is not usually due to lack of information. In reality, doubters must have information in order to doubt. One cannot doubt without having something to question. Doubters receive information, and then question it; that is doubt. Certainly, some doubters may not have all the answers to their questions, but the fact still remains, they must have some answers or some form of information with which to wrestle.

It is said that truth is relative, but the Word of God is not just truth, it is *the* Truth. So, why do the people of God have the spoken Word, the Truth of the one true and living God, but still doubt? There could be an extensive list of reasons why people who say they live by faith in Jesus Christ doubt, but I will address a few that I think are most prominent.

FAILED EXPECTATIONS FROM GOD

Based on my experiences over the many years I've been in the church, I believe a major reason Christians doubt is because they expect God to act in ways other than He has promised to act. If a Christian thinks the Lord should do this or that, but then the Lord does not do this or that, then that Christian might very well question God's promises. That is doubt.

Ofttimes, as Christians, we are expecting God to do this or that because His Word says so. The Word of God does say, "By his wounds we are healed" (Psalm 53:5b, NIV). So, many Christians hold God to these words, expecting Him to heal every sickness they pray about. But those same Christians forget to pay full attention to Psalm 34:19 (AMP), which says, "Many hardships and perplexing circumstances confront the righteous, But the Lord rescues him from them all." Clearly, according to this scripture, believers in Jesus will face hardships, and not a few hardships, but many. Sickness is one of the hardships we will endure, but the Lord does promise to deliver us out of all sufferings we encounter. However, He did not say that the way of delivery would always be healing or a miracle. False expectations like these make a host of Christians question God. It causes some to be angry at God, and indeed, it causes many to doubt God.

John the Baptist is a classic example in the Scripture of a powerful man of God who had bouts with doubt. Jesus referred to John the Baptist as one of the greatest of all prophets (Luke 7:26–28). John the Baptist stands out from the rest. Isaiah predicted he would be the voice crying in the wilderness, and he grew up as a Nazarite. God told him that he would see the Messiah, and God gave him a sign. Indeed, at Jesus' baptism, the Holy Spirit descended upon Jesus like a dove, and then John the Baptist heard God say, "This is my beloved son in whom I am well pleased" (Matthew 3:17, KJV). That is a lot of solid evidence that should never make a person doubt. John himself announced Jesus as the Messiah (John 1:29). So, he knew who Jesus was.

But John the Baptist was imprisoned, and things were not going the way he expected them to go. So, he began to doubt. Even though he heard the voice of God with his own ears declaring Jesus as His Son, and even though he himself had declared Jesus to be the Messiah, he sent some of his disciples to ask Jesus, "Are You the Expected One (the Messiah), or should we look for someone else [who will be the promised One]?" (Matthew 11:3, AMP). In other words, John was saying, "I did not expect things to go this way when the Messiah showed up, so are you really the Messiah?"

With all the irrefutable evidence placed before him, he must have been aware of what was going on, but he was in a hard place then. He was in prison, and it did not look good for him. This state of mind created the right environment for doubt. None of the factual matters he received were proved wrong or false, but he doubted, nonetheless. So, we see having information does not mean one does not doubt.

Even after we have compelling evidence of God's faithfulness, we can still doubt when we pray and things do not go as expected, when we make declarations over our situations and nothing changes, or when we get words of prophecy and nothing changes. When the Lord does not act the way we expect Him to act, our confidence in God tends to wane. We begin to question and doubt God.

68

FALSE EXPECTATIONS

Another contributor to doubt is what I call false expectations. Too many believers have the false expectation of thinking that Christians should not suffer in anyway. They think that because they serve God they will have no family problems, their children will fail at nothing, they will never get a deadly diagnosis, they will never experience extended unemployment or financial challenges, they will never be in a major automobile accident, and on and on. When these Christians go through trials or when other believers go through hardship, they tend to ask, "Where is God?" But in such doubt, they forget that God has already promised to be our Shepherd. Indeed, we shall not want (Psalm 23:1). He also said that He would never leave us or forsake us (Hebrews 13:5), and furthermore, He said He is the same yesterday, today, and forevermore (Hebrews 13:8). When we ask questions such as, "Where is God?", we are doubting God.

I believe many Christians are in this place of delusion because first, in large part, the Christian church has misinformed the people, and second, we fail to study the Word of God ourselves. The false gospel that life will be better, and no suffering will befall us when we come to Christ has fooled countless Christians. Many Christians have been taught to believe that we should not go through difficult times and, thus, are living a life with such false expectation. Therefore, whenever they experience difficult times, they question and doubt God.

It is so that many Christians doubt God, but in fact, we are not really doubting the God of the Bible. When we have these unrealistic or unscriptural expectations, our assumptions of God are false. We think that God is supposed to protect us and our family from all physical harm, and when He does not, we doubt Him. But the one true God did not promise us such protection. Consequently, the god that we are doubting is not the God of the Bible. When we believe that God has made promises that He has not or when God becomes the candy machine in the sky, we are setting ourselves up for unwarranted doubt.

The Word of God tells us that we will go through fiery trials: "Beloved, do not be surprised at the fiery ordeal which is taking place to test you [that is, to test the quality of your faith], as though something strange or unusual were happening to you" (1 Peter 4:12, AMP). There are many other scriptures—James 1:2, 12; 1 Peter 5:10; Romans 12:12, to name a few—that tell us that we as believers are not spared the hardships of life. But what we do know is that God will take us through them and that trials come to make us stronger not to make us doubt God. Romans 5:3–5 (KJV) says:

> *And not only so, but we glory in tribulations also: knowing that tribulation worketh patience; And patience, experience; and experience, hope: And hope maketh not ashamed; because the love of God is shed abroad in our hearts by the Holy Ghost which is given unto us.*

The steps of a righteous man are ordered by the Lord (Psalm 37:23), so we must rest in this Word, knowing that if we are in God's will, whatever happens to us is ordered by Him. God is faithful, He is dependable, and He is steadfast. "God is faithful, by whom ye were called unto the fellowship of his Son Jesus Christ our Lord" (1 Corinthians 1:9, KJV). The Lord our God "keepeth covenant and mercy with them that love him and keep his commandments to a thousand generations" (Deuteronomy 7:9, KJV), so we have good reason to trust Him. We are more than conquerors through Him who loved us (Romans 8:37), so we have no reason for doubt when we face hardships.

EMOTIONAL DISTRESS

Elijah is the champion in one of the most dramatic stories in the Bible. This is the most impressive of Elijah's feats as a prophet. But due to fear of one woman, Elijah, a powerful prophet of God who God had just used to demonstrate His power to a host of idol worshippers, slumped into despair and doubt. We are told in 1 Kings 18 how he confronted the prophets of Baal, confounded their belief, publicly humiliated them, brought them to utter shame, and then destroyed four hundred and fifty of them. Elijah had definitively proven that his God was all-powerful, but what might have been the worst day of his life came on that same day as his greatest victory.

That day should have been his time of triumph. It should have been his moment of celebration and vindication. Yet it was then that he experienced an insurmountable flood of despair and doubt. He quickly moved from a man full of confidence to a man who was engulfed by terror. Hours before his "fall," his courage and conviction were feared and respected. Everyone knew Elijah and what he preached. But now he was fleeing for his life. Right after he killed four hundred and fifty prophets, he became fearful of the death threats from one woman. In that moment, he doubted the presence of God, and he doubted the keeping grace of God. He was feeling abandoned by God. He was emotionally spent.

Emotional distress creates an open door for doubt to creep in. Emotional distress negatively impacts our self-esteem, our self-confidence, our ability to reason, and even our ability to stay in touch with reality. Consequently, Elijah's self-confidence and his ability to reason waned under such emotional distress. Upon hearing the threat, he lost focus. He forgot about the strength and power of the God he had just bragged about and instead held onto a false reality that could bring him no hope.

Stricken with doubt, Elijah fled to the wilderness and begged God to take his life. The following verses in 1 Kings 19 (NIV) give an account of the emotional state of Elijah:

> Verses 3–4 — *Elijah was afraid and ran for his life. When he came to Beersheba in Judah, he left his servant there, while he himself went a day's journey into the wilderness. He came to a broom bush, sat down under it and prayed that he might die.*

> Verse 10 — *"I have had enough, Lord," he said. "Take my life; I am no better than my ancestors." He replied, "I have been very zealous for the Lord God Almighty. The Israelites have rejected your covenant, torn down your altars, and put your prophets to death with the sword. I am the only one left, and now they are trying to kill me too."*

> Verse 14 — *He replied, "I have been very zealous for the Lord God Almighty. The Israelites have rejected your covenant, torn down your altars, and put your prophets to death with the sword. I am the only one left, and now they are trying to kill me too."*

This state of emotional distress brought a strong sense of loneliness upon Elijah. He felt he was the only one upholding God, but not counting those beyond the borders of Israel, there were seven thousand in the small country of Israel who were quietly following God's plan. But unknown to Elijah, God was fully aware of his loneliness and had already provided for his need. Elijah couldn't see it because doubt had clouded his vision.

It is when we are low in spirit, like Elijah, that perplexing questions emerge. It is in these times of doubt that our perception of God and our self-concept unravel, making room for change, be it better or worse. These times can take us deeper into undiscovered truths and drive us to examine our allegiance to God. James 5:17 (NIV) says, "Elijah was a human being, even as we are." In Elijah's case, fear and doubt shattered his self-assurance and self-confidence, but it did not stop there. This experience brought him to a deeper knowledge of God and connected him with like-minded individuals who were also standing for God.

Emotional distress is one of the reasons people doubt, believers and unbelievers alike. Tragic experiences and trauma can evoke doubt:

- Your minor child dies.
- Your spouse of over thirty years dies.
- A parent dies.
- Your business which you invested in for many years fails and you lose a huge sum of money.
- You receive a life-threatening diagnosis from your doctor.
- You lose your job and are finding it extremely difficult to find employment.
- You've been betrayed by someone you trust and least expected to hurt you.
- You're a pastor and one of your ministers led a church split, and you lost a good portion of the membership.

These are but a snippet of the many things that can put a person in emotional distress.

Another subtle emotionally distressing condition that can make us doubt God is when we take on too much. I use the word subtle because being overwhelmed with work does not immediately look like a condition that can contribute to doubt. However, when we take on too much, we run the risk of doing a less than optimal job at anything. And if we have high expectations but do not meet them, the right condition for doubt is then created. Also, when we are worried and stressed about the many things that we are doing all at once, doubt can easily creep in. We must be careful because taking on too much may seem like the right thing to do, but it can be counterproductive to the most important thing, which is our spiritual life.

WRONG FOCUS

Focus is everything. What we keep our eyes on matters a whole lot. Usually, we achieve whatever we focus on, and we end up wherever we set our attention.

The Bible gives an account of Jesus walking across the surface of a lake, and at which time, He invited Peter to get out of his boat and join Him. When Peter stepped out of the boat, he had his eyes on Jesus, but when he changed focus and turned his attention to the raging waves, he began to sink. At first, Peter's confidence in Jesus' power sustained him as he walked on the water, but as doubt quickly crept in, he just as quickly began to sink. As he started to sink, "Jesus reached out his hand and caught him. "You of little faith," he said, "why did you doubt?" (Matthew 24:31, AMP).

Like Peter, we begin to doubt God when we focus on our problems and not the Problem Solver. If Peter had kept his eyes on Jesus, doubt would have no place in him, and therefore he would not have started to sink. If we keep our eyes on Jesus and not on our problems, we will not doubt God.

Doubting God does not mean we don't believe God can deliver; it means we have a divided mind—part of us think the situation is going to kill us and the other part of us think God can deliver us. We only think the situation is going to overtake us when we focus on it. We give way to doubt when we think about how painful, how unfair, how unexpected, or how overwhelming the situation is instead of thinking about God's faithfulness, His omnipotence, and the many prior occasions on which He has delivered us. So, the doubter believes God can, but because they're so focused on the situation, they begin to question *if* God will deliver them. Their mind is in two camps: "God can" and "will God?"

The Greek word for "doubt" in Matthew 14:31 is *distazo,* which is related to the adverb *dis*. *Dis* means "twice" and comes from *duo*, which means "two." So, *distazo*, which is translated doubt, means to have second thoughts, to think again, to waver, or to hesitate. This word is used only twice in the New Testament: Matthew 14:31 and Matthew 28:17. In both texts, it is related to people's opinion about the divine identity of Jesus,[10] and the divine identity of Jesus is the Word of God.

> **John 1:1−2** — *In the beginning was the Word, and the Word was with God, and the Word was God. He was with God in the beginning.*

> **John 1:14** — *The Word became flesh and made his dwelling among us. We have seen his glory, the glory*

of the one and only Son, who came from the Father,
full of grace and truth.

Therefore, if we walk by faith in Jesus Christ—the person of Jesus, the character and nature of Jesus—we must believe the Word of God.

In the Matthew 14 (NIV) account where Peter quickly started to sink after taking his eyes off Jesus, it was not the storm that the disciples were terrified of; it was what they thought to be a ghost which was walking toward them on the water: "When the disciples saw him walking on the lake, they were terrified. 'It's a ghost,' they said, and cried out in fear" (Verse 26). Jesus sensed their fear and "immediately said to them: 'Take courage! It is I. Don't be afraid'" (Verse 27). Then Peter, seeking assurance that this was really Jesus, not a ghost, said, "Lord, if it's you, tell me to come to you on the water" (Verse 28). I propose that when we doubt God while in the storms of life, we are indeed questioning the divine identity, the faithfulness, and the authenticity of the God we serve.

The act of Peter stepping out of the boat in the midst of a boisterous storm, walking on water, and then looking away from Jesus and focusing fearfully on the storm told Jesus he started out with some sense of boldness or some sense of faith and confidence in Jesus, but he doubted shortly thereafter. Jesus' words "You of little faith, why did you doubt?" (verse 31) refer to Peter's short-lived confidence.

Jesus was addressing the duplicity of Peter's mind— "I can walk on this water because Jesus bid me to come" and "this storm is going to kill me." In that moment, Peter questioned whether or not Jesus actually was the Son of God, the Creator and Sustainer who actually had power and authority over the natural elements and could keep him afloat on the surface of a lake in the middle of a raging storm. But to ensure that I give Peter the credit he deserves, he did pray, "Lord, save me!" The fact that Peter addressed Jesus as Lord tells me his faith, although little, was still there. So, you see, doubting does not mean no faith.

The critical question is not do we trust Jesus to do this or that for us, but do we believe that He is the one He claimed to be? As the disciples grew in awareness of the true identity of Jesus, so must we.

Unanswered Prayers

If we believe that God is who He says He is and will do what He has promised, why do so many of us habitually waver in our prayers? Instead of exercising bold faith, we come to the Lord hoping He will hear us and answer our prayers. With this kind of thinking, we cannot expect to receive anything from Him. James tells us that the one who doubts should not expect to receive anything from the Lord. James was speaking specifically about asking for wisdom, but because by nature, God is faithful and all His promises are yes and amen (2 Corinthians 1:20), we can generalize this principle to all requests we put before the Lord.

> **James 1:5–8** (NIV) — *If any of you lacks wisdom, you should ask God, who gives generously to all without finding fault, and it will be given to you. But when you ask, you must believe and not doubt, because the one who doubts is like a wave of the sea, blown and tossed by the wind. That person should not expect to receive anything from the Lord. Such a person is double-minded and unstable in all they do.*

One reason we are so prone to doubt—to waver between "God can" and "will God?"—is because we don't see God at work in our circumstances. Sometimes we ask and we don't get what we ask for, so to us, God did not answer our prayers. God already said that His ears are open to our cry (Psalm 34:15), so He always hear our prayers, and He always answer our prayers. I can assure you that God never reneges on His promises, neither is He ever incapable of doing what we ask of Him. His answer may not be what we want or expect, and thus, we may miss it when it comes, but He answers.

God is not a vending machine. He is not our Santa Claus. Neither is He some cosmic bellhop who jumps in response to our requests. He is omniscient. He sees the past, the present, and the future, and He knows the right time and the right way He should answer every prayer. His invisible hand is always at work on our behalf. He is always arranging situations to accomplish His will, opening hearts, and preparing us to receive what He wants to give, but we often do not see what He is doing because we are looking for Him to answer in the way we expect Him to answer. Some of us are presumptuous enough to tell God what we want, how we want it, and when we want it. God answers those prayers as well, but rest assured, He answers them His way and in our best interest. Even if the answer is no, He answers anyway.

The presumptuous and selfish ways we pray and the way we expect God to answer our prayers are sometimes due to lack of knowledge. We must know the ways of the God we serve. We must know Him. We must not only know about Him and what He can do, but also know who He is. If we don't know God's ways, we will be disappointed in His response. All too often our prayers are accompanied by expectations of how He will work, and when He does not intervene according to our timetable or anticipated method, we start to doubt. But placing our faith in the Lord and trusting in His good and perfect ways will give us unshakable faith as we wait for His answer.

CARNALLY MINDED

I must mention the sinful causes of doubt in this discussion because it is fundamental to why many believers doubt God. When we are not obeying God the way we should or when we have unrepented or habitual sins in our lives, we are going to be susceptible to doubting God at the most basic level. You cannot expect to live in sin and not have your beliefs seriously compromised.

A person with unrepented sin, one who has settled in a life marked by sin is satisfying their flesh, and when our minds are governed by the flesh, we are carnally minded. Therefore, the believer who lives as such is a carnal Christian, and carnal Christians will doubt God. The Scripture tells us that "to be carnally minded is death" (Romans 8:6, KJV)—not physical death, but spiritual death. Living a life that is centered around the satisfying of the flesh is one way to walk by sight and not by faith, and when we walk by sight and not by faith in Jesus Christ, we are carnally minded and are on our way to spiritual death.

The word carnal in the Greek means flesh, which is a reference to our sinful nature. Since all of us still have a sinful nature that dwells within us, we all have the potential to fall victim to becoming carnally minded. The backdrop to being carnally minded is threefold. We see this in 1 John 2:15-16 (NIV):

Do not love the world or anything in the world. If anyone loves the world, love for the Father is not in them. For everything in the world—the lust of the flesh, the lust of the eyes, and the pride of life—comes not from the Father but from the world.

Because the carnally minded lives to please the flesh, they pray and expect God to answer their prayers on their terms. They may say they look to God, but in reality, they have little interest in doing things God's way...whether they are aware of their state of mind or not. Clarence L. Haynes Jr. gives seven warning signs of a carnally minded Christian. These all point to the self-centered nature of the carnally minded:

1. Concern about yourself more than anything else.
2. Obsession with getting more and never satisfied with what you have.
3. Think you are more than what you really are.
4. Unwilling to forgive.
5. Seeking pleasure with no boundaries.
6. Worshipping people and ideas more than worshipping God.
7. Your love for others growing cold.[11]

These warning signs are all reasons the carnally minded pray and expect God to answer on their terms. For example, let us consider warning sign number two: obsession with getting more and never satisfied with what you have. You set your affections on material things; therefore, you will not be satisfied with what you have. You may live in a house that is quite suitable for the family, but you set your eyes on a bigger house, so you pray to God, asking Him to let the bank approve the loan for which you applied to purchase an unnecessarily larger house. However, God does not grant the request because He knows what is best for you and because He knows the end from the beginning. That "unanswered" prayer is not a faith-builder for you because you are blind to the ways of God. Consequently, you doubt God, and you carry that experience into the future and doubt Him the next time you pray.

Also remember that carnal Christians walk by sight— what they can see—and not by faith—what they cannot see in the flesh but know has already occurred in the Spirit. Therefore, the carnal Christian will look at their circumstances and become anxious instead of looking at what the God they serve can do for and through them while in their circumstances. The Christian whose first recourse is anything other than prayer, faith in the Word of God, and resting in Jesus is carnally minded.

We are called to a life of holiness. As followers of Jesus Christ, habitual sin should have no place in our lives. When we entertain sin in our lives, our faith in God will be gradually replaced with doubt. Far too often carnal Christians are unaware of the path they're on and when they get there, they're baffled as to how they got there. Sin will erode your confidence in God, but when you turn away from sin, your doubts will diminish and your confidence in God will grow.

RESPONDING TO DOUBT

Doubt is not the end of faith; it sits between faith and unbelief. Doubt is the lack of sureness of a perceived reality. You know it could be real, but you're not sure about it this time. As mentioned earlier, doubt does not mean no faith. Doubt questions one's beliefs; therefore, the doubting Christian knows God can, but asks, "Will He?" Doubt is natural. It comes to all of us periodically.

Rather than run from it, use it to your advantage. Bring your doubts to God like Asaph did. Seek answers to your doubts like Thomas did. When you do that, your doubts will lead to growth. So, doubt does not have to be fatal. Wrestling with doubts and resolving them can strengthen a Christian's faith. It is like refining a metal by burning off the impurities. The Christian who was strengthened by overcoming doubt can be a source of inspiration to others who are experiencing doubt.

Lack of information is not the cause of doubt, but the absence of sufficient or accurate information does cause doubt. Therefore, when you find yourself questioning some aspect of your faith or the things you believe, it makes good sense to invest time and effort in studying and seeking more and accurate information about the thing by which you are challenged. You must seek to better understand that thing. Perhaps your study will confirm what you believe and remove the doubt, or your study may show you that your belief is incorrect or too shallow. This will then offer the opportunity to grow.

Doubt is a tool of Satan to make you lack confidence in God's Word and question His truthfulness. Therefore, to overcome doubt, you must spend time in the Word to learn God's principles and His ways. As you learn about the ways of God, you will learn that He did indeed answer your prayers those many times you thought He did not. And your faith will grow as you see the unexpected ways that God has answered your prayers. As you learn about the ways of God, you will grasp what He wants to achieve in your life and how He goes about it. The Word of God will help you examine your past from a biblical perspective and will bring you in alignment with the will of God for you.

Remember, doubt is a plan of the adversary. He wants to erode your faith in Christ with this slow-moving weapon of his called doubt. Therefore, it is important to note that when dealing with doubt, you must not isolate yourself and go off in the dark. The devil wants you to cut ties with your Christian community when you struggle. He wants you alone so that he can have his way with you. But I urge you to do the opposite. Stay connected. Stay in the light. Face those challenges within a solid Christian community that can give you support and encouragement. After all, that is what the body of Christ is for: "Two are better than one, because they have a good return for their labor: If either of them falls down, one can help the other up. But pity anyone who falls and has no one to help them up" (Ecclesiastes 4:9–10, NIV).

Faith is the assurance, the foundation, the essence of things hoped for, and the conviction or proof of things we have not seen yet. With faith, we can have confidence even in the things we have not yet seen, because faith guarantees it. Faith releases and reveals what is not seen yet into the visible. Faith brings the unseen into reality. Faith is to light as doubt and unbelief are to darkness. The brighter the light, the less likely it is to see the darkness. Therefore, a means of overcoming doubt is to increase your faith. This is why the father in Mark 9:24 who brought his son to Jesus said, "Lord, I believe; help thou mine unbelief." He needed a faith boost, and therefore was asking Jesus to increase his faith. He was asking Jesus to brighten his light so that he can dispel the darkness of doubt.

So how do we boost our faith? The Bible tells us: "So then faith cometh by hearing, and hearing by the word of God" (Romans 10:17, KJV). In this text, the Greek word for the first "hearing" means hearing sound, and the second "hearing" means giving audience to. Those are two different things, as one can simply hear sound and not pay attention or understand. However, to give audience to something generally means to pay attention. So, faith comes by listening attentively to the Word, not just with our ears but with our heart. By listening with our heart, we will choose to believe God's Word and make the decision to trust Him and not doubt.

Secondly, James 1:5 tells us that if anyone lacks wisdom, they should ask God who gives generously without finding fault, and they will get it. Wisdom is the ability to understand the ways of God and apply the knowledge of His Word rightfully. This will certainly dispel doubt. There is no better cure for doubt than understanding and rightly applying the Word of God.

Chapter Five: Seven Main Takeaways

1. To doubt is to waver between the two, to believe and disbelieve at once, and so be "in two minds."

2. Doubting does not make you an unbeliever, neither does doubting mean you have no faith.

3. Doubt can be spiritually fatal, but it can also spur a person on to spiritual growth.

4. A major reason Christians doubt is because they expect God to act in ways other than He has promised to act.

5. Another contributor to doubt is false expectations. Too many believers have the false expectation of thinking that because they are Christians they should not suffer in any way.

6. Christians have false expectations of the Father because first, in large part, the Christian church has misinformed the people, and second, we fail to study the Word of God ourselves.

7. Many Christians doubt God, but in fact, we are not really doubting the God of the Bible.

SHADES OF DISCOURAGEMENT

We will get discouraged at times, but being discouraged does not mean all is lost. It is when we begin to blame others and stop trying that discouragement will take us under.

The prefix "dis" is negative. It means not or none; therefore, <u>dis</u>courage means not courage or none courage—no courage. To be discouraged is to be dispossessed of courage or self-confidence, to lose hope or spirit, to lose the will to press on, to be disheartened, intimidated, or overwhelmed, or to be beaten down, demoralized, or distressed. The Oxford Dictionary defines courage as bravery, valor, or strength in the face of pain or grief. Courage is further defined as the mental or moral strength to venture, persevere, and withstand danger, fear, or difficulty.

DISCOURAGEMENT AT VARYING DEGREES

Discouragement can be mild, moderate, or severe. Mild discouragement occurs when a person experiences minor problems or pressures that affect their emotions. For the most part, this level of discouragement goes unnoticed by others and is not long-lasting.

Moderate discouragement can happen when we face major problems or pressures. This level of discouragement affects not just our emotions, as emotions can be fleeting, but it affects our spirit, the undercurrent of our emotions. This negative change in our spirit is then manifested in our words and actions, making it easy for others to detect the presence of this inner disturbance.

Severe discouragement is crippling. It disables its hosts, and drains them of their spiritual, mental, emotional, and physical strength. This level of discouragement is very much like depression. When in this state, we have no desire, energy, or ability to go on.

CONDITIONS FOR DISCOURAGEMENT

The following conditions produce discouragement.

WHEN DOING THE RIGHT THING

It is important to state early on that discouragement can come when we are putting energy into something but are not getting the desired results. Such circumstances may rob us of the will or strength to keep trying. Many of us become disheartened and weak, and some of us even become pessimistic when we try and don't see the results we desire. But it is especially true when we are spiritually weak and vulnerable. When we become pessimistic about a challenging situation, we let our guard down, and that is when Satan strikes. We must therefore make good use of the spiritual armor (Ephesians 6:10–18) God has provided to protect us against Satan's attacks.

88

Doing something and, even more so, doing the right thing does not stop the enemy of your soul from attacking. In fact, that is when he strategizes even more to make sure he throws you off course. All discouragement is of Satan or self; it is never of God. God is called the God of all comfort (2 Corinthians 1:3), and comfort here means encouragement. As you forge forward to do the right thing, the devil will try to stop you by way of discouragement. One of the enemy's greatest tools is discouragement, so he will use it at every opportunity. This is the tool he often uses to make you feel bad about yourself, to hinder your progress, and stop you from being successful.

Amid your sincere efforts to do the right thing, Satan will lie to you about yourself and about what you are doing. His lies are the source of every discouragement; they breed self-pity, self-condemnation, self-doubt, insecurity, and more. Note that all the deadly effects of discouragement point to you. Discouragement is accusatory. Due to discouragement, you will doubt yourself and you will lose confidence. The only one to suffer these losses is you. Discouragement is designed to block you from moving forward.

UNMET EXPECTATIONS

Disappointment, which if not addressed can lead to discouragement, generally occurs when our expectations— what we think should happen—do not align with what actually happens.

Sometimes, we become disappointed and ultimately discouraged because we are too idealistic or because our goals are unrealistic. This is especially true for perfectionists. It is also common among believers who take the Word of God out of context or take parts of the Word without considering the whole. For example, the Word says that we shall be like a tree planted by the rivers of waters that brings forth its fruit in its season, and it says that we, being like this tree, our leaves shall not wither and whatever we do will prosper (Psalm 1:3). The Word also says that God will bless the work of our hands (Deuteronomy 28:12). So, the believers who take the Word out of context may be confused when their businesses fail or when their investments do not yield a profit. Bewilderment follows these experiences because these loved ones fail to realize that there is an adversary out there whose main objective is to steal, kill, and destroy. If they do not understand that God calls us to be vigilant and of a sober mind, watching out for the schemes of the devil who roam around like a roaring lion looking for someone to devour (1 Peter 5:8), they will be discouraged when they're attacked by Satan.

Pastors are good candidates for discouragement due to unmet expectations. Warren Wiersbe observes, "The pastor, if he is dedicated at all, is a man of ideals; he wants to achieve for the glory of God. Yet, no matter how hard he prays and works, it seems that his goals forever elude him" (ibid., p. 265).[12] Pastors are prone to discouragement when they invest in someone and nurture them in Christ, and they backslide. They are also prone to discouragement when people leave their church and become members of another assembly. And I'm sure they are challenged by discouragement when they go through the all too familiar church split that is widespread in the body of Christ. Coupled with idealism, discouragement often comes when people disappoint us.

The Apostle Paul might have been discouraged because Demas had backslid.

2 Timothy 4:9–11 (KJV) — *Do thy diligence to come shortly unto me: For Demas hath forsaken me, having loved this present world, and is departed unto Thessalonica; Crescens to Galatia, Titus unto Dalmatia. Only Luke is with me. Take Mark, and bring him with thee: for he is profitable to me for the ministry.*

He asked Timothy to come to him quickly and bring Mark with him because only Luke was with him. Paul wrote this letter from prison. I believe there was a sense of dismay in Paul because Demas had backslid and gone back into the world.

Pastors are a ready target for criticism and slander. Many are always under scrutiny by the public. Consequently, they are at high risk for discouragement if they don't keep their focus on why they do what they do, and for Whom they do what they do. Void of maintaining the mindset that they are working for the Lord with the goal of hearing "well done" in the end, they will be bombarded with and overcome by discouragement.

Steven J. Cole states in Overcoming Discouragement[13] that when Charles Spurgeon began his ministry in London at age 20, he was barraged with criticism in the press, and much of it came from other ministers who were jealous of his success. At the start of his ministry, over 5,000 came to hear him speak each week. "Several pastors wrote that they doubted his conversion. Others predicted that he would be like a rocket that would climb high and then drop out of sight. Another asked for proof that Spurgeon was the Lord's servant and that his ministry was heart-searching, Christ-exalting, truth-unfolding, sinner-converting, church-feeding, and soul-saving" (C. H. Spurgeon Autobiography [Banner of Truth], 1:305). Charles Spurgeon went through this, and many pastors are experiencing the same today.

Disappointment with God is another cause of discouragement. You prayed and worked hard for something, but the results fell far short of your expectations and hopes. From your perspective, it would have been for God's glory if it had happened, but it did not. So yes, you are disappointed with God. The disappointment runs even deeper because you stood on the promises of God. You declared His Word over the situation and prayed in faith. You claimed related promises from the Bible as you prayed and worked, but to you, it looks like God did not keep His promises. This could leave a person wondering whether they should ever try again to do anything for the Lord.

WHEN SATAN LIES TO YOU

Jesus said that the devil is a liar, and the father of lies (John 8:44). He is the originator of lies. Every word that comes out of his mouth is a lie. He is lying even when he is quoting the Word of God.

The devil cannot make us do anything, but he is a master deceiver who is very experienced at making people believe God did not come through for them. The devil came to kill, steal, and destroy (John 10:10). Jesus Christ, in contrast, came to give not just life, but life more abundantly. Jesus is "the way, the truth, and the life" (John 14:6). Satan is the way to death.

You become susceptible to Satan's lies when you lose sight of God's ways or when you do not put your confidence in God's provision for your every need. Ephesians 6:16 (NIV) tells us to "take up the shield of faith, with which you can extinguish all the flaming arrows of the evil one." Faith in the Word of God and faith in the omnipotence and the faithfulness of God will shield you from the fiery darts of discouragement.

When rightly utilizing this shield, the lies of the enemy will not work. At every attempt, you will be able to counteract his lies with the Word of God.

When he tells you that you can't, tell him you can do all things through Christ who strengthens you (Philippians 4:13). The worst thing about this lie is that it can stop you before you even start. It can cause self-doubt as you face life's challenges. Yes, the devil will tell you that you can't handle work and school, so quit trying. He will tell you that you're not good enough to be married to anyone, so stop expecting marriage, let alone a good marriage, but the Word of God says you can.

Sometimes it takes only one failed attempt on your part to make him seize the opportunity to tell you that everything you touch will go wrong, so it's no use trying. He wants you to believe the number one lie: you are a failure. That being said, why even follow Christ? After all, you're not good enough, so just keep living the degraded life you're living. Oh, start a business! That is insane. The devil is ready to show you all the reasons why starting a business is well beyond you. He is a liar. Do not believe him.

Another common lie of the enemy is the words "God won't." It is commonly used as:

- God won't forgive you.
- God won't forgive you again.
- God won't help you.
- God won't hear you.
- God does not love you.

Lies! If you look closely at these lies, you will see that they are the extreme opposite of what our loving Father says in His Word. This is why we must wear the shield of faith, which is the Word of God. If you do not wear—know, understand, and apply—the Word of God, the devil will have liberty to tell you any lie, and you will believe them.

Now let us look at a very small portion of God's Word that outright negate these lies of the enemy. This is what the Lord says in Isaiah 65:24 (NIV): "Before they call I will answer; while they are still speaking I will hear." So, instead of God won't, God will. Matthew 7:7 (NIV) says, "Ask, and it will be given to you; seek, and you will find; knock, and it will be opened to you." And Psalm 46:1 (KJV) says, "God is our refuge and strength, a very present help in trouble." So, God will help you and God will hear you. John 1:9 (KJV) says, "If we confess our sins, he is faithful and just to forgive us our sins, and to cleanse us from all unrighteousness." So, God will forgive you. Micah 7:18–19 says, "Who is a God like you, who pardons sin and forgives the transgression of the remnant of his inheritance? You do not stay angry forever but delight to show mercy. You will again have compassion on us; you will tread our sins underfoot and hurl all our iniquities into the depths of the sea." So, God will forgive you again.

Another lie of the enemy is to tell you nobody cares. This lie is very much like the first recorded lie. His approach to Eve was that God did not have her best interest at heart. According to him, she could have more. She had known only good, but she could have knowledge of both good and evil, and God was withholding it from her. She believed his lie, and it has caused the entire human race much pain and misery.

God cares. He showed His love for man with the ultimate price. He did not spare His own Son but delivered Him up for us all (Romans 8:21). If He can do that, why wouldn't He also freely give us all things?

God also shows that He cares by putting people who genuinely care about us in our lives and in our paths. That may mean you let some people in your life and you share your hurts and discouragements with them when all you want to do is hide. It is natural to withdraw from people when we are discouraged or hurt, even from those who truly love and care about us, but that is counterproductive. Healing will come only when we let God in and when we give way to the plan of God for our lives. And God's plan involves accepting the provisions He has made for us, including people.

The church is a vehicle that the Lord uses to make this provision for us; it is an important function of the church. We must not neglect assembling with other believers, instead, we should exhort one another, and even more so as we see the nearness of the day of the Lord (Hebrews 10:25). We well know that not everyone will respond to our expressed need as God desires, but if we ask the Lord to lead us to the right person, He will. Why? Because He cares.

Another lie of the enemy is to tell you that you don't matter. I think two of the most ridiculous lies the enemy could ever tell a person is they don't matter and that God doesn't love them. When we consider the price God paid just to redeem us back to Himself so that He can have fellowship with us, it seems near impossible for anyone to believe such a lie. But sadly, the enemy of our souls is so cunning that he manages to deceive many into believing these outrageous lies.

Despite when, how, and through whom you came into this world, you matter, and God loves you no less than anyone else. You matter to God. "For God so loved the world, that he gave his only begotten Son, that whosoever believeth in him should not perish, but have everlasting life" (John 3:16, KJV). You are worth so much to God that He took on human flesh, set His deity aside and stepped out of heaven into this sinful world, took the punishment for your sins, died on a cross, and rose again. And His love continues. He lives forevermore to make intercession for you (Hebrews 7:5). You, as a child of God, matter, not because of what you can do, not because of who you are, but because of Whose you are.

He loves you just as much as He loves His Son Jesus Christ (John 17:23). Jesus being the once and for all sacrifice won't need to, but if He had to go back to the Cross of Calvary one more time just for you, He would. He loves you so much that there is absolutely nothing you can do to make Him love you any less or any more than He already does. He already loves you unconditionally, endlessly, and recklessly. If you know and embrace the life-giving truth about the love of God, you will never believe this lie of the enemy and you will not be overcome by self-loathing. God loves you and He wants the best for you. So, it is very sad that, not knowing the loving nature of God Jehovah is a root cause of mankind's problem, even among those who confess to be followers of Jesus.

The final lie I wish to discuss from the enemy that ushers many into discouragement is that it's too late. This is a powerful lie of the enemy because often it appears to be true. You've been diligently trying to achieve a certain goal, but you are not making the progress you desire. Through the natural eyes, it will appear as if it is indeed too late. You made some mistakes early in life, and so you have wasted some precious years. Now you have turned your life over to the Lord and are ready to redeem the time as best you can. Because of the place from which you are coming, the devil will see this as an opportune time to tell you that it's too late, and if you are not grounded in God, you will likely believe it and become discouraged. The devil will bear down on you so hard that the feeling of urgency that should prompt you to action and to make up some of the time you have lost will become his tool to intensify discouragement.

But God says that His mercy is new every morning (Lamentations 3:23), which means every morning you get a new start at life. On the day before, you spent your day's supply of mercy and while sleeping, God refills your mercy account so that you can go on the next day. God's mercies are new every morning, so, it is never too late.

Psalm 103:8 (AMP) adds to this. It says, "The Lord is merciful and gracious, Slow to anger and abounding in compassion and lovingkindness." So, here we see that God is not calling time. He is extending a whole lot of mercy toward you. You might have wasted many years, but He is gracious and slow to anger. It is true that yesterday is gone and will not come again, but you have today. The enemy wants you to languish in yesterday's mistakes. He wants to use guilt, regret, and shame to fuel his assault on you. But you must know and believe that it is not too late. Do not believe the lie of the enemy.

SIGNS OF DISCOURAGEMENT

The enemy knows that if he can dismantle our courage, we will be ineffective at meeting our life goals or accomplish anything for Christ. This lack of courage, namely discouragement, causes us to go back and forth in our minds instead of being steadfast in what the Word of God says. So, we see that the enemy uses doubt—a divided mind—and discouragement together to achieve his destructive goals. The combination of doubt and discouragement affects our ability to make wise decisions and affects our every doing. Therefore, no matter what you're doing, you will feel a heaviness hanging over you as if a dark cloud covers your entire thought life. This is discouragement. This is what makes it so difficult to keep going when one is discouraged.

THE BLAME GAME

When discouraged, people often fall prey to the "blame game." It somehow seems to ease the pain when we point a finger at someone else. Some even blame God, because to them, He has allowed painful circumstances in their life.

Perhaps you made some poor choices in the past. Now you look at your accomplishments and that of others your age. In your eyes, you have fallen short, so, you feel discouraged. The answer is not to blame your parents for a poor upbringing and bad examples. Blaming others will get you no farther in life than you are. Instead, it will only drag you deeper into discouragement, making it even more difficult to overcome. No healing or restoration will come from blaming anyone for the hardships in your life.

It is best to take responsibility for today and stop expecting others to pay for what they allegedly did to you. Gillian Duce says, "You do not blame your shadow for the shape of your body. Just the same: Do not blame others for the shape of your experience."

LOW MOTIVATION TO TAKE ON NEW TASKS

Discouragement will sap your energy or your drive. Discouragement happens because you focus on what did not happen, and as long as you keep looking at the loss, you will be discouraged. Because you are looking at what did not happen, the motivation to try something new will be minimal. Discouragement will drain you of your enthusiasm to get up and go. This then makes a person less likely to take on new tasks.

It is what we think about and what we focus on that really matters. What you did may not have yielded the results you were expecting, but in all your efforts, there must have been something good. To ward off discouragement, you must find that good in a bad situation and dwell on it. Even if ninety-nine percent of what happened was not good, you still have one percent of good. Philippians 4:8 tell us to think upon things that are honest, just, pure, lovely, and of good report, especially if there be any virtue or praiseworthiness in them. So, the remedy is to identify the good in all the losses and think upon it. Now, I'm in no way saying you should totally ignore the fact that your efforts failed. I am, however, saying the way in which we think upon them matters a whole lot. We must think upon the things that did not work to learn from them, not to agonize over them.

Failure to See the Impact of Your Work

Discouragement can make a person want to give up. Failure causes disappointment, which leads to discouragement, and therefore creates doubt about the impact of what you do. But your failed effort does not define you, and it does not represent your work in its entirety. Though you want to take note of the event and learn from it, you must separate the event from who you are and what you do.

FAILURE TO SEE OR THINK YOU HAVE ANY OPPORTUNITY TO ADVANCE

When a person is discouraged, it is very difficult to see an optimistic future, and this is exactly what the enemy of your soul wants. He wants you to give up. He wants you to think all is lost. But think about it; why should one failed event or even a few failed events mean all future events will fail as well? Why not think: I must pay close attention to what happened, how I did what I did so that I can learn from this failed event. I know things did not meet my expectations, but what can I do in the future to have a better outcome? This is the posture we must take.

We must know that there is no finality in a failed event, but instead, there are steppingstones. Find the steppingstones and use them to advance you to your victory.

The indicators discussed above are not what one would expect of a believer in Jesus. However, they are quite prevalent in the church. The Holy Spirit is our helper. He has come to lead and to guide us into all truth. Ask Him to help you and He will. Ask the Lord to search your heart for any trace of discouragement and ask Him to eliminate its destructive power from your life. He is faithful, and He will!

CHAPTER SIX: SEVEN MAIN TAKEAWAYS

1. Discouragement comes when we are putting energy into something but are seeing little or no result.

2. All discouragement is of Satan or self; it is never of God. God is called the God of all comfort, and comfort here means encouragement.

3. Amid your sincere efforts to do the right thing, Satan will lie to you about yourself and about what you are doing. His lies are the source of every discouragement; they breed self-pity, self-condemnation, self-doubt, insecurity, and more.

4. Discouragement is accusatory.

5. Disappointment, which if not addressed, can lead to discouragement. This generally occurs when our expectations—what we think should happen—do not align with what actually happens.

6. The devil cannot make us do anything, but he is a master deceiver who is very experienced at causing people to believe God did not come through for them.

7. The enemy of your soul wants you to believe the number one lie...that you are a failure.

CONQUERING DISCOURAGEMENT

It is God's will for you to overcome discouragement. It is God's will for you to live a life above defeat. It is God's will for you to live a life of stability in Him instead of being up one day and down the next. The only way to do this is to live by God's Word.

Discouragement is a part of life; everyone experiences it at some time in life. It is often preceded by disappointment, and if it is not addressed, it will spiral into depression. Discouragement comes most often when you try to accomplish something and have an expectation to succeed but fail or fall short of your expectation. You are likely to become discouraged when you work hard, but you don't make progress.

A teenage boy can become discouraged if he shows up to practice every day and gives his all to the sport but loses every game. A father can become discouraged if he does his very best at raising his son, teaches him the Word of God, is a good example to him, and goes the extra mile to be the best father he can, but the child rebels and does the very opposite of what the parent has taught him or expects him to do.

Discouragement can be crippling. It can cause one to lose hope, lose their drive, doubt God, and even stop caring, but you can overcome it. People try to deal with discouragement in many ways, some of which are wrong. In an effort to cover the pain, many become absorbed by other things. Sometimes, these things should be constructive, but because of the degree to which some people engage in them, they can be damaging. It could be undue expenses for entertainment and socializing, overworking, overspending, or anything in which the person believes they can find an escape. Some respond even more drastically with such things as drug and alcohol use and abandoning their faith in Jesus. But none of these behaviors or responses will help a person dig themself out from under discouragement; they will only take them deeper into the very thing they're trying to escape. There are, however, some healthy ways we can deal with and overcome discouragement.

Never Forget How Much God Loves You

God doesn't just love, He is love. He has said in His Word in numerous places that He loves you (Romans 5:8; 1 John 3:1; 1 John 4:8, 10, 19; and Jeremiah 31:3). He showed His love for you when He sent His only Son to redeem you back to Him. He said His thoughts toward you are good and He has "plans to prosper you and not to harm you, plans to give you hope and a future" (Jeremiah 29:11, NIV).

The Lord is your Shepherd, and you shall not want (Psalm 23:1). This good Shepherd will supply all your needs (Philippians 4:19). God is your loving Father. The Bible says in 2 Corinthians 6:18 (NIV), "And I will be a father to you, and you shall be sons and daughters to me, says the Lord Almighty." And Psalm 103:13 (NIV) says, "As a father has compassion on his children, so the Lord has compassion on those who fear him." He is a good Father. He is not evil. Look at what Matthew 7:9–11 (NIV) says:

> *Which of you, if your son asks for bread, will give him a stone? Or if he asks for a fish, will give him a snake? If you, then, though you are evil, know how to give good gifts to your children, how much more will your Father in heaven give good gifts to those who ask him!*

When you don't know of or have stopped feeling the love of God, you will get discouraged. When you start focusing on yourself and feeling sorry for yourself, you will get discouraged. You cannot feel discouraged and feel the love of God at the same time; it's one or the other. Some people don't feel God's love because they've been wired to think they're not good enough. Some think God is angry at them. But you cannot earn God's love. So, there is no need to think you must meet a certain standard for Him to love you. Open your heart and receive His love. Let Him love you. When you're discouraged, focus on the relentless love that God has for you, and you will be quickly reminded that He thinks well of you and that He "has plans to prosper you and not to harm you."

BE REAL TO YOURSELF; DO NOT FAKE IT

Discouragement is not a transgression of God's law, so it is not a sin. It is nothing to be ashamed of. One can sin because of how poorly they handle discouragement, but discouragement itself is not a sin. It makes sense to be true to yourself and others when you're discouraged. There is no need to fake it or try to cover it up. It really does not matter who you are or what position you hold. You are prone to discouragement and so is everyone else. The only way to avoid ever being discouraged is to not try and accomplish anything, but such is not the average person. So, you need not pretend that all is well just because you're a Christian or even more so because you are a church leader, the president of a company, the head of a household, or any position of leadership.

The price for being a fake and covering up discouragement is costly. God wants you to "Cast all your anxiety on him because he cares for you" (1 Peter 5:7, NIV). The King James Version of the Bible uses "cares" in place of "anxiety." God is inviting you to throw on Him whatever worries you or makes you nervous or fearful. But to do so, you must first acknowledge and accept the fact that you are indeed discouraged. If you are in denial or pretense, you will close the door to the help that is available to you from your Heavenly Father.

Being real can also help those around you. Perhaps you are a role model to someone. In fact, I believe all of us have what I call a "secret admirer." We all have at least one person who has their eyes on us. We all have a degree of influence on someone. Being real to yourself about your state of discouragement could be helpful to your "secret admirer."

Your transparency could help them understand that what they are experiencing is not a sin and that they are not alone. Also, they can learn how to handle life's challenges just by watching how you handle the hurdles in your life. You must remember that whatever you go through is not only about you. Yes, it is to prune and mature you, but whoever is connected to you will be affected as well. The way you handle discouragement in your life will determine whether your experience is a blessing or not to those who are connected to you.

ACCEPT YOUR LIMITATIONS.

Sometimes we try to do too much and fail, and that can be discouraging. Sometimes our goals are unrealistic or more than humanly possible. The Apostle Paul reminds us of our physical weakness in 2 Corinthians 4:7 when he says we are earthen vessels of human frailty, and God made us that way so that whatever we accomplish will be shown as coming from God, not us. We may appear to be great and sufficient in our own eyes and in the eyes of others, but we are reminded here that we are frail and can be easily broken like a jar of clay. We are reminded that we are limited, but God is limitless.

Pottery can easily crack or even break apart. That is just how weak mankind is, but God chose to put His precious treasure in us, and the One who lives in us is greater than the one who lives in the world (1 John 4:4). So, when you are discouraged, accept your weakness, be honest about your situation, cast all your concerns on God, and the one true and living God of the supernatural will show forth His strength.

In casting your concerns on God, you must be honest and be truthful to God about how you feel. God already knows but He said to throw your cares on Him; lay them at His feet, and to do so, you must tell Him about your cares. You must talk to Him.

In Jeremiah 20, Jeremiah was honest. He felt deceived by God. Clearly, God does not mislead or trick anyone, but Jeremiah felt that God had lured him into the ministry only to make him look foolish. He was being laughed at, and he was offended. His voice was not making a difference. He was crying out for the people to repent, yet they continued toward destruction and judgment. Jeremiah's intense lament—the casting of his cares on God—was private. He did not take his concerns to anyone else; he took them to God.

God wants you to talk to Him. Despite your emotional state, He wants you to come to Him. He wants you to come to him just like a little child goes to their earthly father when they are hurt or need help with something. He wants you to be honest with yourself and with Him. People are dishonest in relationships far too often, even with God, but this does them no good.

Jesus is our example. He poured out his heart to the Father in Gethsemane. We should do the same when we pray. Hold nothing back. "Casting" in 1 Peter 5:7 means to throw upon, to deposit. Secular Greek used "casting" for a man who carried a heavy burden and threw it upon a camel's back.[14] "Casting" carries the idea of throwing or rolling upon. God wants us to roll our burdens upon Him. He wants us to throw our concerns upon Him.

By ridding yourself of your cares, you can enter more deeply into the loving embrace of the Lord. God knows the depths of our hearts. He knows our thoughts, our motives, and our emotions even before we utter them. So, when we fail to give God our cares, we are only hurting ourselves. When we are not honest with God, we are only deceiving ourselves. I implore you, throw your concerns and anxieties upon Him. He cares!

USE YOUR PAIN TO HELP OTHERS

If you have the right perspective, you will know that disappointments and challenging times in life are opportunities in disguise. There are many lessons to learn in the midst of difficult situations. If you learn these lessons, you will be equipped to help someone else who is experiencing difficulties. Because of your experience, you can influence others to avoid the mistakes you have made. You can be a voice of warning against the things that can drag a person down, and you can be a source of guide and inspiration to those who are struggling. Do not waste your pain.

Your pain can also help you to be more compassionate and tenderhearted toward others who suffer, which in turn can lead to some of the most joyous and satisfying relationships. It is an absolute joy when you pour into others only to see them grow and mature in the things you are teaching them. Much joy for you and for others is on the other side of your pain.

There are a myriad of possible reasons why we experience difficulties, but the one we must not forget is that our hard times come to strengthen us so that we can empower others. Even if your discouragement is due to poor choices that you've made, you can use your experience to warn others or let them know that hope isn't lost; disappointment and discouragement are not dead ends. Choose to let your difficulties work for your good and the good of others; that is the Father's plan.

Take Time for Renewal

Discouragement can wear you down; it can wear you out. Therefore, it behooves you to step back and reassess after a bout with disappointment or discouragement. It would not be wise to keep forging forward one failure after another without evaluating the circumstances surrounding the failures. It is very likely that your review of the situations will uncover where you went wrong and even reveal different approaches you can take in the future.

During your time of assessment, you must spend time in God's Word and in prayer. This will undoubtedly recharge and renew you. God will speak to you through His Word and the Holy Spirit when you seek strength and insight from Him. He will be that spring of living water in the desert of discouragement. This is the renewal and refreshing that comes along with the assessment.

As you become aware of the dynamics surrounding the situation, and the Holy Spirit ministers to you, you will be renewed and revived to try again. The Holy Spirit will replenish the strength that has been depleted by discouragement, and you will see new approaches that you can take going forward. Through the assessment, you will see the possibility of success. It will become apparent to you that you can indeed succeed in that thing. That is refreshing! That is renewal!

This step is important because until you figure out your mistakes and until you discover new ways of doing things, you will always be discouraged. Without an assessment, you will continue doing the same things and will continue getting the same result.

BE PERSISTENT; GET BACK TO WORK

When the Jewish people of Judah returned from their exile in Babylon, they were hopeful and quickly began to rebuild the temple, just like Ezekiel told them to. However, after opposition from the Samaritans, they stopped the reconstruction until the second year of the reign of Darius, king of Persia. Progress on the building of the temple stopped completely. Discouragement had led the people to abandon working on the temple for sixteen years. They were not persistent, but the prophet Haggai called them back to work.

Like it was for the Jewish people, we can become discouraged because we become self-focused. Being self-focused can make one feel self-pity and justification for why they quit. The Samaritans might have mocked the people, causing them to feel humiliated, or perhaps they felt unsafe. Humiliation is linked to shame, and shame is self-focused. This is what the Samaritans did that led to the cessation of the building of the temple.

> **Ezra 4:4–5** (NIV) — *Then the peoples around them set out to discourage the people of Judah and make them afraid to go on building. They bribed officials to work against them and frustrate their plans during the entire reign of Cyrus king of Persia and down to the reign of Darius king of Persia.*

It is self-focus that made the Jewish people of Judah stop building the temple. If nothing else, they were afraid to go on building.

Elijah was discouraged as well. He was very honest with God: "I have been very zealous for the Lord God Almighty. The Israelites have rejected your covenant, torn down your altars, and put your prophets to death with the sword. I am the only one left, and now they are trying to kill me too." (1 Kings 19:10, NIV). Elijah, in the midst of his discouragement, was self-absorbed. We cannot see the truth when we are too focused on ourselves. Elijah was so self-absorbed that he thought he was the only one standing for God. Self-absorption will deceive you as it did Elijah. He had no idea that God had reserved seven thousand people in Israel who had not bowed their knees to Baal and whose mouths have not kissed him (Verse 18).

Self-absorption and self-focus will make you sit around and think about your problems. It will tie you down and make you mentally recycle the failures you have had. It will snuff out whatever flame you have in you and prevent you from getting back to work. Self-absorption will make your problems look bigger than they are; it will instill fear in you; it will cripple you. To overcome discouragement, you cannot focus on yourself, you must persevere in the face of opposition.

In overcoming discouragement, you will give a strong witness of your faith in Jesus Christ. Being a witness of your faith in Christ will commit you to doing the right thing amid difficulties, and others who are watching you will see the light of Christ in you and be led to glorify your Father which is in heaven (Matthew 5:16). Matthew 10:33 (KJV) says, "But whosoever shall deny me before men, him will I also deny before my Father which is in heaven." If you will be bold for the Lord, you must know that His eyes are upon you, and He will defend you.

The first thing you need to overcome discouragement is a fresh encounter with God's Word. If being discouraged has caused you to quit, you need to get back to work. And you need to persevere when the inevitable, called opposition, comes. You must know that His eyes are upon you. Persistence means being obedient to your call or your God-given assignment. Keep doing what you've been called to do. Get back to work!

Put Your Hope in God

The Psalmist David wrote in Psalm 42:5, "Why art thou cast down, O my soul? and why art thou disquieted in me? hope thou in God: for I shall yet praise him for the help of his countenance." Verse 11 says, "For I shall yet praise him, who is the health of my countenance, and my God." Discouragement can sadden your countenance, but it is God who can brighten it. David said God is the health of his countenance. God can be the same for you if you hope in Him.

When you hope in God, you will quickly realize that you are not alone. After Jeremiah poured out to God, he realized that he was not alone. He realized God was with him and will fight for him. He said, "But the LORD is with me like a violent warrior" (Jeremiah 20:11, NIV). Jeremiah realized that with God as his defender and warrior, he was not on the losing side. With this understanding, discouragement could not overtake him. He was going to win because the Lord was with him like a mighty warrior, and he knew it.

When discouraged, do not look at the situation. Look to God instead. Put your hope in Him. Despite how you feel, know that God has not abandoned you. He is and has always been with you. He is the lifter of your head (Psalm 3:3). He is your refuge and a very present help in a time of need (Psalm 46:1). He is a present-tense God.

Envision receiving news or a report that was designed to knock out all the joy and strength in you, but instead of becoming downcast or fearful, you don't look at or think about the situation, instead, you think upon and set your eyes on your God of hope and strength. The impact that the situation has on you would be very different than it would if you flounder in fear and anxiety and feel sorry for yourself. Being aware of and entertaining God's presence while going through a storm will help you triumph over discouragement. His presence will give you the tenacity, courage, and strength you need for the journey. It will make you fearless; it will make you persevere.

A. W. Tozer writes: "Living in the glow of God's presence will enable you to fight on despite discouragement." And it is true.

Stay Focused on Eternity

A huge obstacle to many believers that is rarely addressed as such is short-sightedness. Many believers live their life as if this life is their final stop. These beloved ones are short-sighted because they don't focus on eternity. Philippians 3:20 tells us that our citizenship is in heaven, not here on earth. We are simply passing though this life, heading to our final destination. Jesus says:

> **Matthew 6:19–21** (NIV) — *Do not store up for yourselves treasures on earth, where moths and vermin destroy, and where thieves break in and steal. But store up for yourselves treasures in heaven, where moths and vermin do not destroy, and where thieves do not break in and steal. For where your treasure is, there your heart will be also.*

We must lay up our treasures in heaven, not here on the earth. The Bible says, "And as it is appointed for man to die once, but after this the judgment" (Hebrews 9:27, KJV). When we draw our last breath, what we have accumulated here on the earth will go to someone else. After we pass from this life, our fate is sealed, and we will be judged by what is written in the Word of God (John 12:48). This leads me to believe that we must live our lives with our eyes on and our efforts focused on eternity.

Life here on earth is temporary and short, but our next stop is for eternity. James 4:14 says, "Whereas you do not know what will happen tomorrow. For what is your life? It is even a vapor that appears for a little time and then vanishes away." When you live your life as if you will live forever here on the earth, the hiccups in this life will become unmanageable and will overwhelm you. Because of shortsightedness, you will think all is lost and will easily fall into despair. But when you know that better lies ahead, you will have an entirely different perspective of the setbacks of this life.

One day this earth and all its possessions will be burnt to nothing. No one knows when this will be. "But the day of the Lord will come as a thief in the night, in which the heavens will pass away with a great noise, and the elements will melt with fervent heat; both the earth and the works that are in it will be burned up. Therefore, since all these things will be dissolved, what manner of persons ought you to be in holy conduct and godliness" (2 Peter 3:10–11, KJV). Look beyond the present and focus on what is next. The "here and now" can be discouraging, but when you focus on all God has planned for you in heaven, that precious and lively hope will keep you on top of discouragement.

Paul, who had been through unimaginable suffering, wrote:

> **2 Corinthians 4:17–18** (KJV) — *For our light affliction, which is but for a moment, worketh for us a far more exceeding and eternal weight of glory; While we look not at the things which are seen, but at the things which are not seen: for the things which are seen are temporal; but the things which are not seen are eternal.*

The Apostle Paul kept his troubles in perspective, and it helped him persevere. You can too!

GET A FRESH ENCOUNTER WITH GOD'S WORD

To overcome discouragement, you need a fresh encounter with God. Offering up sacrifices, worship, and receiving a word from God through His prophets were common means of encountering God in the Old Testament. The Holy Spirit now lives in you, and you have the written Word of God, so although God still speaks through His servants today, you need not wait for a word of prophecy from anyone. You can encounter God in His written Word, the Bible. Also, you can encounter God in your own time of worship, praise, and prayer.

When we are discouraged, the thing that will most refresh us is to hear God speak to us in our particular circumstances through His Word. God is omniscient. Your situation is not hidden from Him. He is fully aware. Jesus said the Holy Spirit will come as a comforter and guide. The Holy Spirit will comfort you in difficult times. He will direct you to the passage of Scripture that pointedly speaks to your situation. He will bring Bible verses and songs to your memory that will minister to you in the very place you are.

Sometimes the Holy Spirit won't lead you to a scripture that speaks directly to your situation, and you may not feel like reading the Word, but you must go against your feelings and open the Book. Whether you feel like it or not, you need the Word of God. God does speak to us through His Word, and so, you must take the time and effort to read it. The Word of God is a lamp to your feet and a light to your path (Psalm 119:105). His Word will show you the next step to take in life and will light the path you should take.

Hebrews 4:12 tells us that the Word of God heals and in the healing that the Word offers, the Holy Spirit will help you reorient your priorities and submit to the Lordship of Jesus. We are all prone to let the things of this world crowd the things of God out of first place in our lives, and we are significantly more susceptible to discouragement when God does not have first place in our lives. The Word of God is there as a beckon back to the basic priority: seek the kingdom of God and His righteousness first (Matthew 6:33). The Word of God is relevant to all our circumstances. When we read God's Word, it is God speaking to us, so, what better place to go for a spirit adjustment than God?

Praise and worship are powerful tools to overcome discouragement. After praise and worship, Jeremiah's despair turned to joy, his defeated attitude turned to triumph, and his dismay turned to courage. Jeremiah triumphantly proclaimed, "Sing to the Lord! Give praise to the Lord!" (Jeremiah 20:13). This is worship. This is praise, and it broke the heaviness of discouragement off him. Praise is an expression of our acknowledgement that God can and that He is in charge. Praise is the one weapon in the Christian's arsenal against which Satan has no defense. When we praise God, we acknowledge that He is in charge—He can do what He wants, when He wants, and how He wants.

Praise and worship adjust our attitude because it is based on our acceptance of the present as part of God's loving, perfect will for us. Worship is not based on what we think, or hope will happen in the future. We worship God, not for what we expect will happen in our around us, but we worship Him for who He is. Praise opens the door for God's power to move in our lives. The Psalmist wrote, "But thou art holy, O thou that inhabits the praises of Israel" (Psalm 22:3, KJV). God lives in our praise. We summon the power and presence of God when we praise Him.

Rick Ezell gave a modernized version of this story:

The devil had a garage sale. He marked all his tools with their appropriate price: hatred, envy, lust, deceit, lying, and pride. Laid apart from all of these was a rather harmless looking but well-worn tool marked much higher than the rest. A buyer pointed to it and asked, "What is that tool?" The devil replied, "That is discouragement."

"Why is it priced so high?" the man asked.

"Because it is more useful to me than the others. I can pry open a man's heart with that when I can't get near to him with the other tools. Once inside, I can make him do whatever I choose. It's badly worn because I use it on almost everyone. But few know that it belongs to me."

The devil's price was so high that the tool of discouragement was never sold. He still uses it on God's people. But by God's grace and through His Word, we can overcome discouragement. This is why we must be steadfast, immovable, always abounding in the work of the Lord, knowing that our work in the ministry is not in vain (1 Corinthians 15:58).

CHAPTER SEVEN: SEVEN MAIN TAKEAWAYS

1. The only way to avoid ever being discouraged is to not try and accomplish anything, and such is not the average person.

2. You cannot feel discouraged and feel the love of God at the same time; it is one or the other.

3. The way you handle discouragement in your life will determine whether your experience is a blessing or not to those who are connected to you.

4. If you have the right perspective, you will know that disappointments and difficult times in life are opportunities in disguise.

5. Self-absorption will make your problems look bigger than they are; it will instill fear in you; it will cripple you.

6. When discouraged, do not look at the situation. Look to God instead. Put your hope in Him.

7. The "here and now" can be discouraging. But when you focus on all that God has planned for you in heaven, that precious and lively hope will keep you on top of discouragement.

THE DYNAMICS OF DEPRESSION

*Depression is like a deep dark hole into which the devil,
over time, drags his helpless victims.*

D epression is defined by the National Institute of
Mental Health as "A common but serious mood
disorder. It causes severe symptoms that affect how a
person feels, thinks, and handles daily activities, such as
sleeping, eating, or working. To be diagnosed with depression,
the symptoms must be present for at least two weeks."

There are two types of depression: situational depression
and clinical depression. The type of depression that I will be
speaking of here is situational depression. Apart from the
conditions that rightfully meet the criteria for situational and
clinical depression, it is common for people to label themselves
as depressed when having a bad day. Some refer to a bad day
as a blue day. For example, one could say they are depressed
or sad, because "I was really feeling blue after I failed my
comprehensive exams." According to the Macquarie
Dictionary, there is evidence for the use of blue to mean
"depressing" in British English since the 1600s. The

expression blue day meaning "a dismal day" was current at the time. So, it could be said there is a third type of depression.

A blue day, bad day, down day, or the term "depressed" under these circumstances is a type of situational depression, but the symptoms are sometimes not like those of situational depression, and if they are similar, the indicators are significantly less pronounced. The terms "blue day," "bad day," and "down day" covey the brevity of the symptoms associated with this type of "depression." Depression—situational and clinical—is more than just feeling down for a day or two. A "blue day," "bad day," or "down day" is usually short-lived; therefore, I do not consider this condition depression in the true sense of the word but will treat it as such in this discussion.

To ensure we have a clear understanding of depression, a brief distinction between situational and clinical depression follows.

CLINICAL DEPRESSION

According to the Mayo Clinic, clinical depression is also known medically as a major depressive disorder. It is a chronic condition that is severe enough to interfere with one's daily function and can develop into a severe mental health condition if the individual does not recover. Clinical depression can alter a person's thought processes and bodily functions. It is a mood disorder that may happen with or without a specific stressor.

While a specific cause for clinical depression is unknown, it is believed that imbalances in the levels of neurotransmitters, a chemical substance in the body, may be the cause. However, genetic factors are likely to play a role. Genetic factors could influence an individual's response and ability to handle an unexpected experience or life event in a healthy manner.[15] Examples of major life events, which can trigger negative emotions and pose a challenge for an individual with a genetic predisposition for depression include, but are not limited to bereavement, divorce, illness, job loss, a failed business, and financial worries. Uncontrolled anger and alcohol and drug dependence also have links to clinical depression.[16] While the trigger for situational depression is usually a life event, that is not always the case for clinical depression.

Typical depressive symptoms during the time of depression include a deeply sad or irritable mood, lack of interest in normally pleasurable things, change in weight or appetite, change in sleep patterns, fatigue, feelings of worthlessness or guilt, indecisiveness, hopelessness, and suicidal thoughts. But the most common symptom is a depressed mood that the person experiences on most days and for a long time. As expected, some individuals who are experiencing clinical depression will look for a way out, and sadly, many abuse substances such as alcohol or drugs to escape from their suffering. Consequently, clinical depression can seriously affect one's quality of life and threaten their life as well.

Clinical depression is usually more severe than situational depression and typically lasts longer. Situational depression is short-lived, but clinical depression may interrupt one's life for a long time. It may disrupt the person's sleep, eating habits, lifestyle, and work. The higher risk of suicide that is linked with clinical depression points to its severity.

SITUATIONAL DEPRESSION

Situational depression is a short-term form of depression resulting from a traumatic event or change in a person's life.[17] Persons who have difficulty coming to terms with stressful life changes or events are prone to situational depression. Recovery is likely once an individual can come to terms with a new situation. Because situational depression is short-lived, it often improves after a reasonable time following the stressful event. The mood of individuals with situational depression usually improve as the stressful situation starts to dissipate. Some find relief from this condition by talking about the problem.

Situational depression is more common than clinical depression. Situational and clinical depression are similar, but they are not the same. We all experience sadness; it is a natural human emotion. But while a person with situational depression will very likely experience sadness, the person with clinical depression will be subjected to profound sadness. Unlike situational depression, the level of sadness that comes with clinical depression is often crippling. According to the Mayo Clinic, clinical depression is a serious condition that can profoundly impact every part of a person's life, but situational depression is an "adjustment disorder with a depressed mood." Situational depression is a depressed mood, which is a temporary state of mind or feeling, and clinical depression is a chronic or recurring condition.[18]

In addition to sadness, symptoms of situational depression may include anger, appetite changes, constant fear or worry, difficulty carrying out tasks, difficulty focusing, difficulty sleeping, frequent crying, grief, hopelessness, loss of interest in normal activities, and overwhelming feelings from stress or anxiety.

124

Many life events can trigger situational depression. Some are traumatic. Others may be happy events that require major life changes. The symptoms of situational depression are a reaction to a stressful event and may surface within days to a few months, as the person tries to manage the changes that are happening.

Some typical triggers for situational depression include car accident, divorce, experiencing a crime, family problems, a global pandemic like COVID-19, having a baby, illness or difficult diagnosis, loss of a family member, friend, or pet, loss of a job, moving, natural disaster, relationship problems, retirement, school-related issues, starting a new job, and work-related issues.

From this point forward, my use of the term depression will be referring to situational depression and "blue day," "bad day," or "down day."

THE IMPARTIALITY OF DEPRESSION

A read through the Scriptures will quickly reveal that many of the great names and personalities of the Bible experienced depression at one time or another. Job is one of them. God referred to Job as blameless and upright. God Himself said that Job disdained evil; he lived a righteous life. But Job suffered incredible losses along with an excruciatingly painful illness that he did not deserve. After getting the news of the death of all his sons and daughters, Job bowed down and worshipped God: "Then Job arose, and rent his mantle, and shaved his head, and fell down upon the ground, and worshipped" (Job 1:20, KJV). But as seen in Job 6:6–7 (emphasis added), he had some low days:

My days are swifter than a weaver's shuttle, and they come to an end without hope. Remember, O God, that my life is but a breath; my eyes will <u>never see happiness again</u>.

David is another example. The Bible calls David "a man after God's own heart" twice. The first time was by Samuel who anointed him as king to replace Saul. The Bible says that God was with David. God empowered him to accomplish every task he came to. In the Hebrew Bible, King David is famous for slaying the Philistine giant Goliath. With the help of God, David defeated the Philistines who had oppressed and taunted the nation of Israel for years. And through many victorious battles, he expanded Israel into a large kingdom centered in Jerusalem. It is said that David fought several battles and won them all. But there was a time when this great warrior's life was in danger. Due to jealousy and insecurity, Saul desperately sought to kill him, and this brought him to some very low days. The following passage of Scripture gives insight into David's low state:

Psalm 69:1–3 (NIV) — *Save me, O God, for the waters have come up to my neck. I sink in the miry depths, where there is no foothold. I have come into the deep waters; the floods engulf me. I am worn out calling for help; my throat is parched. My eyes fail, looking for my God.*

David is in a dark place here, and he has been there for a while. Now he is saying that he has been sinking in the miry depths, the floodwaters are rising over his head, and he can no longer stand. He is calling out to God for help from the deep, dark hole of depression. In fact, he says he has been calling for

God's help so much that his throat is dry. David has been calling on God for help, and it hasn't been working.

There are 150 psalms, and these psalms contain many accounts of David's cries to God. Like we see in Psalm 69:22, David is crying out to God: "My God My God, why hast Thou Forsaken me?" A depressed person will very likely think that God, the faithful One, has forsaken them. From this dark place, David asks God why He was not coming to his rescue. Time and time again we see David in this position. Being downcast was nothing new to this great warrior. He cried out to God so much that in Psalm 69:3, he said, "I'm worn out. My throat is parched."

Not only has David's throat failed him, but his eyes have also failed him. He has been looking for God in the midst of all the trouble he was facing but could not find Him. But he knew God would never leave him. David wrote in Psalm 23:4, "Yea though I walk through the valley of the shadow of death, I will fear no evil." Why did David say this? "For Thou art with me."

But knowing God is with you and being able to see or feel Him with you are two vastly different things. David did not feel God in these difficult moments and God certainly never left him, but David struggled, nonetheless. David was despondent, but fortunately, he knew what to do amid his despair. David looked to God for help. He kept crying out to God. He placed his trust in the One who made him, loved him, and had always been with him.

Jonah faced depression as well. He was a prophet of God, but he prayed for God to take his life: "Now, Lord, take away my life, for it is better for me to die than to live" (Jonah 4:3, NIV). Only a depressed or hopeless person would pray for God to take their life. Anger drove Jonah to this place of despair.

He became angry and deeply despondent when God did not destroy Nineveh, a people he did not favor.

God told Jonah to go to Nineveh and preach repentance to the people, but Jonah refused to obey. Jonah repented of his disobedience, and God told him again to go to Nineveh and preach repentance to the people. This time Jonah did what God told him to do, and what happened was the exact opposite of what Jonah wanted: the people of Nineveh repented of their sins and turned back to God. Jonah was not happy, in fact, he was downright angry. He did not want those people saved. He wanted them judged, found guilty, and punished. Resentment opened the door for Jonah to become depressed.

The strong and mighty in the Scriptures who had bouts with depression are not limited to Job, David, and Jonah. Others like Elijah and Jeremiah are in the number, and many of us, despite how anointed we are, how long and deeply we pray, or how sincerely we worship, have also had bouts with depression. One writer calls depression "the common cold of emotional disorders." (Quoted by Chip Ingram, I Am Always with You, p. 110.). All of us have spoken words of discouragement and depression. All of us have experienced the overwhelming effects of stress, setbacks, grief, or loss. We are humans. We depend on God as our strength. So, in this flesh, we will find ourselves under the weight of depression at some point in life.

For Christians, depression becomes harder to endure because of the erroneous, yet common notion that Christians don't get depressed. Most times it is not good to throw Bible verses at people when they are down. It's best to relate to them in the love of Jesus Christ and with expressed interest in their wellbeing, not under the camouflage of Bible verses. But many in the Christian community tend to quote Bible verses in untimely ways to the depressed or tend to hurl out clichés, such as, "You just need to have more faith," or "Rejoice in the Lord always," or "The joy of the Lord is your strength." Sometimes they even give an anointed pep talk: "Your life should be a testimony of the goodness of God, get yourself together! What will people think of God if they see you like this?" None of this is untrue, but the depressed need practical advice. Yes, the joy of the Lord is their strength, but how do they tap into that joy?

THE SUBTLETIES OF DEPRESSION

The following are subtleties of depression the believer needs to be aware of.

DESPONDENCY

People fall into depression when they realize they have a problem and at the same time, they believe there is no way out of that problem. The problem or stressor is acknowledged, but the person fully believes that nothing can be done about it. Depression comes out of a feeling of helplessness and despair.

This mindset highlights two things. The first is how the problem is interpreted, and the second is the belief that nothing can be done to resolve the problem. The first problem occurs because of the perspective from which the individual looks at the situation. It is fair to say that the perspective is all but positive or healthy. A person who is emotionally wounded, or has limited information about the situation, or is reactive instead of contemplative will likely take this perspective. Individuals who are disconnected from God, or have a poor relationship with Him, or do not have a significant figure in their life with whom they can consult may also take this perspective.

A person who is heading into depression will interpret their experience from a place of emotional or spiritual deficit. Such a person will wrongfully believe they are destined to live with the undesirable situation forever. This strong sense of hopelessness then overtakes the individual, and their will to go on comes to a halt.

The depressed not only believes nothing can be done to resolve the problem, but also sees options that are not possible, and yet they fix their mind on these impossible solutions. They will see no resolution because, in fact, the options on which they've fixed their mind are not feasible, and this lack of result—lack of change in the situation—only takes them deeper into depression.

PESSIMISM

Negative thinking also sets the stage for depression. People who are pessimistic—those who have a pattern of thinking negatively about themselves, others, and their surroundings—are prone to depression. When a pessimist encounters a problem, their negative thinking will lock them into believing there is no solution to the problem.

The pessimist makes a bad situation worse with their negative thinking. When they encounter a life challenge, they internalize it and interpret it to be a personal assault on them, even when unwarranted. For example, the pessimist had her weekly one-on-one meeting with her supervisor. The supervisor caringly took the time to point out some areas in the pessimist's work that needed to improve. The supervisor made it clear that if the pessimist does not improve in these areas, it

130

will affect her annual evaluation, and if the below-standard performance persists, she must look more closely at her suitability for the position she holds. Instead of the pessimist seeing this as an opportunity to take her supervisor's advice and improve her performance, she convinces herself that the supervisor dislikes her and is preparing to fire her. This becomes her focus, and she becomes angry. And because she is looking at the situation from that perspective, nothing changes, so she spirals into depression. This mindset reinforces the pessimist's negative thoughts about herself. An optimist or someone with a healthier sense of self would take the supervisor's advice and work hard to make sure a meeting of that kind is not necessary in the future and that her annual evaluation is good.

Negative thinking also causes the pessimist to magnify the negative aspects of a situation and ignore all the positive ones. Whatever they are doing—self-loathing or blaming others—will be worsened. Instead of focusing on how to resolve an issue, the pessimist will mentally marinate in it. Their thinking pattern is negative, so as they think about a situation, they sink further into depression, because from their perspective, it is a supremely negative situation.

A person with this mindset fails to see that there is good in every situation, no matter how bad it is. They see the glass as half empty, maybe even empty, rather than seeing it as half full. Sometimes the good outweighs the bad, but because of their negative thinking pattern, they see nothing but bad.

The pessimist also anticipates the worst. This is called catastrophizing. For example, a pessimist is trying to sell her house, and after a couple potential buyers tour the house but opted not to purchase the house, she surmises that the house will never sell. In catastrophizing, the pessimist mentally, and sometimes verbally and behaviorally, goes to the worst outcome and stays there. This negative mental rehearsal breeds fear and anxiety and drags the pessimist down into depression.

Again, the pessimist fails to put things into proper perspective. The extreme is thinking the house will never sell, but that is unlikely. It may not sell by the time the pessimist wants it to sell and they may not sell it at the desired price, but it will sell, nonetheless. Pessimism prevents the individual from seeing potential positive outcomes and from distinguishing between what is reality and what is their catastrophic prediction.

DICHOTOMOUS THINKING

One of the primary causes of dichotomous or polarized—either good or bad, no in between—thinking is anxiety and depression. This type of thinking perpetuates and exacerbates anxiety and depression, so it's an ongoing cycle. Individuals who think this way usually use—or overuse—"absolutist terms." For them, a situation is either entirely bad or entirely good. Therefore, if a stressful life event happens, they are likely to see it as entirely bad, and may use absolutist terms, such as always, never, impossible, disaster, furious, and ruined, when referring to it. The occasional use of these words is acceptable, but that is not the case for a person with a dichotomous thinking pattern.

Persons who think the worst and use absolutist terms whenever something happens will see no way out of the situation, and that creates the right condition for depression. It gets even worse if they say these words to themselves or to others repeatedly. The more they say it, the more they believe it. And the more they believe it, the more the unpleasant situation looks irreversible. This again creates the right condition for depression.

Another implication of dichotomous thinking is its ability to disconnect the person from others, and this is another very fertile ground for depression. Depression is a lonely place. Depression can have its way with you if it can get you all to itself. So, when someone uses polarized words and alienates themself from others or alienate others from them, they are left alone to face the challenge, and then they fall into depression or go deeper into it.

THE STRATEGY OF THE ENEMY

I liken depression to a deep, dark hole into which Satan slowly drags his victims. And as he drags them, they carry all their past mistakes, the demeaning words that their parents said to them when they were children, the abusive language of their spouse, the memories of all the injustice that was done to them, and everything else that was painful and unpleasant that happened to them or that they did. Satan makes sure he drags them through everything they have experienced, all for which Jesus already died and paid the price. As Satan drags his victims through these painful memories and experiences, these things attach themselves to the victims, and the victims carry them with them into the deep, dark hole. It is the weight of these experiences that keep a person depressed.

Satan knows that if he can keep your pain alive, he can keep you down. He knows that by intensifying the pain, he can suppress your joy, your strength, and your faith in God, so he looks for opportunities to bombard you with the things you so desperately want to get away from. Your first reaction to the onset of a challenging or stressful life event either tells Satan you are primed for an attack or not.

Let us say, for example, you're married, and your spouse commits infidelity. You are deeply hurt, and rightfully so. You are devastated, you feel betrayed, and you are angry, but this mindset creates a crack in your spirit for the enemy to bore his way through. He now seizes the opportunity and begins to flood your mind with the words your mother told you as a child: you're ugly, you're no good. Then you begin to recall the words a previous boyfriend told you: you're ugly, no one will ever want you. Now you begin to think: He never loved me, I didn't deserve him, I can never have a good marriage. And as Satan floods your mind with these toxic thoughts, you become buried in them, and they drag you down until you become depressed. This is the process of Satan dragging a person to that deep, dark hole of depression, and as he drags them, they pick up all the things of the past that they wish to leave behind, which dim any ray of hope they have and drain their strength out of them.

Another example: you went to school and got the needed degree. You worked hard and proved yourself to the managers of the company where you're employed. A position two levels above the position you currently hold becomes available. This position comes with a significant salary increase. You apply for the job, and you got it. You accept the job. But instead of being excited about this new venture and the opportunity to grow, you become anxious and worried about whether you can do the job. This creates an opening for Satan to now drag you through the bad memories of your past to wear you down.

As he drags you, you begin to recall how you were ridiculed by your older siblings and your parents never reprimanded them, and you recall how your mother left you in the care of family members who abused you and told you that you wouldn't amount to anything. You remember how you tried in the past and failed. You even remember when you told your teacher in middle school that you wanted to be a school principal, and she said you're not smart enough. All the issues in your life that could possibly contribute to low self-esteem or poor self-confidence flood your mind. You are being dragged by Satan to the deep, dark hole called depression, and with every move, you are picking up bad experiences of the past that are making you anxious and weighing you down.

The process is the same for a blue day or two as it is for depression. If Satan can get your attention or if he can get you to think upon the things he brings to your attention, then he can take you down that dark path. And rest assured, he never brings anything good to your mind, so his objective is always evil. He will even twist the good to make it look bad. He will remind you of times in the past when you prayed and God "did not answer your prayers." This is deception because God did answer your prayers; He always does. He might not have answered them the way you wanted, but He is faithful enough not to close His ears to your prayers. It is Satan's nature to lie to you.

He will even bring times when you were going through a difficult time and you declared the Word of God over your situation and claimed promises written in the Word of God, and nothing happened. Again, it appears as if nothing happened. God always hear the cry of His people. He is a good Father, but Satan's job is to keep an eye out for every opportunity to lie to you and to bombard you with the negative.

Why won't Satan leave you alone? Why is he so determined to ruin you? Let me tell you; he is jealous of you. He no longer has any part with God, but you do, and he is jealous. He hates you for that. You have hope and a bright future, and he does not. You give God the worship that Satan so desperately wants, and he envies that. Satan is wretched and miserable; he is bound by eternal limitations, and he wants you to be miserable too. Do not fall for it.

Chapter Eight: Seven Main Takeaways

1. For Christians, depression becomes harder to endure because of the erroneous, yet common notion that Christians or someone strong in faith do not get depressed.

2. Depression comes out of a feeling of helplessness and despair.

3. Depression starts when we see no viable options.

4. The depressed not only believes nothing can be done to resolve the problem, but also sees options that are not possible, and yet they fix their mind on these impossible solutions.

5. A person who is heading into depression will interpret their experience from a place of emotional or spiritual deficit.

6. Negative thinking sets the stage for depression.

7. Depression is like a deep, dark hole into which Satan slowly drags his victims.

Overcoming Depression: Confront and Fight

Before you can burst forth into light, you
must first confront the darkness.

T he root of the word "depress" means to press down. Depression should be thought of then as a force or a spirit that presses down on the life within a person. That pressing down forces the life or the will to go out of the person. This is why depressed individuals have little interest in or energy to do things, even things that usually are of interest to them. Depression drains its host of its life and energy; it depletes the person's motivation and drive.

So yes, depression is a real phenomenon, and it occurs in the life of many, but how do we overcome it? What can we do to avert those blue days? What can be done to stay out of the deep, dark hole called depression?

MENTAL CONSCIOUSNESS

Many people live their lives without being in touch with their inner man. Everything we do and say is a product of what is inside of us. If we love, it's because love is in our heart, and conversely, if we hate, it's because hate is in our heart. If we buy a new car, it is because we desire a car, and that desire for a new car comes from within.

Proverbs 4:23 (NIV, emphasis added) says, "Above all else, guard your heart, for <u>everything</u> you do <u>flows from it</u>." Because everything we do flows from our heart, we are admonished to guard our heart intentionally and with conscious and concerted effort. We are to guard our heart more than we guard anything else. Satan's strategy is to remind us of damaging memories, and memories come to the mind not the heart, so how does this verse apply to this discussion?

The use of the word "heart" in the Bible refers to the mind in many places. The word "heart" also refers to the inner person, as seen in 1 Peter 3:4, which says, "The hidden person of the heart." I doubt the function of the brain was known in biblical times, so, for instance, thoughts and emotions would be attributed to the heart and not the brain as we commonly would in modern times.

There are several Scriptures where "heart" is used but we can conclude that heart is used in place of mind. For example, Genesis 6:5 (NIV) says, "The Lord saw how great the wickedness of the human race had become on the earth, and that every inclination of the thoughts of the human heart was only evil all the time." From our understanding, we do not think with our heart, we think with our mind. Therefore, the verse is saying the thoughts of the mind of the people were wicked. Another verse is Proverbs 4:4 (KJV), which says, "He taught me also, and said unto me, Let thine heart retain my words: keep my commandments, and live." Our mind gives us the capacity to retain and understand information; therefore, the verse is saying we should keep God's counsel in our minds. Another verse is Proverbs 23:7a (AMP), which says, "For as he thinks in his heart, so is he." We do not think from our heart, we think from our minds.

The heart referred to in Proverbs 4:23 is our spiritual heart, not our physical heart that pumps blood throughout our body. Our spiritual heart is the control center of the soul, which houses the mind, will, and emotions. Therefore, if we guard the heart spoken of in Proverbs 4:23 (and Proverbs 23:7a), we will guard our mind (the way we think), our will (what we want), and our emotions (what we feel). This very important Scripture tells us to guard our soul from any introductions made to us by the enemy. If we do so, we will preserve how we think, what we wish for, and the way we feel. The totality of these three aspects of our functioning is our life. This is why the Scripture says, "For out of it are the issues of life" (KJV).

We run a supremely high risk and put ourselves in a very vulnerable place when we are out of touch with our mental health or our thought life. We must recognize that everything we do and say comes from within. Satan knows that, and so he seeks to reintroduce our painful past to our minds. An unguarded mind is free access to him. After Satan brings back your painful past to your mind, your response in the form of the issues of life—the way you think, what you desire, and how you feel—will come from within you.

Once you recognize this, you can reclaim power over your life. By activating this understanding, you will take the power from your adversary. With an understanding of this verse, you will look at your behavior as symptoms or products of what is happening in your mind. To address undesired experiences, such as a blue day or depression, you will look inside. You will examine your heart—the things you have been thinking about, the things you are anticipating, and the way you feel.

A look on the inside will expose what is causing the depression. The depressive behaviors are not the problem. Those are symptoms of the real problem. It is what's going on in the mind that's the real problem. Therefore, the problem is not the job loss or whatever the stressful event is; it is what the devil is telling you after the event.

Being aware of and in touch with your thoughts at times, but especially in difficult times, is crucial because the devil is an opportunist. He knows that we become vulnerable during these times, so while he is most attentive to detect when we reach these low moments in life, we must be even more vigilant in blocking his entrance. Peter warns us likewise.

> **1 Peter 5:8** (KJV) — *Be sober, be vigilant; because your adversary the devil, as a roaring lion, walketh about, seeking whom he may devour.*

Guard your mind against the enemy of your soul at all costs! Do not let him speak into your spirit. Do not listen to him! Resist him early on to ensure depression does not lay hold of you. Depression by its very nature restricts our ability to act and action is required to overcome a depressed state, so do not let yourself go there.

CRY OUT TO GOD

Asaph was smothered under depression, and in Psalm 77:1–3 and 7–9, he describes how he got from under it. In verses 1 to

3 (NIV), he said, "I cried out to God for help; I cried out to God to hear me. When I was in distress, I sought the Lord; at night I stretched out untiring hands, and I would not be comforted. I remembered you, God, and I groaned; I meditated, and my spirit grew faint." You can hear the despair in Asaph's words. It appears as if he has given up. He said he cried out to the Lord, but he would not be comforted, so it does look like he has given up, but note carefully that he cried out to God. If he had given up, he would not have cried out to God.

Asaph is in a bad place. The word distress in verse 2 describes a feeling of being oppressed as if the walls are closing in. Asaph felt like he was in a dark tunnel, only there was no light at the end. When he says, "I would not be comforted," he means he tried to shake off the depression by the normal means we all resort to, but it wasn't working. It gets worse; in verse 3, he says that when he meditates—when he thinks of the situation to figure out a way out of the problem— his spirit becomes weak. He was so distressed; he could not sleep. He raised his hand to God untiringly, but to no avail.

Things are obviously bad with Asaph, but in his battle with depression, he did not suppress how he felt. He did not pretend he was happy and that all was well, and he did not pretend with God. He was honest with God about how he felt. This is a good example of casting one's care on God. This is the Word of God by which we should be living our lives. This is a life lesson.

Asaph went to God, nowhere else. In modern times, many turn to food, overspending, overworking, drugs and alcohol, gambling, pornography, or any number of other things that are waiting to deceive us. A good way to overcome depression is to be honest with God; hold nothing back. Cry out to Him.

Asaph said in verse 3, "I remembered you, God, and I groaned." The word "groan" can mean anything from a quiet noise to a raging explosion. So let God know how you feel. Talk to Him quietly or in a loud voice; it doesn't matter. The important thing is that you cry out to Him.

I think verses 7 to 9 (NIV) are very revealing. This is what they say:

> *Will the Lord reject forever? Will he never show his favor again? Has his unfailing love vanished forever? Has his promise failed for all time? Has God forgotten to be merciful? Has he in anger withheld his compassion?*

Obviously, Asaph was on an emotional roller coaster, but again, he did not try to hide it. One minute he was crying out to God, and the next minute, he was in doubt as to whether God will show His favor again. This is what depression will do to you. Do not feel you have done anything ungodly if this is your experience when facing depression. Remember, depression is darkness, so, it blurs your sight of the light, the good. Also, note that God did not express any discontent with Asaph's state of mind. God is merciful, and He is touched with the feelings of your infirmities (Hebrews 4:15), so lay it all on Him. He is waiting to hear from you. "The Lord is nigh unto them that are of a broken heart; and saveth such as be of a contrite spirit" (Psalm 34:18, KJV). Pour out your heart to Him in a whisper or with a loud voice and be honest with Him. He can handle it.

HAVE A "THESE THINGS" THOUGHT LIFE

The very common verses found in Philippians 4:8–9 (NIV, emphasis added) provide an incredibly solid remedy and preventive measure for depression. They say:

> *Finally, brothers and sisters, whatever is <u>true</u>, whatever is <u>noble</u>, whatever is <u>right</u>, whatever is <u>pure</u>, whatever is <u>lovely</u>, whatever is <u>admirable</u>—if anything is excellent or <u>praiseworthy</u>—think about such things. Whatever you have learned or received or heard from me, or seen in me—put it into practice. And the God of peace will be with you.*

Not surprisingly, this verse tells us to do the very opposite of what the devil wants us to do. The devil wants us to think upon the lies he tells us and all the bad experiences we have had in the past, but God wants us to think upon what is true. And what is truer than God's Word? His Word is truth, and it is a sanctifying agent (John 17:18). Therefore, as we think upon God's Word, it purifies and blesses us. I must admit that this is not as simple, as easy, or as straightforward as it sounds, because many times, we do not realize it is the enemy that is injecting thoughts into our minds. Many times, we believe we are thinking the way we do because of what we are experiencing, but in fact, the enemy of our souls is lying to us.

As the devil floods your mind with his lies, you can easily get caught up in a cycle of thoughts that continue on and on, like a loop which seems, at the time, difficult to stop. This is what the devil wants, but it is not healthy to stay there for weeks, days, or even a day. Instead of thinking upon and believing what the father of lies have told you about yourself, you ought to think upon and believe what the Word of God says about you.

When the enemy whispers labels in your ears with which you begin to identify and call yourself, reverse them. Tell him you are in Christ; therefore, you are a new creation (2 Corinthians 5:17). Perhaps at one point in your life, you were what he is whispering in your ear, but the old is the old, and now you are in the newness of Christ Jesus. When he reminds you that your mother abandoned you and your husband did the same to you, so you are alone, tell him the Lord your God is with you wherever you go (Joshua 1:9). Tell him you are not abandoned; God has adopted you. Others might have abandoned you, but God decided in advance to adopt you into His own family by bringing you to Himself through Jesus Christ. This is what God wanted to do, and it gave Him great pleasure (Ephesians 1:5). To reinforce your mind, don't relent, repeat this over and over to yourself: "I have been rejected, but God says I am His! Therefore, I will not fear. God has redeemed me. God has called me His own. I am His."

The enemy may say you are unlovable, but God says you are forever loved by God your Father. Tell Satan loud and clear that you are convinced that nothing can ever separate you from God's love—not death, life, angels, demons, the fears of today, nor the worries of tomorrow. Tell him not even the powers of hell can separate you from God's love (Romans 8:38).

When the devil tries to tell you that you are too weak to fight your way out of the bad news you got—the diagnosis, the death of a loved one, the failed examination, the job loss—tell him, yes, you are indeed weak, but the God you serve says He will make you strong. Tell Him the strong arms of the almighty God you serve are with you (Psalm 18:32).

146

When the devil tries to tell you that it's because you are nothing special why you're going through such a difficult time, tell him he's wrong! Tell him you're indeed special because God says you are fearfully and wonderfully made (Psalm 139:14). He may try to convince you that you're worthless, so you might as well give up, but tell him you are not worthless. Remind him that Jesus died for you because you are worth it: "For God so loved the world, that he gave his only Son, that whoever believes in him should not perish but have eternal life" (John 3:16).

In his efforts to keep you depressed, the devil will tell you there is no hope; he will try to convince you to give up. But remind him that God says that, because of Him, you are hopeful: "For I know the plans I have for you, declares the Lord, plans for welfare, and not for evil, to give you a future and a hope" (Jeremiah 29:11). Tell him God created you with purpose; you were created for good works to bring glory to God (Ephesians 2:10), so you cannot give up. Even if what has come about is due to failure on your part, you are not a failure. A failed event does not define you, so do not let the devil lie to you. You might have failed, but God says you are victorious in Christ. Tell him God gives you victory over sin and death through the Lord Jesus Christ (1 Corinthians 15:57).

Satan will try to tell you that you're done; it's over for you. He will want you to believe that the trial you're going through is too much for you and that it's going to take you under. That is the time to lash back and tell him, "Yes, I realize that I'm broken, but instead of turning to you, I will go to my Father. He wants me to come to Him when I'm broken and weak, and He will make me whole." Tell the devil you are complete through your union with Christ, who is the head over every ruler and authority (Colossians 2:10), including him, so

147

he has no dominion over you. Things may look dismal for the moment but tell him that God says He will give you direction: "Whether you turn to the right or to the left, your ears will hear a voice behind you, saying 'This is the way; walk in it'" (Isaiah 30:21).

His most common approach in lying to us is to make us feel unworthy, so he will try to tell you that you are not a good enough Christian; in fact, you aren't even saved; you're a sinner. What a lie! The blood of Jesus has washed you from your sins, do not believe him! Tell him you are the righteousness of God through faith in Jesus Christ. If you are walking with the Lord, you are not a sinner saved by grace. Instead, you were a sinner who has been saved by grace. Be bold! Tell him you are redeemed by the blood of Jesus and that makes you an heir and joint heir with Jesus Christ. Tell him you are a child of God because your sins are forgiven: "I am writing to you who are God's children because your sins have been forgiven through Jesus" (1 John 2:12).

These are examples of how we think upon truth. The truth will counteract the lies of the enemy. Jesus used truth to whip the enemy when he came to tempt Him after His 40-day fast. When you get that bad news or when that undesirable thing happens to you, try not to dwell on it, but instead, try to dwell on what is noble and right. Think about things that are pure, lovely, admirable, excellent, or praiseworthy—all the things that help you stay focused on God's love for you and Christ's sacrifice for you—and your actions will fall in line with your thoughts. Therefore, instead of exhibiting depressive symptoms, you will exhibit the opposite.

In place of entertaining impure thoughts about the dynamics that surround your husband's affair, think about what God designed marriage to be and thank Him for the opportunity to experience it. You must intentionally steer your mind away from where the devil is trying to take it. Instead of thinking about how badly they treated you at work and now you are unemployed, think about the times you were employed and how the Father provided for you abundantly. Thank Him that even in a state of unemployment, you are blessed; you are not forsaken, and you are not begging for bread. In whatever situation you find yourself, despite how fitting the situation is for depression, you can counteract it with the truth. Think upon these things, and as verse 9 says, "The God of peace will be with you." So, you see, in place of a troubled mind, you get peace when you think upon "these things." Peace and depression cannot coexist, so choose peace. Think upon "these things."

Let me direct your attention back to Psalm 77, especially verses 4 to 6 and 10 to 12. This is another go to Scripture to combat depression. Here we see Asaph telling how he pulled himself out of depression. Asaph had a troubled mind and could not sleep. During one of his many sleepless nights, he resolved that God must be keeping him awake for a reason. He said in verse 4, "You kept my eyes from closing; I was too troubled to speak." Asaph was laying there at night wide awake but could not speak. He could have laid there and thought about all the things that had brought him to that downcast state, but instead, he thought about the times when God was good to him. He thought about the times when his spirit was uplifted because of the goodness of God to him. In verses 5 and 6, he said, "I thought about the former days, the years of long ago; I remembered my songs in the night. My heart meditated and my spirit asked." Another version of the Bible uses the words, "my spirit ponders" in place of "my spirit asked." Asaph was intentional in fighting his way out of depression. He went years back to recall God's goodness to him. He deliberately focused his thoughts on the past times when God seemed so near and thus, could sing his way out of the darkness.

In verses 10 and 11, he said, "Then I thought, 'To this I will appeal: the years when the Most High stretched out his right hand. will remember the deeds of the Lord; yes, I will remember your miracles of long ago.'" Asaph forced his thoughts out of the dungeon of depression back to the years when he saw God do great things. He recalled the goodness of God and reflected on them.

It is very important to regain perspective when you feel weighted down by depression, and you must try to do so as quickly as possible. When troubles come, if you are not aware of what the enemy is doing and if you do not mindfully fight against him, you will resort to doing that which is easy. You will bend the ears of your mind toward the mouth of the enemy, and there he will have free will to tell you how bad things are. You will then focus on whatever he tells you, and that could very well lead you to believe there is no way out. That is when it is important to stop and look over your life. That is the time to stop and start counting your blessings of that day, that week, that month, that year. I promise you; this will open your eyes to see that the goodness of God prevails over that unpleasant situation.

PRAISE AND WORSHIP GOD

Praise and worship are powerful means by which we can change our mental state and our perspective. Praise and worship will take your eyes and mind off the problems and put them on the God who rules over your problems. In praising God, you are acknowledging Him for what He can do and has done, and when you worship God, you are acknowledging Him for who He is.

Worship recognizes His character, His nature. Praise recognizes His capabilities. Therefore, when the depressed praises God, their mind must go back to things that God has done for them, and any recollection of the goodness of God can only strengthen their faith to believe for the now. When the depressed worship God, they are honoring God for being the God He says He is. When they worship God, they set their affections on God and turn their attention to the things of God—not to their problems—and give God praise and thanks. This will without doubt remind them that God is present and well able.

Worship and praise are not the first things a depressed person thinks to do. When depressed, it is easy to curl up in a corner and shut the world out; therefore, you must fight against the tides of depression to praise and worship God when in this state of mind. Asaph was in this very place, but he said, "Thy way, O God, is in the sanctuary: who is so great a God as our God?" (Psalm 77:13, KJV). Asaph recognized that he must muster up the energy and go into the house of the Lord, even though he was depressed.

The Father encouraged us not the neglect the assembling of the saints together (Hebrews 10:25) because He knows there are benefits beyond measure that come to us when we gather with God's people. Could this be why one of the first things the depressed think to do is stay away from church? Could this be another strategy of the enemy, of which many are unaware? Based on Asaph's description of his emotional state, I see no reason to think he was excited and running into the sanctuary. I believe he had to muster up the energy to go there, but he did.

Kathryn Greene-McCreight, in her book, Darkness Is My Only Companion, describes her journey through ten years of extreme depression and bipolar disorder and how gathering with God's people helped her. She said, "It is so important to worship in community—to ask your brothers and sisters in Christ to pray for you . . . Sometimes you literally cannot make it on your own, and you need to borrow from the faith of those around you. Companionship in the Lord Jesus is powerful".[19]

Asaph praised and worshipped God from the pit of depression. Starting with verse 13, he acknowledged the greatness of God. He asked the rhetorical question: What god is great like my God? That is to say, God Jehovah is the greatest God. He declared God as strong and the One Who does wonders. He proclaimed God as the redeemer of His people and went on to state all the wonderful things God had done for His people. Asaph's remembrance of what God had done for His people served as a reminder to him that God cares about him too and can deliver him too. His praises to God served as a reminder to him that the omnipotent God can do all that is necessary to fulfill His promises to him, and that God loves him enough to see about him.

I can only imagine the mental shift Asaph experienced as he opened his mouth and proclaimed the goodness of God when he rehearsed some of the acts of God. It is the same Asaph that is talking in verse 1 that is also talking in verse 13, but he sounds very different, doesn't he? The chapter starts with an Asaph that has an enormous problem and a small God; but he did not curl up and hoped to die. Instead, he cried out to God and moved on from there to worship and to praise God. As he praised God, he forced himself to rehearse the past blessings of God's faithfulness, and that strengthened his faith and gave him hope, and so he worshipped. Now he sees God as big, and his problems small.

Asaph obviously had a mind shift. Praise and worship pulled him out of the deep, dark hole of depression to a place where he is overwhelmed by the power and greatness of God.

Now, I do not think a person whose eyes are on God can stay depressed. Try worshipping God. Try telling Him about Himself. Try telling Him He can deliver you and watch Him alter your situation. He will rise up when you praise Him, and at His rising, your enemies will scatter.

ENCOURAGE YOURSELF

In Psalm 42:5–6 (NIV), David recognized he was downhearted, and asked himself, "Why, my soul, are you downcast? Why so disturbed within me?" Then he encouraged himself: "Put your hope in God, for I will yet praise him, my Savior and my God." Verse 6 says: "My soul is downcast within me; therefore I will remember you from the land of the Jordan, the heights of Hermon—from Mount Mizar." The Amplified version of these verses say:

> *Why are you cast down, O my inner self? And why should you moan over me and be disquieted within me? Hope in God and wait expectantly for Him, for I shall yet praise Him, my Help and my God. O my God, my life is cast down upon me [and I find the burden more than I can bear]; therefore will I [earnestly] remember You from the land of the Jordan [River] and the [summits of Mount] Hermon, from the little mountain Mizar.*

Brenton's English translation of the Greek Septuagint gives a deeper understanding of the spiritual dynamics of the Psalmist David's heart: "Wherefore art thou downcast" (NIV), "cast down" (AMP), or very sad means afflicted beyond measure, deeply grieved, deeply distressed, profoundly sorrowful. O my soul? and wherefore dost thou trouble, or "Why so disturbed within me" (NIV), or "disquieted within me" (AMP), which means complete confusion, profoundly disturbed, agitated like a glass of water that is shaken suddenly, causing inward upheaval, made restless, disturbed calmness.

David encouraged himself to hope in God. Hope urgently called David's attention to the God he knew. Hope reminded him that God is his salvation. Hope made him declare, "My Savior and my God" (NIV), or "My Help and my God" (AMP). The help or salvation that David sought was deliverance and the lifting of his countenance. O my God, my soul has been troubled, or "downcast" (NIV), or "cast down" (AMP), which means shaken or stirred up, troubled, distressed, acute mental/spiritual agitation. David was in a low place. His spirit was disrupted. His countenance was sad.

David was in a state of despair, and despair means literally to be brought low and figuratively to be humbled, to have one's arrogance brought down. The word "despair" in the early 14th century stems from the Old French word *desperer*, which means to be dismayed or to lose hope, despair. The meaning of the Latin word *desperare* is not very different: to despair, to lose all hope. The literal meaning of despair is no hope. It is a state of depressed mood and hopelessness.[20] The Cambridge Dictionary says despair is "the feeling that there is no hope and that you can do nothing to improve a difficult or worrying situation."

A close look at the meaning of these words gives a good picture of the mental state of David. He was in a hopeless state. He felt as if there was no way out. The AMP version says that he felt he had an unbearable burden. But David realized his spiritual state; he looked at himself and began to question himself, and then he answered the question. And look where he found the answer for relief from his despair: in praising God. He said, "I will *yet* praise God." So, even though I am in despair, I am going to praise God. He said, "I am cast down, therefore." So, because of my state of mind, I will earnestly remember God.

To pull himself out of depression, David reminded himself of God's goodness and love. He told himself to hope in God and to wait on God. The Psalmist David had lost his joy, and we see him exhorting himself to hope in God and intently recall the God he knows Him to be. He knew that when he looked to God, his joy would be restored.

David was man like you and me, so, if he could do it, we can too. When you feel downhearted, you may need to find a mirror. Look yourself in the eye, and ask yourself the same question, then answer it as David did. Talk to yourself and talk to the Lord. He will meet your needs. He will lead you in paths of love and light and joy where you will find new hope.

This cannot be a mindless exercise where you simply say the words because they are there to be repeated. You must say these words in faith and with expectation that God is going to show up. You must remember God. You must set your thoughts upon Him. That is your way out of depression. You cannot think about the gloominess you're in and think about God and all His glory at the same time. So, it is either you think upon the gloominess, or you think upon the faithfulness of God. Choose life as David did.

The Psalmist David said, "I will yet praise him." Your praise will invoke the presence of God. God said that He inhabits the praises of His people (Psalm 22:3). Praising God will change your mood and lift the spirit of heaviness. Praise is celebrating who God is; it is always joyous. Therefore, praising God destroys depression. Joy is the antidote to depression. The joy of the Lord is your strength (Nehemiah 8:10). Therefore, as you praise God, you are strengthened, and you gain the ability to pull from under depression.

The Holy Spirit will change your circumstances. He, the Holy Spirit, will bring liberty to you and give you joy for mourning and a garment of praise for the spirit of heaviness (Isaiah 61:3). The presence of the Holy Spirit will remove burdens and destroy yokes (Isaiah 10:27). The anointing power of the Holy Spirit will remove and destroy depression. It is like drinking from a never-ending cup of joy when you praise God.

Take the Psalmist David's advice and praise God. Praise silences and stops the enemy (Psalm 8:2). Praise sentences the enemy to his judgment (Psalm 149:6–9). Lift up praise to the Lord! Say this to yourself audibly: "My help comes from God my Father." If you must repeat this statement over and over until your spirit agrees with it, then do so. You are fighting your way from under depression by setting your mind on God and by praising Him.

Chapter Nine: Seven Main Takeaways

1. The root of the word "depress" means to press down. Depression should be thought of then as a force or a spirit that presses down on the life within a person.

2. We run a supremely high risk and put ourselves in a very vulnerable place when we are out of touch with our mental health or our thought life.

3. Guard your mind against the enemy of your soul at all costs! Do not let him speak into your spirit.

4. Depression, by its very nature, restricts our ability to act and action is required to overcome a depressed state, so do not let yourself go there.

5. It is very important to regain perspective when you feel weighted down by depression, and you must try to do so as quickly as possible.

6. Praise and worship are powerful means by which we can change our mental state and our perspective.

7. Praise and worship will take your eyes and mind off the problems and put them on the God who rules over your problems.

OVERCOMING DEPRESSION: KNOW THE GOD YOU SERVE

When you know the nature of the God you serve, while being closed to everyone else, you will open the door to your darkest place to Him. His light will then overcome the darkness of depression.

It is sad to say, but it is true that many in the church know of God, but do not know Him. To know Him is to know His ways. Many have gained vast knowledge about God and still do not know God in His true nature. Having biblical knowledge so that we can push and debate our doctrinal beliefs will not give us the spiritual sustenance we need in times of difficulties. However, when we seek to know the Person, Jesus Christ, the character, and nature of God, for the sole purpose of intimacy with Him, then our anchor will hold in the time of storm. To know God is to know Him personally, to know Him intimately, and to know Him deeply.

We all have a host of people in our lives, some we can say we know more than others. For example, we know our parents, our significant others, and our friends. By knowing them, I mean, first and foremost, we have a relationship with them, but not all relationships are the same. Some relationships are superficial, and others are deep and genuine. It is the people with whom we have the deeper relationships that we know. These relationships allow us to understand the person.

Oxford Languages defines "know" as such: "to be aware of through observation, inquiry, or information; to have developed a relationship with (someone) through meeting and spending time with them; to be familiar or friendly with." Other definitions of "know" include to be aware, to be conscious, to have knowledge, to be informed, and to have information.

Based on these definitions, to go beyond knowing of God to knowing Him, we must observe Him by reading and studying His Word and being sensitive to what He does and how He works. We must be inquisitive about Him, meaning we should have an interest in knowing His Word. As well, we must spend time with Him—in prayer, reading and listening to His Word, and in worship. If we practice these things with a sincere heart to have a deep intimate relationship with God, the relationship we have with Him will be deepened and become genuinely intimate. When we make our relationship with God a clear priority, when we make Him our first love, and when we live with a heart after God, we can truly say we don't just know of God, but we know Him.

When We Do Not Know God

Bear in mind that to know God is to know His ways. To know God is to know how He works. Now, we will never know God to the fullest, but when we know God, we should be able to tell when God and not our adversary is working. Sometimes the work of the enemy is very subtle, and if we do not know God, we will think God is working when, in fact, it is Satan. The same thing applies when the devil speaks. Sometimes he speaks "truth" to us with a slight twist. If we don't know the truth of the Word, we will believe God is talking to us. God's ways are not our ways, and His thoughts are as far from us as the east is from the west, so we will never fully understand Him. However, we should know Him enough to discern when He is speaking instead of the devil or our own selves.

John 1:1 says, "In the beginning was the Word, and the Word was with God, and the Word was God." It is clear here that God is the Word and that the Word is God. They are inseparable. Also remember that Jesus and God are one. Jesus said that if you see Him, you see the Father (John 14:9). Therefore, Jesus is the God; and if God is the Word, then Jesus is the Word. Mike Mazzalongo puts it this way: If A (God) = B (Word), and B (Word) = C (Jesus), then A (God) = C (Jesus).

You cannot separate God from the Word, Jesus from God, or the Word from God or Jesus. So then, the best way to know God or Jesus, if considering them separate, is to know the Word. And I am not speaking of knowing the Word so that we can prove others wrong or defend our position in a debate about the Scriptures, I am speaking of relational knowing.

The degree to which many Christians become downhearted when things don't go their way—more specifically when God does not answer their prayers as they expect—makes one wonder if they know the God they prayed to or if they are, in fact, praying to the God of the Bible. Some Christians believe that because they are believers, then they should never be sick, and neither should other Christians become sick. Others believe that everyone they pray for in the name of Jesus should be healed. There are those who believe that, because they are followers of Jesus, they should not experience any stressful life events—no fatal accidents, no deadly diagnosis or chronic diseases, no divorce, no unruly children, no financial challenges, and I could go on and on. In other words, they expect life to be void of pain.

These dear believers do not know God, and therefore, expect the unexpected from Him. Upon not getting what they expected, they become susceptible to despondency, which could lead to depression. As a reminder, I am not referring to clinical depression. I am speaking of situational depression or what some call a blue day.

If they knew the God of the Bible, they would know that Jesus said in John 16:33, "That in me ye might have peace. In the world ye shall have tribulation: but be of good cheer; I have overcome the world." Also, they would know that the righteous will endure many afflictions, but the Lord delivers them out of them all (Psalm 34:19). Additionally, they would know that believers do have hard times to the extent that they weep, but despite the troubles, joy comes in the morning (Psalm 30:5). Furthermore, they would know that they will have experiences that are so painful that they feel like they are dying, but the God of the Bible assures them that those experiences won't kill them, they are just shadows of death. The Psalmist David said that, although he walked through the shadow of death, he would not fear evil because God was with Him. If believers would get to know their God, they would not expect Him to operate outside of His character, which is His Word, and then blame Him when He doesn't.

When we know God, we do not grapple with the fact that God decides who will be healed and keep on living in this earth, when they will be healed, and how they will be healed. He also decides who will be healed by transitioning to eternal life. Isaiah 55:8–9 says, "For my thoughts are not your thoughts, neither are your ways my ways. As the heavens are higher than the earth, so my ways are higher than your ways and my thoughts than your thoughts." The mystery of God's thoughts and ways offers the opportunity to trust His character and His Word.

Believers who do not *know* God will likely doubt Him, lose faith, and question Him when He doesn't act as they expect. Some even become angry with Him. Others become saddened to the point of depression after asserting the Word, after praying and fasting, and repeating confessions and declarations over their situation and God does not change their situation as they expect. But when we know God, we understand that our steps are ordered by Him (Psalm 37:23), and when directed by Him, we cannot go wrong. It requires *knowing* God to still believe God is in control and that He is ordering your steps even when things seem to be falling apart and the painful experiences run deep. This level of faith comes only by knowing Him.

Some take Scriptures such as the following, and many others, to mean God will give them everything they pray for.

> **1 John 5:14–15** (NIV) — *And this is the confidence that we have in him, that, if we ask any thing according to his will, he heareth us: And if we know that he hear us, whatsoever we ask, we know that we have the petitions that we desired of him.*

> **John 15:7** (NIV) — *If ye abide in me, and my words abide in you, ye shall ask what ye will, and it shall be done unto you.*

Are they wrong to believe verses such as these and expect God to answer their prayers? Should they believe the Word, but not under all circumstances? Is God unfaithful when He does not answer all our prayers? No, they are not wrong to believe the Word and they are not wrong to expect God to answer their prayers. But it is wrong to box God in a corner and expect Him to answer their prayers their way. If you recall, as children when we asked our parents for things, they answered us, but we didn't always get what we wanted. Sometimes, their response was yes, sometimes it was a flat out no, and other times it was wait. As it was with our earthly parents, so it is with our Heavenly Father.

Think about it, if we were to get everything we ask for the way we want it, our faith would never be tried, which means our faith would never grow. If God was like the vending machine that so many want Him to be, then we would never learn to trust Him. If we were to get our desired answer to every prayer, we would not have a testimony and we would not learn the many life lessons that make us stronger and equip us to be a blessing to someone else.

I don't know how long David was on the run from Saul, but I am certain it wasn't a day; it was much longer than that. I am also certain that David prayed numerous times, asking God to turn his enemies back so that he could go back to a normal life. We see many prayers as such in the book of Psalms. But God did not answer David the first time he prayed, and neither did He answer in the way David prayed.

When the teenage boy, Joseph, was ripped away from his family and all that he knew, and was suddenly thrown among strangers, I am sure he was terrified. I am sure he called out to God. The Scriptures say the Lord was with him, so he must have been doing something to entertain God's presence. Joseph went through one tragedy after another, but instead of God delivering him out of them, He carried him through them. And the outcome was far beyond Joseph's imagination, providing an outcome that not only blessed him but many nations.

Could it be that God does not give you what you ask for because He has a bigger plan? Could your trial that is bringing you to a place of depression actually be trying to equip you to be a blessing to many? Joseph could have fallen into depression, but he did not. He allowed God to do things His way, and the end was to the glory of God.

Hannah prayed many times for a son. She was in desperate need for an answer from God as she faced daily ridicule at the hands of Penina. She was so desperate that while she was praying, Eli the priest, thought she was drunk. God did answer her prayers, but not when she expected Him to. Hannah persisted in prayer, praying fervently, but God still moved on His own time. We must learn to trust God that His plans for us are best. We must learn to wait on the Lord. Perhaps what appear to be distressfully unanswered prayers only require that you wait on the Lord and let Him work on His schedule.

The Apostle Paul prayed three times for the thorn in his flesh to be removed, and God did not remove it. His answer was not the one he desired or expected. The Father told him he must bear it, but not to worry because His grace was enough to help Paul bear it. The Apostle Paul was an anointed man of God. If anybody's prayers can shake the desired answers out of heaven, Paul's prayers should, but the anointing that Paul had was given by God Himself. Therefore, the giver of the anointing is greater than the host of the anointing. God had the final say.

My beloved brothers and sisters, God will not give you what you ask for every time, but rest assured whatever His answer is—yes, no, or wait—is best for you. Even when you don't get exactly what you prayed for, know that grace and peace are multiplied to you in the knowledge of God and of Jesus your Lord, seeing that His divine power has granted to you everything pertaining to life and godliness through the true knowledge of Him who called you by His own glory and excellence (2 Peter 1:2–3). So, you already have everything pertaining to life and godliness, and this comes through the true knowledge of God. You must know His ways to enjoy the peace of God and not be anxious when things don't go your way.

When we know God, the Holy Spirit will capture our thoughts, guide our expectations to keep them within the confines of the Word of God, and He will elevate our thoughts by faith to think more like Christ and less like the one who does not know God. In knowing God and by the divine grace of God, through faith, we will develop the mind of Christ to patiently mine out the truth of God found in His Word. And upon finding the truth, live by the truth and treat God like the truth.

God is faithful. He is the good Father, therefore, when we know Him, we can trust Him. When we know that He cannot lie and His promises are yes and amen, we can rest in Him, even when things are not going as desired. A natural fruit of knowing God is faith in Him, even in tumultuous times. When we know God, we aspire to live out the fruit of faith in Christ and not back Him in a corner and hurl His Words at Him with the expectation that He must do things our way. When we know God, we know it is in our very best interest to say, "Not my will Lord, but Yours be done."

Psalm 9:10 (NIV) says, "Those who know your name trust in you, for you, Lord, have never forsaken those who seek you." Knowing God will free you from worry and anxiety. No wonder He said, "Be still, and know that I am God" (Psalm 46:10a). Seek to know the God who loves you beyond

166

measure, the God who has no limits, so that you can better face the storms of life, knowing He is the Shepherd of your life. God loves you!

FIGHT! KNOW AND LIVE THE WORD OF GOD

Depression is heaviness that weighs a person down. It drains its host of motivation and energy. Therefore, the depressed must fight to come out from under its force. Depression will not lift if you do nothing, but at the same time, depression makes you want to do nothing. So, the depressed must resolve to push past the feeling and fight their way out.

You must fight with the Sword of the Spirit, which is the Word of God (Ephesians 6:17). You must turn your heart to the comforting words of Scripture. You must find a promise in the Word and hold on to that promise, knowing that you have a wonderful and faithful God who has promised to be with you in all the crucibles of life. He said He would be your sufficiency in all situations, and He is waiting to do just that if you would only let Him do it.

Depression is a crucible, and a crucible is a test or a challenge. Depression is a battle, but it is not a physical battle, it is spiritual. We cannot fight spiritual battles with physical weaponry. The Word of God is your number one weapon against depression. The Apostle Paul says it very well.

> **2 Corinthians 10:4–5** (NIV) — *For the weapons of our warfare are not carnal, but mighty through God to the pulling down of strong holds; Casting down imaginations, and every high thing that exalteth itself against the knowledge of God, and bringing into captivity every thought to the obedience of Christ.*

The weapons of depression are the lying imaginations and arguments from the enemy. They are the lies that set themselves up against what God has said in His Word. Paul acknowledges that these weapons will seek to ruin us, but he said we can take captive every thought to make them obedient to Christ Jesus. But how do we do this? We must fight with the Word of God, which is the sword of the Spirit (Ephesians 6:17) and with the shield of faith (Ephesians 6:16). For without faith, the Word will do nothing. We must treat the Word of God as if God is standing before us in the flesh saying them to us. We must believe the Word of God unconditionally, and we must make them flesh by walking them out in our daily lives.

As a child of God, you have rights to a host of promises in the Bible. For example, "The righteous cry out, and the Lord hears them; he delivers them from all their troubles. The Lord is close to the broken-hearted and saves those who are crushed in spirit" (Psalm 34:17–18, NIV). It is quite obvious here that the righteous will experience times of trouble, which will leave us brokenhearted and crushed in spirit. It is also clear in the Psalm that God is not uninvolved during our difficult times, but instead, He draws near to the brokenhearted and those crushed in spirit.

If, as believers, we own this Scripture during times of difficulties, we would do a far better job at keeping depression at bay. If, as you feel yourself slipping or even as disaster strikes, you cry out to God, you will have taken the first step toward your deliverance. As you cry out to God, you know that He will hear you and will deliver you, but because you *know* Him, you have no preconceived notion of how He will deliver you. Nevertheless, you trust Him to do it His way, with the understanding that His way is best for you.

Let us look at a few more Scriptures and how you can use them to combat depression.

Psalm 147:3 (NIV) — *He heals the brokenhearted and binds up their wounds.*

If you take this verse as is, without any condition, you will be convinced that you have a good and wonderful God, a God who is entirely able to heal your broken heart and bind up your wounds. You will know that God will comfort you during hardships and then put you in a place where you can use the strength and knowledge you gained from the painful experience to comfort others.

With that understanding, when you are at a low place, you will go to the Healer, no one and nothing else. You will not resort to overspending, alcohol, drugs, overworking, and other ungodly thing. And you will not rely on man to bring resolution to your situation. This Scripture will remind you that the arm of flesh has the potential to fail you, but the God you serve will not. I am not saying you should shut people out or refuse professional help if needed, but I am saying you must let God be the place from which your healing comes. Even if you talk to someone, you must understand that they are simply a conduit that is used by God.

The Word of God is true and trustworthy; His Word is perfect and pure, and His promises to you endure from one generation to another. And God has promised to heal your broken heart and bind up your wounds.

Philippians 4:6−7 (KJV) — *Be careful for nothing; but in every thing by prayer and supplication with thanksgiving let your requests be made known unto God. And the peace of God, which passeth all* *understanding, shall keep your hearts and minds through Christ Jesus.*

I call these two verses free therapy. Here you are told to be anxious or worry about nothing. Anxiety and worry are opposites of rest. Nothing means nothing. So, no circumstance in life should give you the okay to worry. Therefore, the Father who holds your life in His all-powerful hands is telling you that despite the situation, He has things in control, so do not be anxious. He is saying, instead of being anxious, you should pray, and not only pray but supplicate. When you worry or are anxious about anything, you think constantly about what has or may go wrong. You recycle checklists and scenarios in your mind, and this gets you nowhere. You cannot rest in God and worry or be anxious at the same time.

Next, the instruction is to pray the prayer of supplication. Supplication is to kneel before the Lord and humbly petition—appeal, plea, beg—God to intervene. You cannot make talking to God a secondary plan when going through a tough time. He must be your only plan and your only source. Also, you cannot proudly approach Him and throw His Words back at Him and presumptuously expect Him to do exactly as you command. This is not the time to name it and claim it. It is time to humble yourself before God and plea to Him to move on your behalf.

The next instruction is to couple the prayer of supplication with thanksgiving. So, you are not only asking, but while you are asking, you are thanking Him for the answer: His answer. Thanksgiving will steer your mind from the problem to the solution. Therefore, you cannot stay depressed while giving God thanks, especially if you're thanking Him for something you haven't even seen or experienced yet. This is what Hebrews 13:15 (KJV) calls the sacrifice of praise: "By him therefore let us offer the sacrifice of praise to God continually, that is, the fruit of our lips giving thanks to his name." This kind of praise will put you in a mode of expectancy, definitely not depression or gloominess.

Then verse 7 says, "And the peace of God, which passeth all understanding, shall keep your hearts and minds through Christ Jesus." You must first put away anxiety and worry, then take your requests to God, and while asking Him, give Him thanks for His gracious move on your behalf *and then* the peace of God will flood your soul.

This peace is no ordinary peace. This peace will pass human understanding. So yes, given the situation, you should be curled up under a blanket, but instead, you are thanking God. That is not humanly possible, so such a behavior will be confusing to you and to those around you.

Praying with thankfulness is the pathway to peace, and peace and depression cannot coexist. That is why this prescription is free therapy. It is the remedy for depression. This peace, although mysterious, is not an ambiguous theoretical idea. It is an actual force that can significantly impact your situation. Have you ever heard a believer who is facing incredibly hard or sad times say that they feel peace? I can assuredly say that the believer facing a difficult time but also has the peace of God in their heart is not angry, not ungrateful, and is not complaining, but is grateful and is resting in the Lord. This is God's peace, and it is appropriately clear that this peace comes from God, not from their circumstances. We get the peace of God when we thank and praise Him, and thus we have good reason to give Him the praise that He well deserves.

You can have this peace too. Depression is not your portion. Follow this protocol and you will have God's peace in place of anxiety and worry.

> **Psalm 37:23** (AMP) — *The steps of a [good and righteous] man are directed and established by the Lord, And He delights in his way [and blesses his path].*

This verse excites me! It tells me that if my ways please the Lord, I can "blame" Him for whatever happens to me. The qualifier to the promise is a righteous man. A righteous man lives a life that aligns with the Word of God. If you live your life in accordance with God's Word, you too can claim this promise. Therefore, you can look up to God from your low dark place and say to Him, "God, You directed me down this path because my steps were ordered by You; therefore, I am waiting on You to get me out of this situation."

This should give anyone who meets this criterion great peace. The Lord is in control of the life of a righteous man, and the Lord takes joy in the course of his life. What better person to be in control of your life than the God of gods and King of kings? Rest in Him with the assurance that He is in control of your life.

> **Deuteronomy 31:8** (NIV) — *The Lord himself goes before you and will be with you; he will never leave you nor forsake you. Do not be afraid; do not be discouraged.*

Here is another powerful promise in the Word of God that can pull you out of depression: God will never leave you or forsaken you. It may not look that way while in depression, but your loving Father does go before you and clear the way. Think about it, the situation that is causing the depression could be worse. It might have been designed to kill you, but God went ahead of you and cleared the way. He is with you even in your dark place. Remember, He is close to the brokenhearted. That is you while in depression. The Lord is nigh, and He said that He is not going anywhere. He will always be with you.

If you can own that promise and act like you do, you will shake off depression. If you can own this promise, you will not be afraid or discouraged.

> **Psalm 40:1–3** (NIV) — *I waited patiently for the Lord; he turned to me and heard my cry. He lifted me out of the slimy pit, out of the mud and mire; he set my feet on a rock and gave me a firm place to stand. He put a new song in my mouth, a hymn of praise to our God. Many will see and fear the Lord and put their trust in him.*

Ofttimes, we read the Scriptures and we detach ourselves from what the Father has done in the lives of the Bible characters. But we must remember that these were people just like we are. David was a man like you and me. So was Moses, Elijah, Jeremiah, Peter, Catherine, Vicky, Jeremy, Nathaniel, and the list can go on. Here David said that he was in a low place—a slimy pit of mud and mire. He cried out to God from this low place and God heard him. God not only heard him, but He pulled him out, put him standing on a firm place, and put a song of praise in his mouth.

When you're depressed, you're in a slippery place, and without help from God, the only place you will go is down. God heard David's cry and pulled him out. He will do the same for you if you cry to Him. Too many of us cry to others. We tend to cry to people who can do nothing for us. Some of these people are in similar situations as we are or even worse. Cry to God. He is your way out.

God will put a song of praise in your mouth. Praise comes from the Latin word "pretium," meaning price. Prize is also a variation of this word. Originally, it meant "to set a great price on." So, when we praise God, we are placing an immense value on Him and His acts. According to Dictionary.com, "Praise is the act of expressing approval or admiration; commendation; laudation." It is the offering of grateful homage in words or song as an act of worship or a hymn of praise to God.

The song of praise is paramount, because your singing will tell God that you highly regard Him and what He does and can do. When you sing praises to God or speak well of Him, your mindset will change and the circumstances that surround you will adjust to the will of the Father for you. You cannot speak well of God and still be depressed. Praise will focus your mind on God.

Your song of praise is a weapon. It will silence the enemy. Praise confuses the enemy. In the Bible, there are several examples of how praise was used in battles to help secure victories. Praise will break the grip that the enemy has on you. If you cry out to God, He will give you this weapon so that you can use it to help you fight this spiritual battle called depression, and your life will be a testimony to others.

So, you see, your troubles are not all about you. If you don't walk out this Word, you stand the chance of blocking someone's blessing. When you cry out to God and He puts a song of praise in your mouth, you will change and "Many will see and fear the Lord and put their trust in him." Many who know where you were and probably didn't expect what the Lord has done for you will see the work of God and, as a result, fear and trust Him. So, I encourage you today to make your trials count. Let God work through you and bring you to a place of victory, so that others can be blessed.

Psalm 32:10 (NIV) — *Many are the woes of the wicked, but the Lord's unfailing love surrounds the one who trusts in him.*

As you read these words, I want you to say out loud, "I'm so glad trouble doesn't last always." My dear brothers and sisters, like everything else, your troubles are only for a season. You may see many afflictions, and it may not look like they're going away, but believe the Word of God: joy will come.

This is a verse of hope. You will weep, but you won't weep forever. This should lift your spirit. The night may look quite long sometimes but hold on to the fact that morning is coming. God's Word is true, your low state will not kill you. It will not last forever. Things will change. Joy will come. Your job is to take God at His Word. Believe Him!

2 Corinthians 1:3–4 (NIV) — *Praise be to the God and Father of our Lord Jesus Christ, the Father of compassion and the God of all comfort, who comforts us in all our troubles, so that we can comfort those in any trouble with the comfort we ourselves receive from God.*

Is your God "the Father of compassion and the God of all comfort"? Compassion and comfort embody the God of the Bible. In Hebrew and Greek, compassion in the Bible means "to have mercy, to feel sympathy, and to have pity."[21] God is "a compassionate and gracious God, slow to anger, abounding in love and faithfulness" (Psalm 86:15, NIV). His compassion is limitless and unending. His compassions never fail; they are new every morning (Lamentations 3:22–23).

God will comfort you in your troubles. Note, the verse does not say He will rescue you from your troubles. There are times when He will do so, but it is important to know that sometimes He will bring comfort to you *in* your troubles. This is very important, because God "comforts us in all our troubles, so that we can comfort those in any trouble with the comfort we ourselves receive from God" (2 Corinthians 1:4, NIV). We experience hard times so that we can teach others from what we learned in our own experience. God will comfort you so that you can comfort those in trouble. Maybe you won't know how to comfort others if you don't go to a low place so that you can be comforted by the Father. So, your pain is purposeful and should not be wasted.

This is very important for the church to hear. Sometimes, our first recourse is to go into spiritual warfare or call our prayer partner to pray us out of the storm that the Father wants to join us in. I'd rather be in a storm with God than to be in a place of peace but absent from Him. He sometimes wants us in the storm so that we can learn something to later build someone up. This is a device that the Father uses to equip us to work the ministry effectively.

A good understanding of this Scripture will save you from depression. In fact, walking out this Scripture should make it easy for a person to praise God while in the struggle. Why? Because they see that God is working out a plan. They see that God is preparing to use them. What greater joy there is than to know that God is working through you?

> **Hebrews 13:8** (KJV) — *Jesus Christ the same yesterday, and to day, and for ever.*

I think this is a fitting verse with which to end this discussion. We have looked at several Scriptures, but they will mean nothing if you don't see the steadfastness or the unchangeability of these Words coming from your Father. The Scripture here tells us that the God we serve is unchangeable. He is the very same yesterday, yester-month, and yester-year, He is the same today, tonight, this morning, and this afternoon, and He will be the same forever.

So, without doubt, you can always trust and believe the Word of God. No matter what the situation looks like and no matter what dispensation you are living in, the Word of God stands forever. He is His Word, and His Word is Him so, if He is unchangeable, then His Word is unchangeable. Trust the God you serve. Trust the God you worship. Learn to look to God and not at your circumstances. Stand on His Word. Exercise your faith. Do not make His Words conditional. They are not circumstantial. They never change, and He never changes.

PRACTICAL STEPS TO MANAGING DEPRESSION

The following steps are practical things every believer can do to manage depression.

MAKE A DIFFICULT CHOICE

Ofttimes, the person facing depression must make a difficult choice to make their way out of depression. For example, you may need to accept the fact that your marriage has ended. You may have to accept the fact that your spouse has chosen someone over you, and you must choose to forgive him. Unforgiveness will keep you tied to depression, so, this is a must. You may even have to accept how you contributed to the ongoing conflicts in your marriage. Then you need to choose what is necessary to build a new life without your spouse. When things don't go as we hoped, we need to be strong and make new choices.

Be In Touch with Your Feelings

It is particularly important that you are in touch with your feelings when dealing with depression. This will help you ward off depression and help you get out of depression. By being aware of your feelings, you will know that your spirit is becoming gloomy well before depression sets in. You must listen to yourself. What words are you saying? With what emotions or feelings are you speaking? You cannot ignore what you hear. You must accept what you hear and deal with it early on. This will keep you from spiraling into depression.

Deal with Your Feelings

In dealing with depression or any other situation, the healthiest thing to do is deal with your feelings. Maybe, you will need to give yourself the time and space to express your feelings. For example, you may need to cry or maybe you need to express the anger you feel about the situation. You can cry. Crying does not mean you are weak. And you can show anger—only be sure to do so without sinning. Whatever the emotional response, express it, but do so in a godly manner. The worst thing to do is pretend the feeling is not there. That will make room for it to intensify.

It is also very important to realize that your state of depression will not last forever. Even the worst situation will come to an end. However, depression will last longer and will worsen if not addressed or if not faced with the truth. If you feel fear, sadness, confusion, shock, anger, or any other emotion, face it and do the needful to address them. Sometimes by allowing yourself to feel these emotions, you can uncover what is going on more deeply under them.

DO SOMETHING

The worst thing you can do besides ignoring your feelings is not do anything. Action and movement are the rivals of depression so you must do something to get out of depression. It will not be easy, but you must think carefully about what you can do with your time and energy. As hard as it may feel, you must devise a plan for what you will do and even more importantly, you must follow through even if you don't feel like it. You must fight to get out of depression, or it will not lift. This is the crucible of the fight.

One thing you can do to get out of depression is to write down all the things that have gone right recently. This exercise will quickly reveal to you that things are not as bad as they seem. Another is to set your needs aside and help someone while you yourself need help. The mental shift that this can bring is unimaginable and it gets God's attention. Job was in misery but "The Lord restored the fortunes of Job when he prayed for his friends, and the Lord gave Job twice as much as he had before" (Job 42:10, AMP).

Believe it or not, you have control over depression. Depression does not have control over you. When the depressive feelings start, you may feel like you cannot control it, but if you are caught in the rain, you can put up an umbrella, get out of the rain, or stay in the rain uncovered and blame the weather. When depression visits you, will you let it in? What will you do to avoid being submerged in depression?

Chapter Ten: Seven Main Takeaways

1. The degree to which many Christians become downhearted when things don't go their way—more specifically when God does not answer their prayers as they expect—makes one wonder if they know the God they prayed to, or if they are, in fact, praying to the God of the Bible.

2. When we know God, we do not grapple with the fact that God decides who will be healed and keep on living in this earth, when they will be healed, and how they will be healed. He also decides who will be healed by transitioning to eternal life.

3. Because many believers do not *know* God, they doubt Him, lose faith, and question Him when He doesn't act as they expect. Some even become angry with Him.

4. Depression will not lift if you do nothing, but at the same time, depression makes you want to do nothing.

5. The weapons of depression are the lying imaginations and arguments from the enemy.

6. Praying with thankfulness is the pathway to peace. This peace, although mysterious, is not an ambiguous theoretical idea. It is an actual force that can significantly impact your situation.

7. Believe it or not, you have control over depression. Depression does not have control over you.

A MENTAL PICTURE OF THE FRUSTRATED

Expectation is the mother of all frustration.
—Antonio Banderas

L ike how discouragement, if not dealt with, can lead to depression, frustration, if not addressed, can lead to helplessness and failure. Frustration results from small annoyances in our lives. When taken independently, they seem insignificant and unimpactful, but cumulatively, they can be devastating. The intent of the devil is for us to ignore the small irritations while he piles them on, and by the time we become cognizant of what is happening, we are buried in frustration and failure.

We are all busy doing multiple things. Some of us are overly committed, and consequently, have created ample opportunities to be frustrated. When we have more to do than time allows, more to do than we can complete in a spirit of excellence, or more to do than we have the knowledge, skills, or experience for, we will without doubt be frustrated. Frustration is not good for our mental, emotional, or spiritual wellbeing. But as we try to respond to the many demands that are placed on us by this fast-paced world in which we live, we often unintentionally create an environment in which frustration can proliferate in our lives.

There are also cases in which we do not contribute to the frustrations that seep into our lives. Many of us have healthy and realistic goals that we seek to accomplish, but things do not always go as planned. Sometimes we work at our best, yet our efforts appear to be fruitless, and often it is not a major event that averts our goals. These are frustrations.

You should know as well that the more you achieve or even the more you seek to achieve, the more frustration will knock at your door. Typically, the more important the goal, the greater the frustration. This is so, mainly because frustration is a tool that the enemy uses to divert you from your calling and purpose in life. Therefore, the more you strive to fulfill the call of God upon your life—be it in ministry, your family, your career, or your relationships—the more the devil will seek to frustrate you. His aim is to frustrate you enough so that you give up. He wants you to abandon your calling. That is failure.

Oxford Languages defines frustration as the feeling of being upset or annoyed, especially because of an inability to change or achieve something, the prevention of the progress, success, or fulfillment of something. Frustration is experienced whenever the results you experience do not fit the effort you have made; for example, your actions produce less and fewer results than you think they should. Generally, whenever we reach our desired outcomes, we feel pleased and whenever we do not reach them, we may become frustrated, we may feel irritable or annoyed, or we may even become angry. Repeated inability to achieve our desired outcomes will result in a loss of confidence, and ultimately failure.

Frustrations also occur because we lose something that is needed to achieve our goal. This could lead to failure, and we all will fail at some point in life, but because of the prevalence and the wide use of frustration by our adversary, a person will be frustrated far more often than they fail. Frustration is as effective as it is because it is incremental. It seems small and is almost unnoticeable; and as a result, many times we are frustrated, and we think little of it. But each time we are frustrated, we lose focus, time, and energy needed to accomplish our goals.

THE DYNAMICS OF FRUSTRATION

All healthily functioning human beings want to achieve something. And if we want to achieve something, we must act upon our desire to achieve that thing. Once we begin to work toward the thing we want to achieve, we have created the perfect environment for frustration. Therefore, it is fair to say that life is full of frustrations. This can range from the minor irritations of losing something replaceable to the major problem of continually falling short of accomplishing a desired goal. Since many of the things we truly want attract frustration, it is in our best interest to understand it so that we can manage it effectively. And in understanding frustration, we must also consider the underlying forces of frustration.

An eye-opening fact of life that we all must keep in mind is we all have an enemy whose aim is to use pain and pleasure to make us blind, foolish, and miserable. The Bible calls him "the devil and Satan, the deceiver of the whole world . . . the accuser" (Revelation 12:9,10), "the ruler of this world" (John 12:31), and "the god of this age" (2 Corinthians 4:4). He is the adversary of the believer, and he roams around like a roaring lion, looking for someone to devour (1 Peter 5:8). Satan uses various means to devour his prey. Some are overwhelmingly harsh, sudden, and can be readily seen, and others, like frustration and distraction, are subtle and can go unnoticed.

I think it's worth introducing here that all things—all actions, thoughts, words, desires, or emotions—are fueled by one of two spirits: the Spirit of light or the spirit of darkness. There is no in-between, no gray spirit. A spirit is either of God or the devil. Even though one could argue that a spirit could be of oneself, the question then becomes which spirit is controlling the self? I say this because due to the seemingly harmlessness of frustration, some may hesitate to attribute it to the works of Satan. But once we consider the purpose and outcome of frustration, we will quickly see that it is not of God. Some would even argue that often we cause our own frustration. But I would rebut with the same question: which spirit is influencing the self to function in a manner that causes them to be frustrated?

If you drop a small pebble in a pond, it will produce ripples on the surface of the water. The ripples will spread in all directions and create circular waves that increase in radius across the surface of the water. If there is a light drizzle and you stand uncovered in it long enough, you will eventually be drenched with rain. If you put a frog suddenly into boiling water, it will jump out, but if the frog is put in lukewarm water which is then brought to a boil slowly, it will not perceive the danger and will be cooked to death. This is how Satan uses frustration against us.

The enemy of your soul can pile it on in a single day, over the course of a few days, or longer. For example, you have an especially important presentation to make at work. Your plan was to get to the office at least an hour early so that you can review your presentation at least one more time. But your nine-year-old daughter decided to go back to sleep even after you woke her. She moved the slowest in getting ready, and you were not able to drop her off at school in sufficient time to get to the office as early as you had planned. You are frustrated.

You got to the office and, in your haste, to get to your desk, you bumped into a colleague while carrying your cup of coffee and spilled it all over your dress. Your dress now has an obnoxious coffee stain on the front, and you do not have enough time to change your clothes before the presentation. You spend time trying to remove the stain as much as you can, and by the time you're done, it's time for the presentation. You are further frustrated and are losing confidence because one, you feel like you do not look professional and everyone is looking at the stain on your dress, and two, you do not feel prepared because you did not get to review the presentation.

You start the presentation, but because you are distracted by all that has happened and you have lost confidence in your ability to make a stunning presentation, you make several small mistakes, you are repetitious, you use a lot of fillers, and you do not engage your audience. This frustrates you even more because you know you can do better, and you know that failure to perform well on this presentation could cost you a good performance review and even a promotion.

If we take each of these incidents independently, they are not so bad, but taken together, the impact is great, and it's the impact that our adversary is seeking to achieve. All of what happened could gradually lead up to this person getting a poor performance review and being overlooked for a promotion for which she had worked all year.

Here's another example: you are scheduled to facilitate a workshop at the annual women's retreat that your church hosts.

You have been praying about the retreat and specifically about your role as a facilitator, and you have high expectations for the retreat. The week before the retreat you planned to minimize your activities on other things so that you can spend more time with the Lord and focus your mind on the task ahead. But during that week, several things happened that demanded your attention, making it impossible for you to be as focused as you wanted to or for you to spend the time you wanted to in prayer.

First, the car you planned on using to transport you and three other ladies to the retreat started leaking. You took it to the mechanic the moment you detected the leak. The mechanic told you it's fixed, and as required, you pay for the work that was done on the car, but the next day you notice that it's still leaking. You then had to go back to the mechanic and spend more time there while they work on the car. In addition, your six-year-old daughter caught the flu. She is clingy and needs mommy's tender loving care. You have given her home remedies and have prayed for her, but there are no signs of improvement. You're now spending most of your time back-and-forth with the mechanic or caring for your daughter. In fact, it is very difficult to get any time to yourself because your daughter, due to being ill, is clingy.

These incidents hindered you from preparing for the retreat the way you had planned, and now you are frustrated. If not careful or aware of the strategy of the enemy, you could become angry with the mechanic, and you could become annoyed and impatient with your daughter who needs you. Furthermore, if not careful, you could take this same spirit of frustration and discontent to the retreat. This is what the adversary was after all week, as it would then interfere with your ability to facilitate the workshop under the leading of the

Holy Spirit and could hinder the work of the Holy Spirit among the women at the retreat.

Frustration is a sinister threat that arises gradually rather than suddenly. Its gradual emergence makes us underestimate it, and thus we are less likely to respond to it as we should. This is a strategy of the enemy. However, we should not be ignorant of Satan's devices so that he does not outwit us (2 Corinthians 2:11).

THE EFFECTS OF FRUSTRATION

Frustration is not necessarily bad. It can point one to the problems in one's life and, as a result, it can be a motivator to change. However, frustration is destructive when the result is worse than where you were before the onset of the upsetting situation. When we are not aware of the strategies of the enemy, some of the usual responses to these unsettling situations include distraction, irritability, anger, stress, loss of confidence, destructive thinking, and quitting.

DISTRACTION

I liken the little annoying situations that frustrate us to the uninvited bugs and the little gnats that buzz around us continuously. A picnic in the park, a hike, a walk through the trails, or a cookout with friends and family are all fun-filled summer activities that can be ruined by annoying gnats that never leave us alone. There are different types of flies and there are different types of annoyances in our lives. Some flies are after the proteins, carbohydrates, salts, and sugars that are naturally present on our skin. Other flies are probably after our blood.

That is the nature of the annoyances that cause frustration. They inject themselves into our daily activities—work and play—to spoil the fun and to make our work futile. Annoyances come to take from you and in taking from you, they distract you from your focus.

Let us go back to the scenario with the mother who was scheduled to facilitate a workshop at the annual women's retreat. The annoying incidents that happened during the week before the retreat distracted her from focusing on the task. When the car she was planning on driving to the retreat began leaking and when her six-year-old daughter became ill, her attention was turned away from preparing to minister, focusing instead on these unexpected and unpleasant situations. Instead of spending her time and mental efforts on the task at hand, she was redirected to unplanned situations, and in doing so, she did not achieve her goal.

As discussed in an earlier chapter, distraction by nature takes you off course. Distraction changes the focus of our energy, effort, and attention to whatever it presents. Therefore, we must understand that we cannot take the little annoyances that present themselves in our lives lightly. They may look like gnats, but they have big intentions against us. They are big thieves, and we must treat them as such.

IRRITABILITY AND ANGER

There is a saying: "Frustration begets anger and anger begets aggression" (Quoted by Dr. Vincent Berger in Psychologist Anywhere Anytime, 2005). Ofttimes, when we are frustrated, we become angry with and aggressive toward the object or person perceived as the cause of the frustration.

As a part of your morning routine before going to work, you go to the kitchen to make your smoothie, and after filling the canister and placing it on the base of the Magic Bullet, you find that it is not working. The machine has seen all its days. You become irritated and angrily throw the now useless Magic Bullet in the trash. You are even more irritated because all the ingredients for your smoothie have gone to waste.

You're in line at the grocery store and the salesclerk is a teenager who recently got the job, so he's not moving as quickly as you would like. In addition, there's an elderly woman with just a few items checking out, but she is fumbling through her purse for coins and whatever else to pay for the few items. You cannot understand what is taking so long. By the time you get to the cashier, your mood has changed and you're not as courteous as you should be. The Christlikeness in you has left. You are frustrated and you are projecting it onto the cashier.

Some sources of frustration are mild and will not push you to the point of anger or aggression, but some will. Sometimes, we express anger or aggression directly to the source of the frustration, and sometimes we don't, but usually the thing or person closest to us gets the brunt of it. That could be your husband, your wife, your children, your coworkers, or employees. If the target is not the direct source of frustration, it is often redirected toward a less threatening and more available object.

When we act angrily in ungodly ways, we are not allowing the will of God to be done in and through us. When we act out of anger, we have given in to the frustration and the annoying situation now has no restraint. When we act out of anger, we give the spirit of frustration full rights to our spirit, mind, and emotions.

Anger is not always bad. It is one of the many emotions that the Father has given to us. We are told in Scripture to be angry and sin not (Ephesians 4:26), so we are allowed to be angry. But we should control our anger. Anger must not control us. While being angry, our ways must still please the Lord. If handled in a godly manner, anger can motivate us to take positive actions. However, we know that far too often, the actions we engage in when angry are destructive. This is what the enemy of your soul wants. He wants to destroy you, but you must fight back by diligently guarding your heart.

STRESS

According to SecondsCount®, a registered trademark of The Society for Cardiovascular Angiography and Interventions, stress is a psychological and physical response by our body to anything that is perceived as a threat or a challenge. Stress can be caused by either a negative challenge (i.e., job loss) or a positive challenge (such as a wedding). When you experience stress, your body acts like an alarm system. It makes hormones, such as adrenaline and cortisol, which give you a burst of extra energy. This helps you get through temporary periods of stress until you can relax again.

The human body and mind are created to respond to stressful or threatening situations in two ways: by fighting or fleeing, called the "fight or flight" response. However, when confronting threatening situations, the stress hormones that make us either fight or flee are thought to be harmful to our health in many ways. And when we are stressed, our spiritual, emotional, and mental behaviors and lifestyle will deteriorate.

You cannot completely avoid stress, but the way in which you respond to stress will help you minimize its effect. First, you must know the intent of the adversary. Second, you must know that things will never go right or go your way all the time. An understanding and openness to this will help you maintain a positive approach to life and will help you set realistic expectations of yourself and those around you. Just think about how much stress you would have already avoided if you had realistic expectations of yourself and of others. You can start doing so today.

Knowing yourself and how you typically respond to challenging and uninvited situations will help you deal with the stress that frustration induces. Get to know yourself more by identifying any unhealthy ways you typically use to cope with unpleasant situations. Use the Word of God as your standard for appropriate and inappropriate responses to frustrating events, and upon identifying your habitual responses, face and accept them and seek God for healthier ways of functioning.

It is impossible to separate life from stress. Therefore, it is in our best interest to find healthy means of dealing with stress. Stress induces the gradual breakdown of our body, mind, and spirit as we deal with the irritations and annoyances that come with the daily demands of our continually changing environment. Our job is to do the needful to avoid the excess build-up of the daily stress we encounter.

LOSS OF CONFIDENCE

Repeated frustrating events can wear you down and drain you of your inner strength. After looking at and going through one frustrating situation after another, you may begin to think something is wrong with you. You may begin to think these things happen because you lack the ability to ensure better outcomes. You may begin to question yourself: Can I do this?

Am I the person to do this? Am I ready for this? These questions point to a lack of confidence, and a lack of confidence means the inability to perform.

With self-confidence you have a positive yet realistic view of yourself and the situations that are happening in your life. Self-confidence gives you the courage to admit your limitations, and therefore, deal in a healthy manner with what would otherwise be frustrating. Therefore, because frustration is often a result of unrealistic expectations and self-confidence gives you a realistic view of yourself, self-confidence naturally protects you from frustration. Also, self-confidence prepares you and makes you fearless in the face of challenges that normally lead to frustration.

We all have areas in our lives where we have self-confidence and there are other areas in our lives where we do not have self-confidence. Having an accurate sense of our strengths and our weaknesses and acting accordingly will protect us from reckless behaviors and unnecessary frustrating situations. But it also means you are not afraid to take risks on tasks that you are able to do, and you do not get paralyzed by fear and anxiety when faced with things you want or need to do.

Loss of confidence is a terribly frequent side effect of ongoing frustrating situations. When we lose confidence, we no longer trust in our ability to perform. You must understand that frustration will wear down your self-confidence—the very fuel you need to keep ploughing through life. A loss of self-confidence could mean you quit easily. Some won't even try, so they never have to quit. Loss of confidence means you no longer believe in the power of the God you serve and Who lives in you. This can become a self-destructive attitude, but that is not the life that Jesus came to give you. He came to give you a more abundant life, and you are to start living that life now while on earth.

Intrusions on Our Thoughts

Of all the things that happen in our bodies, I think what happens in our minds is the most important. We are what we think. Proverbs 23:7 (AMP) says, "For as he thinks in his heart, so is he." Your thought life is supremely powerful. The enemy of your soul knows that, and this is why he invests so much in attacking your mind.

Only you and God know what you are thinking about at any time. The devil does not know your thoughts. He cannot read your mind, but he can gauge your thought pattern by the words you speak and by your behavior. Based on what he hears and observes, he can then inject situations to further frustrate your thinking. Our thoughts inform the words we speak, and the words we speak inform our behavior. The battle is in the mind. If we can win the battle there, we will have won the war. So, everything starts with our thoughts.

When we focus on and mentally recycle the annoying things that happen in our lives, we begin to speak words that agree with those situations, and if we continue to speak those words, we will eventually begin to act accordingly. As we repeat those negative words to ourselves, we will convince ourselves that the negative situation is insurmountable, and the self-doubting negative voices will get louder and louder. So, whatever you think about—positive or negative—will create your experiences and perspectives. You don't only experience what you think, but you become what you think. If you get it right inside, you will get it right outside.

The mind is where strongholds begin. You just graduated from college and are seeking employment. You applied to three companies and none of them offered you a position. Based on how you verbally and behaviorally respond to the rejections, the devil begins to put thoughts in your mind: you're not smart enough, it was a waste spending the time and money to go to college, remember what your elementary school teacher told you, she must be right and that is why none of the companies hired you.

Those thoughts, if meditated on, will produce strongholds which shape your words, and ultimately, your behavior. So, now you are hesitant to continue looking for employment. No one has to doubt you because now you already doubt yourself. This only happens because you listen to what the devil says about you and not what your Heavenly Father says.

The devil will seize every opportunity to lie to you about who you are in Christ, but you must believe what God says about you. To manage frustration is to feed your mind with the Word of God so that you can remain mentally positive and keep trying, even in difficult circumstances.

Give Up

No one decides to give up after one frustrating experience. We usually come to this fatal juncture after repeated frustrating experiences. This is the goal of the adversary. He wants you to quit. He wants you to lay down and play dead so that he can steal from you, destroy you, and kill everything you have.

When we give up or quit, we surrender to frustration. Repeatedly frustrating experiences can make a person drop out of school, quit jobs, stop attending church, abandon the ministry to which they are called, file for divorce, or physically move away or relocate to avoid frustrating situations. Repeatedly frustrating situations can also make a person stop caring. This is a form of giving up. They are still in the situation, but they are no longer trying to make it work. They are now apathetic. They have given up on their goals and are no longer trying to accomplish them.

We are all surrounded by difficulties, and the enemy of our souls is relentless. Consider how many projects you started, and then gave up on them because you became frustrated and lost patience. This is the plan of the enemy. Napoleon Hill says, "A Quitters never wins and a winner never quits". I cannot agree with him more. We must fight the good fight of faith (1 Timothy 1:18). We must resist this merciless enemy (1 Peter 5:9, James 4:7), we must refuse every day to give him an opportunity (Ephesians 4:27), and we must stand daily against his schemes (Ephesians 6:11).

Chapter Eleven: Seven Main Takeaways

1. Like how discouragement, if not dealt with, can lead to depression, frustration, if not addressed, can lead to helplessness and failure.

2. The intent of the devil is for us to ignore the small irritations while he piles them on, and by the time we become cognizant of what is happening, we are buried in frustration and failure.

3. The more you achieve or even the more you seek to achieve, the more frustration will knock at your door.

4. Frustration is a sinister threat that arises gradually rather than suddenly. Its gradual emergence makes us underestimate it, and thus we are less likely to respond to it as we should.

5. Loss of confidence is a terribly frequent side effect of ongoing frustrating situations.

6. Of all the things that happen in our bodies, I think what happens in our minds is the most important. We are what we think.

7. When we focus on and mentally recycle the annoying things that happen in our lives, we begin to speak words that agree with those situations, and if we continue to speak those words, we will eventually begin to act accordingly.

FRUSTRATION: TREAT IT FROM THE INSIDE OUT

No one is emotionally spent due to an initial onset of frustration. Frustration starts small, and therefore can go unnoticed. But though small, it is continuous, and it intensifies while aiming at complete emotional exhaustion.

It is unrealistic to believe you can rid yourself of frustration forever, but you can learn to do things to minimize your frustrations and to make sure you do not engage in unhealthy responses to frustration.

One of the best ways to overcome frustration is to understand how it works. Frustration does not have its impact due to one big event. A tragedy or disaster is a single event that could have the same effect that repeatedly frustrating events have. Frustrating experiences are often not dreadful. They usually are not tragedies. Therefore, I call frustration a subtle attack of the enemy.

A response that is closely linked to frustration is annoyance or aggravation, which if not addressed, will turn into anger. These emotions—aggravation, frustration, and anger—are present only in the absence of the peace of God. They cannot coexist with the peace of God. So, you see, frustration is intended to rob you of the peace that Jesus has given you. Jesus Himself said, "Peace I leave with you; My [perfect] peace I give to you; not as the world gives do I give to you. Do not let your heart be troubled, nor let it be afraid. [Let My perfect peace calm you in every circumstance and give you courage and strength for every challenge]" (John 14:27, AMP).

We become frustrated when we walk by sight and not by faith. When we are frustrated, we start questioning God and the people around us, we get angry, we become unpleasant; we give the enemy an entryway into our lives. Instead of responding in such ways, here are some more effective means by which we should respond to frustrating situations.

WALK BY FAITH AND NOT BY SIGHT

To walk by faith and not by sight is to trust God, not yourself, not man, not anything else. To "walk" is to live. To live by faith is to have confidence in the promises given to us by God in His Word. To walk by faith is to walk with God and we do this by letting His Word navigate every step we take in life. That is the essence of following Jesus our Lord.

True believers are the people who trust and walk with God. To trust God is to leave everything in His care without worry or concern. We become frustrated when we try to handle matters that are beyond us. The resolution to this is to leave these unmanageable things to the Lord and let Him handle them.

When the Apostle Paul says, "We walk by faith, not by sight" (2 Corinthians 5:7), he is not telling us how we should walk, but instead, he is telling us how we walk. This is how a believer should live their life. This is like saying a fish does not walk, they swim. Simply put, believers walk by faith. Those who believe in God walk by relying on God even when we don't know what will happen next.

Under the right circumstances, children trust their parents enough to go with them wherever they take them, they go to wherever they send them, and they do whatever they tell them to do. Children are dependent on their parents. They expect to be fed, clothed, and housed by their parents. Children also expect their parents to guide and counsel them, and usually are not surprised when disciplined by their parents.

We are to relate to Christ our Lord, God our Heavenly Father in the same manner that earthly children relate to their earthly parents. Jesus said, "Verily I say unto you, Except ye be converted, and become as little children, ye shall not enter into the kingdom of heaven" (Matthew 18:3, KJV). Another verse says it is impossible to please God if we have no faith. Faith and trust are synonymous and can be used interchangeably. Even Merriam-Webster defines faith as "belief and trust in and loyalty to God." So, there is no practical difference between faith and trust. Any differences that exist between the two are insignificant.

When we trust the Lord—that is, when we walk by faith and not by sight—we know that, while the situation itself may be upsetting and unpleasant, we do not have to be frustrated. Knowing and accepting the fact that God is sovereign, that He cares about you, and that nothing is impossible with Him will help you steer clear of frustration.

I am not saying you should ignore annoyances that are injected into your life and therefore subject you to a substandard life. I am saying you should not be disturbed when annoyances come. You should never settle for living beneath your God-given privilege. You must trust God enough to know that He is in control of your affairs. Therefore, if a frustrating situation occurs and the circumstances are entirely out of your control, you will ward off frustration if you throw that care upon God and let Him handle it.

Some situations that cause frustration are simply unavoidable. It is just the way life is. There is simply nothing you can do about these things, but though they can be frustrating, you can choose not to be frustrated. Your goal in dealing with these situations is to recognize the wisdom of Neibuhr's Serenity Prayer: "God grant me the serenity to accept the things I cannot change; courage to change the things I can; and wisdom to know the difference." Serenity means peacefulness, tranquility, calmness, stillness. If you can accept the things that you cannot change and give them to God, you will experience serenity—peacefulness, tranquility, calmness, stillness, not frustration.

I admonish you to know the nature and character of your God. Know Him; don't know of Him. Do you know Him enough for Him to earn your trust? If not, take the admonition given by Simon Peter, the chief apostle of Jesus Christ: "Grow in grace, and in the knowledge of our Lord and Saviour Jesus Chris" (2 Peter 3:18, KJV). As you grow in the knowledge of God, your trust in Him will grow. As you grow in grace and come to know your God, you will see Him work out your situations daily. This will help you get to the point where you trust Him in everything. This is an iron clad guard against frustration...trust God! With this kind of covering, nothing will frustrate you.

BE REALISTIC

A lot of people become disappointed and frustrated because of unmet unrealistic expectations. Realistic goals and expectations are those that are within reach, those that one can sensibly expect to achieve. This does not mean we should not set goals that are challenging. We should always challenge ourselves, but the challenges should not be entirely out of our reach or completely against standard protocols. For example, if you want to be a pilot, it would be unrealistic to set a goal to obtain your pilot license within ninety days. Pray all you want; it is extremely unlikely that you will achieve this goal.

An unrealistic goal or expectation could be what you expect of yourself or of others. It is unrealistic to expect your ten-year-old son who just gave his life to the Lord to never get in trouble at school. Simply because he is now a believer like you, you cannot expect him to never sin, even though you do. Children—regenerated and unregenerated—mess up. They lie to us, they're sneaky, they don't listen, and they know how to push all the wrong parent and teacher buttons. You will set yourself up for undue frustration when you have such unrealistic expectations.

A perfectionist will probably be frustrated more often than a more relaxed, easy-going person. Perfectionists set their sight on something and often cannot settle for anything less. And when things don't turn out as expected, they become frustrated.

To guard against frustration due to unrealistic expectations and goals, you must learn to distinguish between what you expect will happen, what will possibly happen, and what actually happens, and you must be open to all three. This is the "Thy will be done" posture in a believer's walk. It is the best frustration-free life to live. With this mindset, you leave things in the hands of the Lord. Yes, you do your best to achieve your goals, but you also know that if you achieve them, it is God who gives you the strength to do so, and you also know that if you don't achieve them, the will of the Father will be manifested in your life when He opens an even better door of opportunity. When you start learning to truly accept this reality, you will be one step closer to being able to deal with frustration in a healthy way.

One may ask where Ephesians 3:20 (AMP) fits into the discussion. The verse says, "Now to Him who is able to [carry out His purpose and] do superabundantly more than all that we dare ask or think [infinitely beyond our greatest prayers, hopes, or dreams], according to His power that is at work within us." Doesn't the Scripture clearly say the Father will far exceed what we ask for or even think, so isn't it reasonable to expect Him to meet our unrealistic expectations? Isn't it fair to expect Him to give us the extraordinary?

Most of us go wrong by believing the Father should give us everything we ask for in the way we pose our requests to Him. He does say, "Whatever you ask in My name, that I will do, that the Father may be glorified in the Son" (John 14:13, NIV). It pleases the Lord to give us what we ask for, but we must note that whatever we ask for must be couched in the name of the Lord Jesus Christ, meaning it must be according to the will of the Father. The key here is to ask in His will. When we ask to satisfy our own lusts, we ask amiss, and He does not answer those prayers (James 4:3). Additionally, He cannot give us everything we ask for, because if He does, we will never learn to trust Him, our faith would not grow, and we cannot please Him if we have no faith (Hebrews 11:6).

God is supernaturally powerful. There is nothing that He cannot do if it is His will to do so. He is the Creator of everything that exists or will ever exist. He holds the universe in the palm of His hand. He created the laws of nature and can break them whenever and however He wants to; no one else can do that. He is sovereign and powerful, so He has the capacity to answer your prayers and immeasurably do more than what you ask or think. But God's answer to your prayer does not depend on His ability, but rather, on His will. Anything you pray according to the Father's will shall be done (1 John 5:14–15) because He is able:

> *Now this is the confidence that we have in Him, that if we ask anything according to His will, He hears us. And if we know that He hears us, whatever we ask, we know that we have the petitions that we have asked of Him.*

So, here's another question: Isn't it His will to heal my sick child? I've been praying and fasting for the healing of my child. I've even gotten the prayer warriors at my church to join me in prayer, but my child is still sick. Is praying for healing not according to His will? Aren't we healed by His stripes (Isaiah 53:5)?

Many believers become frustrated and lose faith under circumstances such as these because we fail to line up Scripture with Scripture. The same God also said He purifies us with fire (1 Peter 1:7). We cannot come out as pure gold if we don't go through the fire. We will not have a testimony if we're not tested. Testing is unpleasant, and it may come in the form of a sick child, a sick spouse, or any form of devastating situation.

Whether we see or believe it or not, "unanswered prayers" are in His will sometimes. Why? Because there are greater lessons to learn in the storm than in escaping the storm. We always want to escape the storm, but sometimes it is His will to take us through the storm. There is no limit to God's power, so there is no limit to His ability to give you enduring strength through the storm. Understanding these principles will keep your faith and expectations of the Father realistic and in accordance with the Word and will save you from much frustration.

Do Not Worry

Learning that you cannot control everything, and therefore, taking things calmly will help you be more content and happier which, in turn, will help you keep frustration at bay. If you are frustrated, you will have less patience and tolerance for everything and everyone around you.

Bible verses like Isaiah 26:3, Proverbs 3:5–6, Romans 8:28, Proverbs 3:6, and Ecclesiastes 7:9 are powerful antidotes to frustration. Some of these are well known throughout Christendom, but to what degree do we really walk them out in our daily lives?

Isaiah 26:3 (AMP) tells us that the God we serve is faithful and gracious enough to "keep in perfect and constant peace the one whose mind is steadfast [that is, committed and focused on Him". God will keep frustration away from those who keep their thoughts focused on His ability to do all things and not on what could potentially frustrate them. God will make peace a regular companion of those who trust and take refuge in Him. His Word is true. He will keep you in His perfect peace.

The world is seeking peace, but many do not understand that it will not be found in idolatry. This peace comes through

206

Jesus Christ alone and it prevails in good and in bad times. We get it by having a steadfast, firm mind that is set on the character of God. When you set your thoughts on Christ Jesus, you will be filled with an inner peace, an incomprehensible peace, the perfect peace that only comes from above.

Solomon the wisest man ever lived admonished us in Proverbs 3:5–6 to "Trust in and rely confidently on the Lord with all" your heart and do not rely on our own insight or understanding. He also added that we should recognize and accept the Lord in everything we do, and if we do that, God will order our steps. People often quote these verses as a source of comfort when they are going through a dark season or a situation they don't understand. But I am encouraging you to make this your way of life in good times and in bad times.

As followers of Jesus Christ, we must learn to rely on God and include Him in whatever we do. By doing so, we give Him a chance to keep us on the right track. We do not always know what lies ahead, but He does. Many of us speak these words but do not do them, and as a result, we suffer unnecessary frustration. Paul Baloche the writer of the song, "What a Friend We Have in Jesus," said it well, "O what peace we often forfeit / O what needless pain we bear / All because we do not carry everything to God in prayer." Many of us get beat up by frustration simply because we do not give our cares to God. We try to manage what is out of our control with our own intelligence and abilities, and of course we fail, and that spirals us into worry.

Sometimes it looks like we have things in control and problems are resolved, and while that may be good, our spiritual life is of much more importance. This is so because if there is spiritual soundness and a humble dependence on God, the issues of life will also be taken care of. Not relying on God will cheat you of the opportunity to know Him more deeply and the experience to establish true faith in Him.

The Apostle Paul in Romans 8:28 (AMP, emphasis added) encourages us to know with great confidence that the God who loves us deeply will "causes <u>all</u> things to work together [as a plan] for good for those who love God, to those who are called according to His plan and purpose." This is a very reassuring promise, but it will do us no good if we don't believe it and live by it. A key word in this verse is "all." All simply means everything, the whole quantity or extent of a thing. There is no other meaning for this powerful three letter word. The other thing to observe is that there are two conditions required for one to capitalize on this promise: You must love the Lord and you must be called according to His purpose. Without doubt, God loves you and like everyone else, He has called you. The question is whether you have answered His call. If you love God and have responded affirmatively to His call, you should be able to trust that He is working for your good and is always looking out for your welfare.

By following Jesus Christ, you have submitted to His purpose for you. This is not as complicated as some may think. It does not mean you have to be an ordained minister, a pastor, or have some notable ministry. As a disciple of Christ, you are automatically called or submitted to His purpose, and He holds your life in His hands. In fact, these two qualifiers—loving God and experiencing His call—are inseparable; they are one. Your love for God is a qualifier for being called by and submitted to Him. One cannot be called according to God's purpose and not love Him, and one cannot love Him and not be submitted to His purpose for their life. Jesus said in John 14:15, "If you love me, keep my commands." So, love for God and submission or obedience to Him are inseparable.

208

Being called according to God's purpose means that it is not our comfort or worldly success that matters. It is the furthering of the purpose of God through us that really matters. Therefore, when potentially frustrating things happen, we ought to look for how the Father can use those things for His purpose and His glory while working them out for our good. An understanding of this would save many from being frustrated.

AVOID ANGER

James 1:19–20 points our attention to anger. Anger is closely tied to frustration. Frustration is mild anger that, if not controlled, could turn into outright anger. There is righteous and unrighteous anger. I am speaking here of unrighteous anger. The Bible says a lot about unrighteous anger. James 1:19–20 (NIV) says, "My dear brothers and sisters, take note of this: Everyone should be quick to listen, slow to speak and slow to become angry, because human anger does not produce the righteousness that God desires." and Ecclesiastes 7:9 (NIV) says, "Do not be quickly provoked in your spirit, for anger resides in the lap of fools."

You cannot be angry and live the righteous life that God desires. Neither can you host anger and consider yourself wise. Anger is as big a problem because it is a gateway to a host of other problems. It's been said that "anger is one letter short of danger," and that is a good warning to keep in mind. Anger can cause great damage, not only in your life but also in the lives of those around you. So, think about it, if frustration, which we think so little of, leads to anger, and anger is as dangerous and spoken against so strongly in Scripture, isn't it worth avoiding frustration at all costs?

Anger can cause relational problems in many areas of our lives—marriage, family, friends, work. If not managed, it can cause job loss, lawsuits, damage to property, damage to others, and it can even lead to murder. We see this on the news every day. Anger can cause emotional problems. If you are an angry person, anger will affect you emotionally at every level. Also, anger can cause physical problems. According to the Jed Foundation, high blood pressure, heart disease, headaches, stomach problems, ulcers, colitis, and insomnia have all been linked with unresolved anger. This one thing called anger can cost you your emotional, relational, physical, social, financial, and spiritual health. It is to be avoided on every front and it starts with avoiding frustration.

Rest In the Lord

Psalm 37:7a (KJV) says, "Rest in the Lord, and wait patiently for him." The Amplified version says, "Wait patiently for Him and entrust yourself to Him."

Frustration does not come upon us in a physical form and neither does rest. When the psalmist says, "Rest in the Lord, and wait patiently for him," he's not talking about physical rest that involves taking a break from an activity, relaxing, napping, or stopping to regain strength to continue or complete a physical task. Rest in the Lord refers to a spiritual rest from confusion, worry, stress, useless human effort, and a break from all internal, external, mortal, and spiritual enemies.[22]

This rest connotes peace. One cannot be at peace and be frustrated at the same time. The Hebrew meaning of the word "rest" in Psalm 37:7 is "to be at peace," "to be still," or "to be quiet or calm." In place of "rest in the Lord," the English Standard Version (ESV) and New International Version (NIV)

Bible translations say, "Be still before the Lord." The Christian Standard Bible (CSB) says, "Be silent before the Lord." The God's Word (GW) translation says, "Surrender yourself to the Lord." And the New Living Translation (NLT) says, "Be still in the presence of the Lord." In every translation of the verse, we see an exhortation to surrender to the lordship of Jesus Christ.

We become frustrated when we try to reach an objective or when we try to achieve an outcome but fall short. We also become frustrated when things get in our way that we do not favor. It could be how a person communicates with us. It could be a "bad" habit of your spouse or your child, or delays in traffic, the bank, the doctor's office, the post office, or the grocery store. It could be an issue that persists even though you have done everything in your power to fix it. This verse is not telling you to lay still and do nothing when faced with a challenge, but it is telling you not to do what you do in your own strength. You must trust the Father enough to come under His power and wisdom and endeavor to do whatever you do in His strength.

It is like hand-over-handwriting. This is where the person teaching a child to write places their hand over that of the student and directs the child's hand with their own. So, it is like having the Father's hand over your hand wherein He directs you to do whatever you are doing. Your hand may be moving, you may be working, but make sure He is moving your hand; make sure He is doing the work, not you. A glove can do nothing if a hand is not in it. Make yourself the glove and make Him the hand. That is resting in the Lord. That will protect you from frustration.

In Matthew 11:28 (NIV), Jesus invites us to rest in Him. He says, "Come to me, all you who are weary and burdened, and I will give you rest." Jesus also said in John 15:11, "I have said these things to you so that my joy may be in you, and that your joy may be complete." It gives the Lord joy and you as well when you rest in Him. It makes Him happy when you depend on Him. The Lord wants you to depend on Him. He wants to give you rest from frustration. Cares of life can easily weigh you down. There could be financial concerns, health concerns, concerns for your family, your children, or even the ministry, but your first recourse should be total reliance on God your Father.

There are a few widely used adages that may be influencing some of us to operate in our own strength and thereby cause unnecessary frustration. One is: "If it's going to be, it's up to me." Another is: "Stand on your own two feet." And the final one is: "God helps those who help themselves." This last one is most misleading because many actually believe it is a Bible verse. Let me be clear, this adage is not in the Bible.

The counsel given to us in the Word of God is not to help ourselves, but instead, it is to rest in the Lord (Psalm 37:7, Psalm 62:1, Matthew 11:28-29). When we are tired, the natural thing to do is rest. Have you ever been so tired that you couldn't wait to get off your feet or fall into bed? Usually, we are so tired that we don't question or wonder if the chair or sofa or bed we collapse into will bear up our weight.

Rest is trust. Rest means quieting all our racing thoughts, the over-thinking, the worries, and concerns, and giving them to God. When we want to rest, we trust the bed we lie in will bear us up and give us the rest we need. In other words, we trust the object enough to put our safety and need for comfort in it. This is what the Lord requires of us. He wants us to trust Him without hesitation and without questioning His capability. He wants us to enjoy the peace that He came to give us.

Challenging situations with unexplainable peace are in His will for you, but frustration is not, and He has given you the formula by which you can get this peace. It's in His Word. It's in His nature.

Jesus certainly came to save us from our sins. He came so that we may have a relationship with our Heavenly Father and obtain eternal life. But He also came to give us abundant life, and that is to be experienced here on earth in this life, not later in eternity. Frustration will deplete your life and leave you to exist—not live—trying to work your way through one frustrating situation after another in your own limited strength. Do not let that be you.

PRACTICAL STEPS TO REDUCE FRUSTRATION

We commonly respond to situations that are out of our control with frustration. The source of frustration could come from within or from the world outside of us, and no one is immune to the negative impact of feeling defeated, unsupported, or that the world is not "on our side." But there are some practical things we can do to emotionally educate and equip ourselves to reduce or evade frustration.

BE AWARE OF THE SOURCES OF YOUR FRUSTRATION

Don't just go from one thing to the next, one unpleasant situation to another without taking note of potential patterns or sources of the unpleasant situations. Spend the necessary time identifying your triggers. Perhaps it's the way your supervisor speaks to you, or maybe it's the way someone does something. Or maybe it's a person's point of view on an issue that you see very differently. Once you've identified the source of frustration, decide whether this is something you can or cannot control. If it is something you cannot change or control, let it go. The appropriate thing to do is change you—change how you respond. For example, you cannot control another person's point of view, but you can control whether you engage this person in a conversation or not. You have the power to turn off this source of frustration.

Adjust Your Attitude Toward Frustration

Frustrating situations are going to arise, and there is nothing you can do about some of them. For example, you are divorced and are co-parenting your five-year-old son, but your ex-spouse is unreliable, combative, and is simply not doing his/her part to help raise the child. Ideally, you would love to have this person out of your life, but that is not an option because no matter what, he/she is still the child's parent.

In a case such as this, your best option is to mentally adjust to the situation because you cannot remove or replace the source of frustration. The devil would want you to blame yourself, think nothing is going right in your life, or think every problem has a solution so you should be able to resolve this issue. But it is to your disadvantage to think about yourself as such or to assume responsibility for someone else's behavior. The appropriate thing you can do to effectively manage the situation is adjust your expectations, focus on addressing what's within your control, and make sure you respond to associated moments of frustration in a manner that pleases the Lord.

Problems of this nature may very well be there to stay, so do not evade them. Instead of trying to evade frustrating situations that will not go away, try to focus on cultivating a

214

helpful attitude toward them. Understand why they exist in your life and be open to facing and learning from them.

Pick Your Battles

Some of us wear ourselves out by trying to make everything and everyone perfect. We want things to go our way, and we become frustrated when that does not happen. And guess what? It will never happen that way; therefore, you will always be frustrated. When we want things and people to operate our way, we end up manipulating them whether we are aware of it or not.

When you feel yourself getting frustrated, pause and ask yourself if what you are getting frustrated about will matter tomorrow, or next week, or next year. You can even ask yourself how this will improve your life or you as a person. And since we should care about others, another question to ask is how this would help the next person. If the situation is not somehow linked to your deeper values, you will quickly see that the situation is not worth your emotional investment. Perhaps it is not a battle worth fighting.

Handle Frustration Healthily

If we get permission in Scripture to be angry— "Be angry, and do not sin" (Ephesians 4:26, NKJV)—then, we must have permission to be frustrated, but that too must not lead us to sin. A healthy way to handle frustration is to deal with it in such a way that it does not harm you or those that are in its path.

I am not suggesting you suppress your frustration, because by doing so, it goes unaddressed. It is these suppressed issues that cause us to behave in unexpected ways that surprise us and others and, in fact, are often displeasing to the Lord. Suppressed issues are lying in wait for triggers, and when triggered, they respond without restraint or rationale. Sometimes frustration is more effectively dealt with by expressing anger in a godly manner instead of acting like it's not there.

Be Thankful for the Little Things

Frustration directs us to what we think is not working right, which in turn is why we are frustrated. Therefore, I would suggest refocusing your mind on something for which you can be grateful, no matter how small it is. Your husband frustrates you immensely. In fact, both of you argue far too much. But this very annoying husband always makes sure your car is clean and the gas tank is full. He knows your favorite foods and seems to know just when to come home with the right carryout. And without any of this, when you are not arguing, he is the best person with which to spend time. Although he is a source of frustration, if you refocus your mind, you will find plenty of things for which you can be grateful.

We so often overlook the little things and become frustrated because that thing we consider so very important did not turn out the way we expected. Your son has been getting in trouble at school almost every day. The teacher and principal make regular calls to you about his behavior, so of course, you are frustrated. But this week, he only got in trouble two days, and on neither of those days was he sent to the principal's office or was suspended. I would suggest that this is an occasion to be thankful and not be frustrated.

With a heart of gratitude, you will find solace in the little things. It is difficult to get frustrated if you are amused by and

216

thankful for life's sweet little gifts, like your husband who brings you your favorite carryout. Use an attitude of gratitude to redirect you when you see yourself becoming frustrated.

STAY UNDER THE ANOINTING

I must close this chapter with this analogy. In the previous chapter, I likened frustration to the little pesky gnats that fly around us with an annoying buzzing in our ears. They land all over—on our face, on our food, on our legs, our arms—and it is very difficult to avoid them.

Like the gnats that bother us, bugs and insects bother and frustrate sheep. These annoying creatures buzz about the sheep's heads and try to lay eggs on the moist membranes of their noses and ears. If a fly successfully hatches larvae and burrows into the soft flesh of a sheep's nasal passages, it can cause irritation, inflammation, and infection. Also, sheep are distracted and obsessed with keeping the bugs away. Their sometimes-frantic efforts to get away from the insects can cause them harm.

The shepherds' remedy is to anoint the sheep's head with oil. Shepherds have been putting oil on sheep since before biblical times. In fact, the twenty-third Psalm is actually an extended metaphor that compares shepherding techniques of the times to the shepherding available to us through Christ. The shepherd cares for all the needs of the sheep. Like it is with the earthly shepherd and the sheep, so it is with our Heavenly Shepherd, Jesus. If you let Him, He will anoint you with His anointing oil so that the frustrations of life will find no place to land in your mind or spirit. The smell of the anointing oil will repel frustration. The oil will create such a slippery place that frustration cannot attach itself to you. An all-cure for frustration is to stay under the anointing of Jesus your Shepherd.

Chapter Twelve: Seven Main Takeaways

1. To walk by faith and not by sight is to trust God, not yourself, not man, not anything else.

2. We are to relate to Christ our Lord, God our Heavenly Father in the same manner that earthly children relate to their earthly parents.

3. To guard against frustration due to unrealistic expectations and goals, you must learn to distinguish between what you expect will happen, what will possibly happen, and what actually happens, and you must be open to all three.

4. Whether we see or believe it or not, "unanswered prayers" are in His will sometimes.

5. Learning that you cannot control everything, and therefore, taking things calmly will help you be more content and happier which, in turn, will help you keep frustration at bay.

6. Some of us wear ourselves out by trying to make everything and everyone perfect. We want things to go our way, and we become frustrated when that does not happen.

7. With a heart of gratitude, you will find solace in the little things. It is difficult to get frustrated if you are amused by and thankful for life's sweet little gifts.

FAILURE: THE COMMON DENOMINATOR

There is no failure except in no longer trying.
—Chris Bradford

F ailure is said to be the absence of success. It is a common denominator to everyone who walks the face of this earth. The only way a person lives this life and avoids failure entirely is by never trying to do anything, and such a person would not be normal. We will all try to do something at some point in life. But the moment we try to do something, we stand the chance of failing.

While some people find success almost as soon as they set out to look for it, many successful people must try numerous times before achieving it. For example, Mozart found success quickly. By age six, he was performing as a child prodigy at the Imperial Courts in Vienna and Prague, probably before he had any concept of what the word success even meant. Vera Wang decided at the age of forty that she wanted to be a designer. She designed her own wedding dress that year and opened her first bridal boutique just a year later before becoming internationally known.[23] Neither Mozart nor Wang experienced multiple failures before achieving success, but some of the world's most highly successful people experienced epic failure before coming into success.

For example, many of the Wright brothers' models failed before they successfully built an aircraft, but they persisted. They first became interested in aviation in the late 1890s, and by 1903 they made history by building the world's first man-powered aircraft that flew 852 feet in fifty-nine seconds. Even with this accomplishment, it took a while for the world to notice. Local newspapers dismissed their achievements as unimportant, and even with photos, the authenticity of subsequent longer flights was questioned as fake. It was in 1908 when public demonstrations were made that the brothers began to get the credit they deserved.

The films of Walt Disney and those from his studio produced after his death are an integral part of many people's childhood. But Walt Disney experienced multiple failures, including one point at which he was in such a financial dearth that he allegedly ate dog food to survive. His first studio, the Laugh-O-Gram Studio, lasted just two years before going bankrupt in 1923.[24]

By 1926, he had created Oswald the Rabbit, a successful and well-known cartoon character. But when he tried to negotiate a higher fee for producing the series, his distributor informed him that his fee was to be reduced. Even worse, to his surprise, he did not own the intellectual property to the character. He was given an ultimatum: accept the reduced fee or lose the character and staff. He declined, and most of his staff left him. But the loss of the Oswald character was ultimately to his benefit. The next character he created, the famous Mickey Mouse, will be remembered long after Oswald.[25]

Sir James Dyson created a whopping 5,126 failed models of his vacuum cleaner over the course of fifteen years before creating the self-titled best-selling bagless vacuum cleaner that led to a net worth of $4.5 billion. If he had given up, he would not have been a winning entrepreneur who has successfully manufactured some of the best household appliances.[26]

Steven Spielberg's filmmaking career has grossed more than $9 billion and brought him three Academy Awards, but the master of the blockbuster was rejected twice by the University of Southern California's School of Cinematic Arts. In addition, Spielberg also struggled with dyslexia which made it harder for him to cope with school. To date, he has won eleven Emmys, three Oscars, and seven Golden Globes, and he is one of the most successful directors of today's time.[27]

J.K. Rowling, the author of the Harry Potter series, says, "It is impossible to live without failing at something, unless you live so cautiously that you might as well not have lived at all—in which case, you fail by default." Rowling came from a past of being on welfare. She was a broke, depressed, divorced single mother simultaneously writing a novel while studying.[28] Seeing the popularity of Harry Potter today, it is hard to believe that a lot of publishers rejected Harry Potter, but Rowling is now one of the richest women in the world. This is not an endorsement of Harry Potter. The point here is that failure has no discrimination. We all experience it, but it should not stop us from achieving success.

Success is relative. Not everyone will experience it at the levels like Walt Disney, Steven Spielberg, J.K. Rowling, or Sir James Dyson have. Oxford Languages define success as "the accomplishment of an aim or purpose" or a "favorable or desired outcome of an undertaking." Therefore, a person will achieve success when they accomplish whatever they set out to do, be it small or great. If most people set their level of success at that of these famous people, they will not reach it, and will therefore think they have failed even when they have succeeded. Success is within reach for us all, but failures will be markers along the way to it.

PERSPECTIVES ON FAILURE

A change in perspective can help a person through the worst of situations. If we look at or think about some situations differently, we will experience them differently. Photographers do just that when taking pictures. They move their camera lens around to get different angles of the same object.

Two things that I will discuss here that can change our perspective on failure are one's level of skill and knowledge and seeing failure as a learning opportunity. With the right perspective, a teenage girl who failed her driver's test can learn a lot about handling failure in a healthy manner. First, she will be less likely to beat herself up because she had very little skill in driving to begin with. Second, she could learn that she must be better prepared when taking on future tasks.

One must consider their level of knowledge when determining if a situation is a failure or not. When you are new at something—like the teenage driver—success is less likely. It would be just as unrealistic to expect a ten-year-old boy to drive a car at all, or if he does drive the car, to expect him to do so perfectly the first time. To give another example, it is unfair for you to hold yourself to the standard of a tenured professor when you just got your doctorate degree and are completing a fellowship. You set yourself up for failure when you hold yourself to the standard of the expert when you're still a novice. Having a beginner's mindset and reminding yourself that you are a novice will give you the right perspective on failure.

The fear of failure is one of the biggest barriers to learning. One example is outlined in the classic Harvard Business Review article, "Teaching Smart People How to Learn." Chris Argyris points out that many highly successful people fear failure. I would add that many perfectionists also fear failure. Highly successful people fear failure because they have very little experience with it. As a result, they tend to respond defensively to failure. And they try to avoid it or stubbornly deny it.

In the process, they miss out on the opportunity to learn and grow from their failures. When something happens that is different than what we expected, if we have the right perspective, we can learn a lot about the situation and our assumptions. We can also learn about ourselves and how we handle setbacks and the unexpected. If you find yourself feeling defensive about a failure, change your perspective by asking yourself what you can learn from the experience.

Perfectionists tend to label things as failures when they are not. For example, you may make a mistake during a presentation at a high-level meeting with top organizational leaders. Despite excellent feedback from all in attendance, you fixate on the one moment that didn't go exactly as planned. By being so critical of yourself, you miss the opportunity to learn. This could be the perfect time to review your performance so that you can identify where you went wrong and determine how you can avoid the same mistake in the future. The idea is to learn from the mistake but not dwell on it. In a scenario like this, there is plenty more to celebrate than there is to lament over. A simple review of your performance will show you that a flawless presentation is not the sole criterion for success.

Thomas Edison had a healthy perspective on failure. This is what he said about inventing the light bulb: "I have not failed. I've just found 10,000 ways that won't work." Don't be afraid of trying and failing. Know that, as you fail, you can learn from the failure. This mindset embraces failure as a natural part of personal growth. When you see your failures as steppingstones, you create a new opportunity for advancement. Sometimes, our failures become the setback that motivates us to pursue a goal. You may have subconsciously put the goal aside or maybe you've been distracted by other priorities, but a failure could turn your attention to the very thing you have set aside. With the right perspective, you will come to know that what looks like a failure may very well be a picture of an unfinished process.

Many have the wrong perspective on failure, and therefore, failure is as detrimental as it is to them, because far too often, they see it as a threat to their success or an attack on their self-worth and self-esteem. Some even struggle with self-acceptance because of failure. But if you cannot accept yourself for who you are, others will not. You must accept your strengths and weaknesses to have the inner force to push past failures.

Low self-esteem and lack of self-worth are often linked to past experiences where significant figures in people's lives were overly critical, failed to affirm them, or failed to draw attention to what's good about them. Despite how flawed we all are, everyone has something good about them. It is paramount that, as children, we hear that we are good enough. It is especially important that those who mean the most to us—like parents and teachers—underscore our strengths. Void of that, we will often find ourselves searching for something to

226

make us feel good about ourselves or wondering why we can never feel worthy.

The person with low self-esteem and poor self-worth will be easily overwhelmed by failure. This is so because they already think they will not succeed. Poor self-worth overshadows the strengths and assets in an individual, so failure will only confirm their false beliefs about themselves. No one goes around announcing that they expect to fail, but some in their subconscious and out of anxiety have mentally created and accepted failure and have already resolved that their attempts will not succeed, and as expected, they fail. This mindset sets the stage for failure; it is called self-fulfilling prophecy, also known as interpersonal expectancy effect.

The most damaging attitude toward failure is to believe that failure defines you. Having failed at anything does not mean you are a failure. There is a huge difference between the two. One is an event—something that happens *to* you, an external force. The other is what happens *in* you, an internal force. It is what happens *in* you that defines you. Therefore, you could fail at something, but it is how you respond to the failure that defines you, not the failure itself.

For example, let's say you got a full scholarship to college. You were ecstatic. Your parents were super proud of you. But in the second semester of your freshman year, your grades began to fall, and you were placed on probation. Then later in the semester you got pregnant and had to drop out of college. These failures do not define you. That is not who you are. These failures are the manifestations of the interaction between your inner state and how you responded to your environment, so they happened to you, not in you. What will define you is what you do with these failures or how you respond to them. These failures are a part of your story, not the end of your story. What you do with the failures and turn out to be after dealing with the failures is the end of your story, and that is what matters most.

Another example: you are in college, but you quickly find out that a four-year degree or even a master's degree is not for you. You drop out of college and start your own business flipping houses. Things are going well the first year or so and then business begins to decline sharply, and you lose everything. The business has failed, but you are not a failure. The failed business does not define you. The true you will show in your response to the failure.

You could be that person who confronts the failure—the loss of the business—with resilience, learns from it, and uses it as a steppingstone. Or you could be the person who grieves the loss of the business, tell yourself you're good at nothing, and give up on trying. It is your perspective of and your reaction to the failures that define you, not the failure.

Failure is a teacher. It is like fertilizer to your life; it stimulates growth. If you do not experience failure, perhaps you are not taking big enough risks. If all your endeavors are easy to do and turn out exactly as planned, maybe you aren't stretching yourself. And if you're not stretching yourself, you will not grow. Failure is an asset, not a deficit, but we must have the right perspective.

Many people beat upon themselves because they think they have failed, but we must remember that failure is subjective. Said differently, like beauty—which is also subjective—failure is in the eye of the beholder. Like what is one man's trash is another man's treasure, what is failure for one person is a huge success for another. Consider these three scenarios, which one, if any would you consider a failure?

Example #1

An experienced marathon runner sets a goal to run her next marathon in four hours. This goal is 15 minutes shorter than the best time she has ever run that same marathon. She ran the marathon and completed it in four hours and six minutes, nine minutes shorter than the best she has run in the past.

Example #2

The executive director of a nonprofit organization retired, and the deputy director applies for the position. This would be a well-earned promotion, she thought. She competed against other internal candidates as well as external candidates. She received positive feedback from the hiring committee but was not offered the position. She was told that the hiring committee and the organization's leadership team felt that hiring an external person would bring some well needed change and innovation to the organization.

Example #3

The executive assistant for the president of a large company was asked to prepare talking points for a speech the president would be making at the company's annual fundraiser event. The executive assistant gave it her best effort and compiled what she thought would inform a moving speech and presented it to the president. The president complimented her for a job well done, but upon listening to the speech, the executive assistant observed that the president made several significant changes to the talking points she prepared.

Notice that the subject in each scenario had a specific target. Simply because they did not achieve their goal, they could consider it a failed event. But that would not be accurate.

In scenario number one, the runner beat her fastest run. That is not failure.

In the second scenario, the applicant got good feedback, and it had nothing to do with her skills as to why she did not get the job. They were simply looking for an outsider.

In the third scenario, the executive assistant prepared excellent talking points; the president of the company told her so. But she could not discern exactly what the president wanted, so based on her knowledge, she provided what was best. It is not that the talking points weren't good; it was because they did not reflect what the president was thinking.

Some people would contend that there are grounds to consider all these scenarios as failures, but to me, there are no grounds for such a conclusion. Because we tend to set a specific mark for success, we consider some results a failure when they are not. Goals should be objective, but sometimes they are subjective, and when they are subjective, they should be treated as such, especially when defining success and failure.

Another example: if your eighth-grade son's math test scores are routinely in the thirty and forty percentage range, he is failing the course. But if he brings home a score in the sixties, though by normative standards he is still failing the course, he has indeed succeeded in raising his grades. Obtaining that score on a math test might be a failure for another student, but for him, it would be a huge success. Perhaps that common definition of failure as "not achieving a goal" is not as accurate and straightforward as we think.

Surya Bonaly did not fear failure and she had the right perspective of success and failure. In her 1998 final Olympic appearance, she skated through an Achilles tendon injury. She knew this would be her last performance as an amateur athlete, and thus, she perfectly executed her signature backflip, even though she knew it was an illegal move. For her, at that moment, she did not see herself as an injured victim, but instead, seeing herself as pushing the boundaries of the sport and expressing herself were more important than scores from the judges. The audience gave her a standing ovation and the judges gave her low scores. In her eyes, she succeeded, and in the eyes of the judges, she failed.[29]

EMBRACE FAILURE

Failure is probably the one thing in life of which most people are afraid. Thus, it is natural to try to avoid things that could end in failure. But there is no need to be afraid of failure. Failure is all too common to be feared. Everyone has failed, and everyone will fail again. If you want to succeed, you must first know that you will fail, and second, you cannot stop after experiencing failure. You must get back up and try again and again. So do not be afraid of failure; it is a part of your road to success.

Why should you not fear but embrace failure?

FAILURE TEACHES GREAT LIFE LESSONS

Ralph Heath, author of Celebrating Failure: The Power of Taking Risks, Making Mistakes and Thinking Big, says, "The quickest road to success is to possess an attitude toward failure of 'no fear.' In order to grow, you must fail and learn the necessary lessons taught by failure. So, it is in your best interest to have the right attitude toward fear, and that is the 'no fear' attitude. This does not mean you should expect to fail, but you should accept it when it happens."[30]

More than anything else, failure will get you to know yourself better. If taken with the right attitude, failures can teach you new things about yourself. They can make you rethink, reconsider, and find new ways and strategies to achieve your goals.

FAILURE CAN BE THE CATALYST TO YOUR POTENTIAL

To reach your potential or your personal best, or to make the "impossible" possible, you must push yourself to your limit and you must not fear failure. Ralph Heath says, "One of the biggest secrets to success is operating inside your strength zone but outside of your comfort zone." Too many of us do not reach our potential because we fear pushing ourselves beyond our comfort zone. Fear is robbing many of the life they were created to live, the person they were meant to be, and the difference they were created to make on this earth. Fear is stealing not only from you, but it is also stealing from the people you are here to impact. The "no fear" attitude will motivate you and give you the determination and perseverance you need to succeed.

FAILURE BUILDS CHARACTER AND HUMBLES YOU

No one wants to fail. It does not feel good, and it does not look good to the onlookers. Failure will force you to look closely at yourself, and it can be a humbling factor. The arrogant athlete

232

who proudly thinks no one can outrun him will be humbled when a younger runner, new to the team, outruns him. If he wants to succeed at the sport, he must now turn his attention to himself and make the necessary adjustments. A failure such as this will likely humble this arrogant athlete and might make him evaluate his approach to the sport and his performance.

Pride can make us waste the pain of failure that should be a lesson and springboard for the better. If you are proud, your response to failure will be shame and humiliation, and that will prevent you from seeing the lesson you can learn from the experience. The proud always want to be right and always want to look impressive. Pride will get in the way of both you and your success. To be successful, you must accept failure when it comes; then evaluate, learn, and keep going.

FAILURE REVEALS YOUR CHARACTER

There are people who take failure personally. They see it as a permanent situation and give up. Then there are people who use it as a lesson. They do not take it personally but see it as a temporary setback and a steppingstone to success. The latter group has the right perspective and has embraced failure as part of their road to success.

It is natural to feel downcast after we have failed, but how we respond to personal failures is what determines our road to success. The idea is not to stay in that low place. You must acknowledge the fact that no one is perfect, that no one gets it right all the time, and everyone will fail. Ask yourself what you can learn from that experience and how you can use the experience to help someone else in the future. Questions like these will get you back on track.

Your true character will show when you fail. When you fail, do you curl up and wait to die? Do you blame someone for your failure? Do you quit trying? My mother embedded this adage in me. She said, "Rosie, only your best is good enough." She has taught me that if I have done my best but fail, I must know that I have done my best and that it is good enough.

Failure does not give us the right to beat upon ourselves or point fingers at others. If you know you have done all you could, but you still fail, it may mean you need to learn some other strategies and come back and try your hardest yet again, but it certainly does not mean you stop trying.

I recall when I was studying for my doctorate. I overcomplicated my dissertation to the point that my committee chair said my dissertation was a noble attempt. This is not a good character trait, but I'm an overachiever, so I tend to complicate things. I worked the hardest I could on my dissertation: the data collection, data analysis, and the writing of the dissertation. The time came for me to defend it and at my first defense, I failed. There were so many data to be presented in so many different ways that the main critique of the committee was that I had not presented a comprehensive report of all the findings. I failed after trying my best. To say I was devastated is an understatement.

I had applied to graduate in the spring of 1997, but I had to pass my defense to graduate then. Failing my defense meant I most likely would not graduate in the spring, meaning I had to wait until December 1997. I had several options: quit pursuing a doctorate degree, accept the failure for the time being and wait to graduate in December, or push on and graduate in May. I chose the latter.

I think I cried all the way home. I got home midafternoon that day and went straight in my bed and pulled the cover over my head. I did not eat dinner, and I did not talk to anyone. But while lying there after soaking in my grief for a while, I told myself, "I am graduating in May." I got out of bed after two the next morning and while everyone else in the house was sleeping, I got back on the computer and started to address, one by one, all the comments I received from the committee.

I also sent my committee chair an email first thing the next morning with an appeal for another opportunity to defend my dissertation so that I could graduate in May. This is not the norm. One failure meant a student had to wait for the next round of defense the following semester. But perhaps, due to my persistence, he granted me the opportunity to defend a second time within the semester. I spent many nights, many long hours, and many days at my computer perfecting my data analysis and reporting. I defended my dissertation not long thereafter and passed with stellar comments.

You need a never-give-up fighting attitude to overcome failure. You must be persistent to overcome failure. You cannot criticize yourself, have a bruised ego, or doubt yourself when you fail, especially when you know you have done your best. Failure will press hard upon you and will expose the real you. It will expose what you are made of. What will others see when you fail?

CHAPTER THIRTEEN: SEVEN MAIN TAKEAWAYS

1. Failure is a common denominator to everyone who walks the face of this earth. The only way a person lives this life and avoids failure entirely is by never trying to do anything, and such a person is not normal.

2. Many have the wrong perspective on failure, and therefore, failure is as detrimental as it is to them, because far too often, they see it as a threat to their success or an attack on their self-worth and self-esteem.

3. The most damaging attitude toward failure is to believe that failure defines you.

4. Failure is a teacher. It is like fertilizer to your life; it stimulates growth.

5. Failures can make you rethink, reconsider, and find new ways and strategies to achieve your goals.

6. Fear steals not only from you, but it also steals from the people you are here to impact.

7. Your true character will show when you fail.

FAILURE ISN'T FINAL

Failures are finger posts on the road to achievement.
—*C.S. Lewis*

F ailure does not feel good, but it is not inherently bad. As painful as it may be, there is good in failure. All is not lost when we fail. It is not final. We often miss this very important truth, but most failures provide amazing opportunities to gain new insights about ourselves and for growth. Eventually, everyone will experience failure. Even Bible heroes, God-appointed people, like King David, Simon Peter, Abraham, and King Saul failed.

KING DAVID

God made David a king, and David was reckoned by God as a man after His own heart, yet he committed adultery and then had the woman's husband killed. The story is told in the eleventh and twelfth chapters of Second Samuel as well as in the first and second chapters of First Kings. Bathsheba was the wife of Uriah, one of King David's generals. While she was bathing, David saw her and was overcome with lust. He later found out she was married to Uriah—a man who was out on the battlefield risking his life for the king and the king's people—yet David selfishly proceeded to summon her to come to his chambers where they conceived a child. King David was not in the battle fighting for his people, but instead he was resting at home and taking another man's wife for his own sexual gratification.

David was the king and no woman in his kingdom had the power to deny his sexual advances. But that was not enough for David. He further abused his regal power to cover up his adulterous rape and its ensuing pregnancy by having Uriah, Bathsheba's husband, murdered in cold blood. And that was after he tried to manipulate the man into disloyalty to the troops on the front line. This exposes David as a ruthless, narcissistic ruler concerned only with satisfying his own carnal desires.

David failed, but that was not the end of him. David was "called to the carpet" on this morally reprehensible behavior by the prophet Nathan. David then repented. He felt the sting of his tremendous spiritual and moral failure and wrote the fifty-first Psalm as a poetic lament for the disgrace he'd brought upon God and all the people of Israel.

David's tragic story is told in Scripture so that we can truly understand that, despite the gravity of our errors, we can be restored. God can still create a new spirit within us after our failures. Failure is not final.

Simon Peter

Peter was so sure of his relationship with Jesus that he said to himself and others, "Even if I have to die with You, I will not deny You!" (Matthew 26:35, AMP). Jesus called Peter "the rock" and said of him, "Upon you I will build my church." No wonder Peter "the rock" became the leader of the disciples and the early church, but he nevertheless failed and denied Jesus three times.

Peter was so staunch in his denial of Christ that he denied Him, not one, not two, but three times. He went as far as to tell his accusers, "I do not know Him" (Luke 22:57). That is flat out denial. Peter had failed tragically, and he knew it. Not only did he deny Christ, but he forsook his calling and went back to fishing. Peter had given up. At this point, he thought he could no longer go on in the faith.

To prove failure is just a steppingstone, Peter cried bitterly, repented of his denial of Jesus, and was fully restored to the Savior's love. After a time of fishing with his friends, he saw Jesus on the shore and there he had a turnaround experience with Him. Jesus asked Peter, "Simon son of John, do you love me more than these?" (John 21:15, NIV). Jesus asked Peter the same question three times and Peter gave the same answer three times.

It is important to note that Jesus did not remind Peter about his failure or tell him to repent or warm him about watching and praying against the wiles of the devil. Jesus instructed Peter to feed His lambs. In essence, Jesus was telling Peter that He had forgiven him, now he must forgive himself, forget about his failure, and go out there and minister to the needs of His people. Our failures are not final with our Lord and Savior, and they should not be final with us either.

ABRAHAM

Abraham is included in Hebrews 11—the faith chapter—because "when he was called to go out into a place which he should after receive for an inheritance, obeyed; and he went out, not knowing whither he went" (Hebrews 11:8, KJV). God told Abram to go to a land that He would show him and that He would bless him greatly. Abram trusted the Lord and obeyed, not knowing where God would take him. This was a show of great faith in God, but it was not long before things looked very different for him. Abram failed when he faced famine (Genesis 12:10), when he faced danger (Genesis 12:11–20), when he faced delay (Genesis 16:1–6), and when he faced danger again (Genesis 20:1–2).

Facing drought (Genesis 12:10): Abraham arrived in the promised land to find an ongoing famine. He became fearful and began to wonder how his family would survive. Instead of trusting God, he took matters in his own hands and trusted his own resources and abilities. He could have trusted God and waited for God to fulfill verse 2 of the same chapter— "And I will make of thee a great nation, and I will bless thee, and make thy name great; and thou shalt be a blessing."—but instead, Abraham chose to leave Canaan and went to Egypt. To no surprise, this plan did not work out. He went from drought to a greater threat.

Facing danger (Genesis 12:11–20): The Egyptians were known to kill foreigners who have something they want, and Abram had something every Egyptian wanted, and this was the beautiful Sarai. Abraham was faced with a choice. He could trust God or take matters into his own hands. Once again, he took matters into his own hands and crafted a plan, but he failed. Out of fear for his own life, Abram led the Egyptians to believe that Sarai was not his wife. In essence, he lied to them. This means that just a few verses after Abram showed great faith in God, he literally handed over his wife to Pharaoh just to save his own skin.

Facing delay (Genesis 16:1–6): Years have passed, and Abraham has no child despite the promise God made to him. Sarah crafted a plan and Abraham went along with it. Neither Sarah nor Abraham asked God for direction. That was not the means through which Abraham's heir should come, so the plan failed. Hagar, Sarah's handmaid, became pregnant and gave birth to Ishmael; but he is not the son of promise (Genesis 17:18–19).

Facing danger, again (Genesis 20:1–2): Fear made Abraham repeat the same error he did in chapter 12. He again did not leave it up to God to protect him and Sarah.

Abraham faced four trials and he failed all four trials. Each time he had the choice of trusting God or relying on his abilities, and each time he chose to rely on his abilities. Abraham failed miserably each time, yet the Bible says, "And he believed in the Lord; and he counted it to him for righteousness" (Genesis 15:6, KJV). Failure is not final!

KING SAUL

King Saul had four problems that caused his downfall: pride, the fear of man, envy, and an evil spirit from the Lord. Three of these were self-induced problems. The fourth was given to him by the Lord because of the first three. King Saul had three key failures:

1. He defied God by performing the duties of a priest when he offered sacrifices. He lacked patience and prudence, and therefore stepped outside of his role.

2. He did not obey the command of God to destroy all the plunder from the Amalekites.

3. He was insecure and therefore unnecessarily protective of his office as a king.

The main difference with Saul and all the other great men of God discussed here is that Saul did not repent. So, we see that failure can be final if we make it so. By not repenting, Saul closed the door to the Father's redeeming grace toward him and faced the consequences of his failure.

Saul started out as king, thinking little of himself. The Prophet Samuel reminded him of his self-perception in 1 Samuel 15:17 (KJV): "So Samuel said, 'When you were little in your own eyes, were you not head of the tribes of Israel? And did not the Lord anoint you king over Israel?'" He appeared to be humble, but during his reign, it became evident that he was immensely proud.

When he stepped out of line and offered the sacrifice at Gilgal, he justified his wrongdoing by saying, "The people were scattered from me" (1 Samuel 13:11). After failing to keep the commandment of God in the battle against the Amalekites, Saul said, "I have performed the commandment of the Lord" (1 Samuel 15:13). Even after he was proven wrong, he said, "I have obeyed the voice of the Lord" (1 Samuel 15:20). It was pride that made him use "the worship" of God to bring himself personal honor (1 Samuel 15:30). Saul used the Lord—false worship—for his own glory.

Saul was grossly self-centered. When he was rejected by the Lord, he asked Samuel, "Honor me now, please, before the elders of my people and before Israel" (1 Samuel 15:30). When David escaped to Adullam, Saul complained to his men. He said, "All of you have conspired against me, and there is no one who reveals to me that my son has made a covenant with the son of Jesse; and there is not one of you who is sorry for me or reveals to me that my son has stirred up my servant against me, to lie in wait, as it is this day" (1 Samuel 22:8, NKJV).

Saul started out as a good man (1 Samuel 9:2). While a young man going about his own business, the Spirit of God came upon him (1 Samuel 10:10), and the Lord gave Israel victory in battle through him (1 Samuel 11:6–13). God then laid out His conditions for Israel's continued success (1 Samuel 12:14–15). But Saul feared the people, not God. So, he offered a burnt offering to appease the people (1 Samuel 13:11). When Saul disobeyed the commandment of the Lord in his battle against the Amalekites, he confessed that he did so "because I feared the people, and obeyed their voice" (1 Samuel 15:24). He justified his decision by offering to sacrifice some of the spoil to the Lord (1 Samuel 15:21). Fear of people and the need to be liked and accepted by people are rooted in a warped and unhealthy need to please people. And this was an underlying cause for Saul's failure.

The last impetus for Saul's failure to be discussed here is a huge one: envy. In Saul's eyes, only he should get any credit for Israel's victories. When Jonathan attacked the garrison of the Philistines and won, Saul took the credit (1 Samuel 13:3–4, AMP):

> *Jonathan attacked and defeated the Philistine garrison which was at Geba, and the Philistines heard about it. Then Saul blew the trumpet throughout the land, saying, "Let the Hebrews hear." All Israel heard that Saul had defeated the Philistine garrison, and also that Israel had become despicable to the Philistines. And the people were summoned to join Saul at Gilgal.*

When God used Jonathan and his armorbearer to bravely overtake the Philistines in 1 Samuel 14, driven by jealousy, Saul was ready to kill his own son Jonathan (1 Samuel 14:39, 44).

The degree of envy and rage Saul had for David was way worse. Saul was outraged against David after he killed Goliath and then performed valiantly in battle (1 Samuel 18:7–9). And as David continued to prosper, Saul only grew increasingly bitter against him (1 Samuel 18:28–29). Envy made Saul hunt David down for many months like a dog.

The Spirit of the Lord left Saul, and God caused a distressing spirit to come upon him (1 Samuel 16:14). It appears as if this evil spirit made Saul very unpredictable. On the one hand, he loved David (1 Samuel 16:21) and was glad to have him with him (1 Samuel 18:2, 5). He even called David his son (1 Samuel 24:16). But, on the other hand, he was obsessed with killing David. He would relentlessly pursue David to kill him and then repent (1 Samuel 19:16, 24:16–22). This strange, inconsistent behavior was the work of that evil spirt in Saul. Saul had failed.

God was not surprised when any of these great men failed, and He is not surprised when we fail. God knows all things. He is the author and finisher of our faith. He is the Alpha and Omega, the beginning, and the ending. He has already written the full script of our lives, so our failures do not surprise Him. But why do so few of us include Him in our failures? God sees and knows about our failures, and yet He is often the last person we turn to.

Joshua 7 tells of the time when Joshua sent his army against the city of Ai, and because they had recently routed their enemies, they underestimated Ai and were unequivocally defeated. Many lost their lives. In response to this huge failure, Joshua fell on his face before God and cried out to Him in prayer. In doing so, Joshua invited God into the midst of his failure.

When David first tried to bring back the Ark of God to Jerusalem, he failed because he did not follow God's instructions. David's mistake resulted in the death of an innocent man. "David was afraid of the Lord that day; and he said, 'How can the ark of the Lord come to me?'" (2 Samuel 6:9). He then invited the Lord into his failure. David went back and studied the Word of God. He familiarized himself with the strict protocol that he must follow when transporting the Ark and was successful on the second attempt. We can be successful on the second attempt when we invite God into our failures.

So often, when we fail, we turn to our spouse, a friend, a co-worker, or a relative when the person we need to turn to first is God. When we involve God in our failures, we can draw on His wisdom and strength and that will allow us to keep the right perspective. Remember, man seeks success, but God seeks faithfulness. If you focus on success, you increase the risk of striving in your own strength. But if you remain faithful to God by making Him your source of everything—even in the midst of your failures—He will honor your faithfulness.

FAILURE IS AN EVENT NOT A PERSON

William Brown said it best: "Failure is an event not a person." When the inevitable called failure strikes, not only do some people feel like they have failed but some feel like they are a failure. Unfortunately, and wrongfully, some let failure define them; they wrongfully let failure characterize them. There is a vast difference between failure, the event, and a person being a failure. You are not defined by the mistakes you make. Instead, you are defined by your response to failure, and your response to failure determines your level of success and accomplishment in life. Your response to failure determines who you become as a person but more importantly, who you become in Christ.

The purpose of failure is to prune you. Gardeners only prune plants when they are actively growing. Pruning removes dead and dying branches and stubs, allowing room for new growth. It also deters pests and animal infestation and promotes the plant's natural shape and healthy growth. Jesus said, "Every branch that does bear fruit he prunes, that it will be even more fruitful" (John 15:2, NIV). Isaiah 5:6 (NIV) says, "I will make it a wasteland, neither pruned nor cultivated, and briers and thorns will grow there."

Like pruning, failure is unpleasant, but we must take note of three things here:

- First, the criterion to be pruned is active growing. Therefore, you will not be pruned in the form of failure if you are not doing something for advancement or if you are not moving in the right direction.

- Second, failure occurs in our lives for us to grow more than we are already growing. Failures come so that we may bear more fruit. So, people who fail did not really fail. You must be on to something to fail. Perhaps what we call failure is not failure. I think this gives us a good reason to think well of ourselves, at least in this context, when we fail.

- Third, in the absence of failure, your life will be like a wasteland; it will be like a desert. Thorns and briers will grow up in your life only to choke out whatever good you have in it.

These three things tell me that failure is a necessity, and we should view failure as an opportunity to grow, not as a death sentence. Failure is the gift of another starting point.

If you have the right viewpoint on failure, you will rise above failure to become something better and greater. That is failing forward. The wrong point of view will only keep you down, and when down, your life will only be a shadow of what it could have been. That is failing backward. Which will you choose?

GET THE RIGHT PERSPECTIVE ON FAILURE

As followers of Christ, we must have the right perspective on failure because our response determines the path of our life and our spiritual growth. A few practical things we can do to respond to failure healthily include the following:

PERSONALIZE THE WORD OF GOD

Many believers read the Word of God, but they do not see themselves in them. They read the Word and the words sound good, but they fail to intentionally apply the Word to their lives. For example, the Bible contains many promises for the righteous. How many of us own those promises? The Bible also describes the righteous in may passages of Scripture. How many of us see ourselves in those Scriptures?

The Scripture that is quite fitting here is Proverbs 24:6 (NIV), which says, "For though the righteous fall seven times, they rise again, but the wicked stumble when calamity strikes." If you see yourself in this verse, you will know that you will fall. You will know that failure is coming, but you will also know that you will get back up. You will be assured that failure for you will not be a calamity.

You must remember that you do not have to stay down. Oliver Goldsmith says, "Our greatest glory is not in never failing but in rising each time we fall." You may not be able to reclaim the loss, undo the damage or reverse the consequences, but you can start afresh as a stronger, wiser, more astute person who is renewed by the Holy Spirit and more determined to succeed. This is why the Scripture says tribulation worketh patience (Romans 5:3).

People who fail forward look for opportunities out of what could be a tragedy. The old phrase, "When life gives you lemons, make lemonade," is widely used by elder folks. When they say this, they are essentially encouraging us to fail forward. They are telling us to look ahead, not at the present or the past. Kyle Rote, Jr. said, "There is no doubt in my mind that there are many ways to be a winner, but there is only one way to be a loser and that is to fail and not to look beyond the failure." The Apostle Paul put it this way: "But one thing I do: Forgetting what is behind and straining toward what is ahead, I press on toward the goal to win the prize for which God has called me heavenward in Christ Jesus" (Philippians 3:13–14, NIV). So, when you fail, make up your mind to press on.

The very widely known Philippians 4:13 (AMP) is another verse: "I can do all things [which He has called me to do] through Him who strengthens and empowers me [to fulfill His purpose—I am self-sufficient in Christ's sufficiency; I am

248

ready for anything and equal to anything through Him who infuses me with inner strength and confident peace.]"

I chose the Amplified version of the Bible because it specifically says, "I can do all things which He has called me to do." So, this is not talking about doing things outside of His will. If it is within the Father's purpose for you, rest assured, He will give you what you need to get it done. Many of us quote this verse, but we walk in fear of failure. Many of know this verse, but we yet are quick to say, "I can't." The question then is: if you are a follower of Jesus Christ, why not own this promise? We must understand that our doing is not of our strength or knowledge, it is through Christ. Put your name in place of "I" and declare that Christ will work through you to do the things He has called you to do.

ACCEPT YOUR FAILURES

Instead of blaming others for your failures, face them and take responsibility for them. Instead of looking to someone else as the reason you failed, honestly look at yourself. You will only fail in direct proportion to the excuses you make for failure. Excuses are the exits off the freeway of life and every time you take one, you invite failure and slow down your progress.

Many of us hate admitting our failures, but this is the first and crucial step to failing forward. A part of what can help you failing forward is to recognize that everyone fails. Failure is not exclusive to you. It's not even exclusive to the weak. The strong and powerful fail as well, so why not you? Romans 3:23 (KJV) says, "For all have sinned and fallen short of the glory of God." And James 3:2 (NIV) says, "We all stumble in many ways." Realizing you are not alone can help you to honestly face your failures.

LEARN AND GROW FROM YOUR FAILURES

As mentioned above, David successfully brought the Ark of God to Israel on his second attempt. Why? Because he learned from the mistakes that he made on the first attempt. The first attempt cost Uzzah his life and David was confused. He probably wondered, how a person could lose their life when he was trying to do a good thing. But David did not stop there. He went back and studied the Word of God so that, on the next attempt, he could follow God's guidelines for transporting the Ark, and he did it successfully.

IBM founder Tom Watson guided the company for over forty years. One of his most impressive moments in leadership occurred when a junior executive lost $10 million on a risky venture for the company.

Watson called the man into the office who nervously blurted out, "I guess you want my resignation."

And Watson replied, "You can't be serious. We've just spent $10 million dollars educating you."[31]

Mistakes are great teachers that provide us with invaluable lessons if we allow them to do so. So, don't waste your failures. Learn all you can from them. When Joshua and the Israelites experienced defeat, Joshua ripped his clothes, fell on his face, and began praying to God asking God what can be done. Joshua's actions are an example to us that in the middle of a failure we should ask God what we can learn from the experience. We should be seeking to know what the experience can teach us. A prayer like this could change the course of your life and can spur your spiritual growth. But for that to happen, you must go to God in prayer and ask Him to teach you what you need to learn from the failure.

The good news for almost all of us is that failure is rarely a matter of life and death, although it sometimes feels that way. I am not suggesting that you seek out failure, but I am suggesting that you allow failure to be a possibility, and when it happens, you should embrace the opportunity to learn from it. Winston Churchill said it well, "Success is the ability to go from one failure to another with no loss of enthusiasm."

DO NOT WASTE YOUR FAILURE

God can use your failures if you let Him. Some time ago, I read a story about a preacher who went to a small town to preach a series of sermons in a revival. His attempt was to evangelize the little town. He preached every night for two weeks and during that whole time, only one little girl gave her life to Christ. He thought he had failed. The preacher left dejected thinking the revival was a failure, and for years, he lamented the great effort he had expended with such little result. But that little girl grew up to be a strong, faithful Christian woman. She married a Christian man, and together they produced several sons, all of whom became preachers of the gospel. Through their sons' work in the ministry, thousands of unbelievers converted to Christ.

This preacher thought he had failed, and he thought he couldn't recover from that failure. But what we do and what he did for the kingdom will not fade away. We are responsible for planting the seed and God will take care of the rest. Only God is responsible for the harvest. This preacher planted the seed, but unknown to Him, God watered it and there was much more growth from it than he ever imagined.

Tim Timothy tells the story of Pastor Randy Kanipe who told his story of a sabbath time away from his church while he was struggling with failure. He happened to be walking by a cow pasture and stopped to gaze over the fence while imagining God leading him through the green pastures. He stated that his attention was drawn to a big, round, flat area that was covered with dried cow dung. But in the center of the pile of dung was a single, beautiful flower. It was blooming and doing its best to grow, but it was surrounded by a foul stench, and a horrid mess.

The contrast between the beauty of the flower and the stench of its surroundings was striking. Yet somehow, God gave the flower the ability to bloom where it had been planted. Obviously, the seed was there before the cow dung was put there, and the flower had to push its way up and through that mess. But it eventually did, and it brought forth great beauty.

On looking around further, the pastor spotted several more flowers trying to grow in the middle of a pile of cow dung. Then he thought, there are precious souls in his church who know all about the failures in the ministry. The people (the flowers) know about the failures (the mess) but can do absolutely nothing to move from under it, yet they push their way through it and bloom anyway. In spite of their surroundings and in spite of the overwhelming stench surrounding them, they bloom.

The virtue he deduced from this picture is this: Sometimes our lives can seem like we're doing our best to bloom where planted, to grow despite the stuff heaped upon us and the stench that overpowers our best efforts to make the world a better smelling place, yet we bloom because the power of God enables us to do so.

There is much to learn from your failures. When you focus solely on or are driven by success, you overlook the big picture and miss the lessons that failure can teach you. When you succeed, you're only motivated to repeat what you did so that you can succeed again. I am not encouraging you to pursue failure, but I am saying there is more to learn from our failures than from our successes. When we succeed there is less of an incentive to grow than when we fail. Failure will give you a lot to think about and a huge incentive to learn a lesson, to change, and to get better. Henry Ford said it very elegantly: "Failure is simply the opportunity to begin again, this time more intelligently."

Chapter Fourteen: Seven Main Takeaways

1. All is not lost when we fail. It is not final.

2. There is a vast difference between failure, the event, and a person being a failure.

3. The purpose of failure is to prune you.

4. You must be on to something to fail. Perhaps what we call failure is not failure.

5. Failure is not as a death sentence. Failure is the gift of another starting point.

6. If you have the right perspective on failure, you will rise above the failure to become something better and greater. That is failing forward.

7. Mistakes are great teachers that provide us with invaluable lessons if we allow them to do so.

FEAR: THE PAPA DEMON

Fear keeps us focused on the past or
worried about the future.
—Thich Nhat Hanh

T he idea to write this book was born from a sermon I preached several years ago at the church I was attending at the time. The title of the sermon was the same as the title of this book: Ds and Fs Won't Do. As I was preparing for the sermon, the Lord revealed to me that fear is the papa demon. All the Ds and Fs addressed in this book have a demonic root, and fear is the source. Fear is the father of them all.

Fear, by definition, is a response which seeks to avoid threatening danger. Psychologists claim there are three types of fear: rational fear, which occurs when there is a real, imminent threat or danger, primal fear, which is innate to humanity, and irrational fear, the fear that cannot be sensibly explained. Irrational fears (fears that go beyond the scope of common sense) are sometimes called phobias.[32]

The mere fact that there is such a thing as rational and primal fear tells us that fear is not always bad. Our brains are

255

hardwired for fear. It is an innate capacity that helps us identify and avoid threats to our safety. The fear-wiring in our brain is linked to our emotions and memory. Therefore, upon encountering a threat to our safety, we react emotionally by fleeing from the threat and that potentially dangerous situation is registered in our memory so that if we experience the same situation again, we recall it as dangerous.

While I acknowledge the reality of rational and primal fear, I want to discuss two types of fear: fear of the Lord and fear of the unknown.

Fear of the Lord

Fear of the Lord is reverential fear. This is a holy fear. It is really an awe and respect for the majesty and holiness of God, our Heavenly Father.

Fear of the Lord comes from a good or healthy place, but fear of the unknown comes from a bad or unhealthy place. Fear of the Lord will do you good, but fear of the unknown will damage you. The source of fear of the Lord is the Holy Spirit, but the source of fear of the unknown is Satan, the father of lies.

A recurrent command that was given to God's people in the Old Testament is to "fear God" or "fear the Lord." Like the children of Israel, we have the choice to fear the Lord and be free from all destructive and satanic fears or not.

To fear the Lord, we must know who He is. We must know His nature, His character. When we fear the Lord, we acknowledge and appreciate His unending love and everlasting mercies, but we also are aware of His capacity for wrath and judgment. The fear of God makes us recognize that He is loving, merciful, and forgiving and that He is holy, just, and righteous. Proverbs 2:5 (AMP) tells us just that: "Then you will understand the [reverent] fear of the Lord [that is, worshiping Him and regarding Him as truly awesome] And discover the knowledge of God."

Fearing the Lord means to be in reverent awe of His holiness, to give Him complete reverence and to honor Him as the God of great glory, majesty, purity, and power. When God revealed Himself and his great power to the Israelites at Mount Sinai through "thunder and lightning, with a thick cloud over the mountain, and a very loud trumpet blast. Everyone in the camp trembled" (Exodus 19:16, NIV). Trembling before the Lord was fear of the Lord expressed. They even begged Moses to tell them what God had said so that they would not have to face God Himself (Exodus 20:18-19; Deuteronomy 5:22–27). Also, we see it recorded in Psalm 33:8–9 (NIV): "Let all the earth fear the Lord; let all the people of the world revere him. For he spoke, and it came to be; he commanded, and it stood firm." The fear of the Lord will make our jaws drop. It will take our breath away.

Because fearing God incites knowing God, when we fear Him, we place our faith and trust in Him alone for all our affairs. Psalm 115:11 (KJV) shows us that fearing and trusting the Lord go together: "Ye that fear the LORD, trust in the LORD: he is their help and their shield." The psalmist encourages all who fear the Lord to trust in the Lord. Why? Because He is their help and shield. Therefore, fearing God produces confidence, hope, and trust in Him.

In knowing God and understanding His character, we accept the fact that due to His justice and holiness—His purity, perfection, and abhorrence for evil—He judges and punishes sin. Undoubtedly, God is loving, merciful, and kind, but a holy reverence for God will be a constant reminder that He is also a

God of judgment. Therefore, fearing God involves recognizing that He detests sin and requires holiness of us. The fear of the Lord will teach us that He has the power to punish those who are proud and those who are hard hearted toward Him and break His laws and precepts presumptuously.

We have numerous evidence in Scripture where God punished sin. For example, Adam and Eve were evicted from the Garden of Eden and life-long penalties were placed upon humanity when they disobeyed God (Genesis 3:16–24), Cain was punished when he murdered his brother (Genesis 4:11–12), King Saul was punished when he disobeyed God (1 Samuel 15:28–29), King David was punished when he raped Bathsheba and murdered Uriah (2 Samuel 12:10–12), and Ananias and Saphira were punished when they lied to the Holy Spirt (Acts 5: 1–11). The fear of the Lord will teach us that the God who punished sin in the days of old will do the same today.

We should fear and be in awe of Jehovah, the God of all gods and King of all kings because of His matchless power and because He is the Creator of all things and all people. The amazing power that He incessantly exercises over His creation is cause for fearing Him. The ever-flowing blessings and new mercies, especially the forgiveness of our sins, that we receive from God every morning are undeniably good reasons to fear Him.

FEAR OF THE UNKNOWN

Fear of the unknown exists in the absence of faith and trust in God. If there is faith in God concerning a potentially fear-producing situation, fear cannot exist there. In other words, fear and faith cannot coexist; it must be one or the other.

True faith in God is to know that He does not and cannot change (Numbers 23:19). True faith in Him is to know that He is forever faithful (Psalm 89:2). True faith is to leave everything in His hands. True faith in God is to cast all your cares upon Him and leave them there. It is to trust and believe that God indeed knows the beginning, middle, and ending of all things concerning you. Faith in God is a solid conviction that His thoughts toward you are good (Jeremiah 29:11) and that He will not withhold anything good from you if you walk uprightly before Him (Psalm 84:11). This kind of faith will override fear in challenging times.

The unknown produces fear because we walk by sight and not by faith. Fear presents itself because we function based on what we can see with our natural eyes, not what the Lord is showing us in the Spirit. When we walk by faith, we close all openings to fear because we embrace the fact that even though we may not see things working out on our behalf at the moment, we trust and believe that God is working them out in the Spirit realm and that His desire toward us will be accomplished in our lives.

We fear the unknown because we fail to trust in the Lord and lean not on our own understanding, and this only makes it more difficult to deal with life's circumstances. And yes, it becomes more difficult because, when in fear, we try to manage things on our own versus handing them over to God and trusting Him to take care of them. We could live a "care-free" life, a life void of anxiety and worry, but because of our lack of faith, fear has moved in and has robbed many of us of the abundant life that is available to us.

Fear of the unknown produces unwarranted distress and anxiety surrounding that which is unknown or uncertain. For example, you have an upcoming job interview. Of course,

259

unless the Holy Spirit shows you, you do not know the outcome of the interview. But if you do not rest in the Lord, knowing that you have prayed about the matter and are trusting God to do on your behalf what is best, you will spend unnecessary emotional resources being anxious and distressed about the matter.

Fear of the unknown makes you imagine what could or will happen, and because fear of the unknown is from the devil, these imaginations are never positive. These negative imaginations will then cause greater levels of anxiety and worry, and thus tighten the grip of fear upon you. Therefore, the interviewee will imagine a totally disastrous interview and not being offered the job. The young lady with one of the most beautiful voices who is slated to sing a solo will imagine herself making mistakes, missing notes, forgetting the words of the song, and could even imagine people ridiculing her. This could all happen while the masses consider her an anointed singer and are looking forward to hearing her sing.

Adam did not know how God would respond to his act of disobedience to Him. As a result, Adam ran and hid himself, and when he was asked why he was hiding, he said, "Because I was afraid" (Genesis 3:10). Because he had disobeyed God, Adam had good reason to be afraid, but this was fear of the unknown, it was not reverential fear. Reverential fear would either make him obey God instead of disobeying Him or run to Him and repent when he sinned. Reverential fear drives us to God, not away from Him.

In Numbers 14:9, it was fear of the unknown that was expressed by the children of Israel when Joshua and Caleb tried to convince the children of Israel not to fear the people of Kadesh-Barnea. The people of Kadesh-Barnea were a resource to the children of Israel but because of fear, the children of

Israel could not see that. The people of Kadesh-Barnea had no defense, but Yahweh, the God of Israel, was with the children of Israel yet fear blinded their eyes to His presence.

I have read that the words "fear not" are in Scripture as many as 365 times. Whether the exact number is 365 or not, God's Word addresses our fears again and again. This might be so because so many of us are consumed by fear.

"Fear not" is a command of the Bible that we all do not obey at times. We are never warned before fear shows up. Fear appears uninvited, and it often comes forcefully. It comes with negative predictions and "what if questions" that bombard us and override all sense of reasoning and rationale. Fear will rob us of peace and confidence because it is a thief.

FEAR IS A THIEF

Satan, the father of fear is a thief; therefore, fear, being an offspring of its father, is naturally a thief. Fear will rob you of your spiritual inheritance as an heir and joint heir with Jesus Christ. Fear will stop you from doing what the Father wants you to do and from receiving what the Father has for you. Fear will steal your freedom, your peace, your hope and expectations, your time, your motivation, and your focus. Fear will take so much from you that it immobilizes you. It will stop you from accomplishing anything.

Fear will keep you from taking risks. It will keep you from trying new things and from trusting the God in you who has already empowered you to do what He has assigned to you. Fear will even keep you from obeying God and growing in Him. It will keep you from enjoying life.

Once, while at the orthodontist, I saw a woman in the waiting room with three young children. The Holy Spirit directed me to go over and minister to the woman. I hesitated and bargained with the Father, saying if I saw her in the lobby of the building when I left the office, I would talk to her. Well, after seeing the orthodontist and I got off the elevator in the lobby, there was the woman with her three children. My heart started pounding in my chest, and I walked right past her to my car.

Fear stopped me from trusting the God in me to do what He told me to do. I've grown quite a bit in the Lord since then, so I would readily obey the Holy Spirit today. But fear not only robbed me that day it also robbed the woman. The Holy Spirit would not have directed me to minister to the woman if He did not see a need and wanted to use me to fill that need. I was robbed because my faith and spiritual giftings will only grow when I exercise them, and I did not exercise them that day. Fear restrained me that day, so I did not have the opportunity to grow from the experience that would have encouraged me and given me the boldness to obey the Lord more readily next time.

I've mentored several young believers and almost always, my focus is to instill in them the discipline of personal prayer and devotions as well as confidence in praying publicly—for example to open or close a service or gathering or to pray for and with another individual. The area that I see the most fear is in praying in public. These loved ones always doubt themselves and overthink the task, yet when they pray publicly, they do well.

We know that the more we do something, the more proficient we become in that thing. If these loved ones let fear stand between them and praying publicly, they will never grow in that area and the contributions they could make to others and the ministry will not be to the fullest. This is one of the many ways that fear sneakily steals from us.

Fear's natural companions are worry and anxiety, and these two spiritual parasites are slow killers. They slowly deplete your joy which is your strength, so in essence, they make you weak. Worry and anxiety are antonyms for peace and contentment. Fear is indeed a thief and a killer.

FEAR IS A LIAR

The Word of God tells us that perfect love casts out fear (1 John 4:18). God's love is perfect, unconditional, relentless, and complete. He loves you more than you can ever imagine or understand. You will close all openings to fear when you know and accept this fact. By basking in the love of God for you, you will embrace the truth of the Word of God about you and your circumstances, and that truth will shield you from fear.

Nonetheless, Satan, being the all-time liar that he is, will try to lie to you by highlighting your flaws and failures and will try to convince you that God does not love you and God does not care about you. He will even tell you that God does not hear your prayers and that God will not answer your prayers. The most frequent lie he tells is that God doesn't forgive you even when you asked Him for forgiveness. He tries to keep you tied to your past and make you think you've gone too far for God to forgive you. Even those who are saved, he tries to convince them that they are not saved.

All these are attempts to make you doubt the love of God. They are his attempts to make the love of God appear imperfect to you. If you doubt or mitigate the love of God, you will then make room for fear. Fear cannot touch you if you understand and believe that the love of God is perfect and complete. The devil knows that, so his recourse is to lie to you about the God who loves you beyond measure.

There is no truth in the Devil. He is the father of lies (John 8:44). Every word that comes out of his mouth is a lie. Lying is his nature. Even when he quotes Scriptures, he lies. Yes, the Word of God is truth, but Satan uses Scripture for his own destructive purposes, and therefore, whatever he says is a lie. He is the deceiver of the whole world (Revelation 12:9). When we are told any lie, it is of Satan. He lies to us because he is trying to dishearten us, and unwarranted fear is one of his tools.

Fear is also a deceiver; it's a cheater and a swindler. It tricks you to make you think there is a threat when there is no threat. Fear also makes you feel issues are worse than they really are. Sometimes the fear you experience is worse than the very thing you are fearful about. In truth, fear makes you believe the unreal to be real. I've seen it said that the meaning of FEAR is False Evidence Appearing Real, and I agree. By making the false look real, fear will shift your focus from the positive and constructive to the negative and destructive and from what's actually happening to a worsening situation or outcome that you have conjured up in your mind.

Fear closes the door to peace and contentment and offers anxiety and worry. With worry and anxiety, many will never step into the blessings that the Father has for them. Worry and anxiety will overwhelm you with concerns about what might or will not work and will inhibit you from taking the needed step forward. We never know what will happen tomorrow, and we never know what other people are thinking. But those who fall prey to fear are often trying to predict and control what others are thinking and what will happen tomorrow—things they do not know and cannot control. The ill-fated attempt to control these things gives way to the lies of the enemy about the things that concern them, and in fear, they believe them.

Fear will then drill those lies into their mind, and that heightens the fear even more. It's a vicious cycle.

The enemy lies to a person who is facing a challenge by telling them that God has forgotten them or that God does not love them. These lies directly contradict the promises of God. Psalm 115:12a says, "The Lord remembers us and will bless us." In Isaiah 49:15, the Word says He will not forget us, and in Deuteronomy 31:8 He says, He will never abandon you. There are a host of scriptures that give us the assurance that our God will never forget or leave us. God wants you to have a life of peace and contentment here on earth, but fear, being the liar that it is, can steal the life out of your life.

Many people never live up to their full capabilities because of fear. Some never enjoy healthy relationships with people whose lives they could enrich and whose lives could enrich their own significantly. The lies of fear can lead to a substandard life that is marked by instability, unhappiness, and a lack of contentment. Fear saps spiritual vitality, and it can cause spiritual, emotional, and even physical paralysis.

Fear demands emotional energy that is poorly invested in something that often never happens. In Matthew 6, Jesus instructed His disciples to not be excessively anxious about providing for their basic needs. In other words, they were advised not to worry about how their needs will be met. Verse 33 admonishes us to seek the Kingdom of God and His righteousness first and then all these things—food, clothing, and shelter—will be added unto us. When we live with fear—worry and anxiety—we spend a whole lot of emotional energy but reap no rewards.

Fear Hath Torment

The Bible says in 2 Timothy 1:7 (AMP), "For God did not give us a spirit of timidity or cowardice or fear, but [He has given us a spirit] of power and of love and of sound judgment and personal discipline [abilities that result in a calm, well-balanced mind and self-control]." Fear is a spirit sent by Satan, but power, love, and a sound mind come from the Spirit of God. The spirit of fear is sent to torment you and the spirit of power and love is sent by God to give you peace.

There is no peace in torment, and there is no torment in peace. So, you see, Satan's aim is to offer you the very opposite of what your Heavenly Father has for you. Satan is offering you fear and torment. But instead of fear, God is offering you peace that will be expressed in the form of love and a sound mind.

The carriers of the torment, which comes with fear, are worry and anxiety. We worry and become anxious when we don't know for sure what will happen next, and instead of entrusting the matter to God, we concoct the outcomes ourselves. Naturally, in the absence of trust in God, whatever outcomes we anticipate are inherently bad, and the anticipated negative outcomes in turn cause more worry, hence the torment.

Worry is tormenting because you anticipate the worst, and you want to remedy the matter, but you can't. Therefore, you feel defenseless and powerless. You're doing all you can—usually in your mind—to control the perceived impending bad outcome, but it is out of your control, and you are troubled by that fact. You are tormented.

When people worry about a situation, they play and replay their negative predictions about the situation in their mind. That alone is torment, because as they live and relive the perceived negative outcomes, they are repeatedly faced with an issue that is entirely out of their hands. Truthfully, due to their degree of concern about the matter, if the matter was under their control, they would have done something about it. But although the situation that concerns them is not in their control, they continue to think upon it and anticipate the worst. This is the formula for increased worry and anxiety, and the result is torment.

Out of fear, people may go to great lengths to gain certainty about an unknown situation but find no answer. Some will try to be certain about their future, even if it costs them personally, but to no avail. That is torment. Job was overcome by fear concerning his children, and ultimately, the very thing he feared happened to him. Job in Job 3:25–26 (NIV, emphasis added) said, "What I feared has come upon me; what I dreaded has happened to me. I have no peace, no quietness; I have no rest, but only turmoil." Job was tormented. He had no peace, no quietness, no rest…only turmoil, instability, and confusion. This is what the presence of fear and the absence of God's perfect love looks like—torment, anguish, pain, suffering, instability, and confusion. Worry is torment. Anxiety is torment.

Torment is a weapon Satan uses to cause you to think that God is not going to help you. But I am encouraging you to firmly push back. Do not accommodate fear. You mitigate your faith in God when you let fear in. You cannot walk in fear and, at the same time, be spiritually, interpersonally, or emotionally healthy. Fear comes with torment, and torment will kill your peace. Torment comes with unrest, helplessness, and turmoil. You must choose faith and trust in God over fear.

CHAPTER FIFTEEN: SEVEN MAIN TAKEAWAYS

1. We fear the unknown because we fail to trust in the Lord and lean not on our own understanding.

2. Fear is a thief.

3. Fear will keep you from taking risks.

4. Fear is a liar.

5. Fear closes the door to peace and contentment and offers anxiety and worry.

6. Fear demands emotional energy that is poorly invested in something that often never happens.

7. Fear is torment.

OVERCOMING FEAR

Fear is crippling; it stops effort, and production. Thus, the cure for fear is action. The courage to keep trying will break one free from the grip of fear. Do not stop trying!

A host of materials about fear and overcoming fear are available. This is so because it is a common phenomenon in humanity. Our brains are hard-wired for fear. It is a protective factor, an instinct that if used wisely can keep us from danger. That is one of two types of fear. The other is the fear that deceives us and keeps us from what is good for us. So, the in-born, God-given fear protects us from harm and the fear that is of our adversary is intended to be harmful to us. The fear that comes from our adversary is the fear we must overcome.

Because the aim of this fear is to keep us from experiencing the good that is intended for us, it is naturally crippling. It has the capacity to paralyze us and thus restrict us from moving forward and into the greater things that the Father has for us. This fear distorts reality and makes things that are promised to us look like they are not ours. It makes things that are good for us look dangerous, and it makes things that we can do look impossible.

To many, fear looks like a giant that they cannot conquer, and they are partially right. Indeed, fear is a giant and we ourselves cannot conquer it, but the God in us, the God Who is greater than the one who is in the world, can conquer fear through us.

In fact, we do not actually have a fear problem, but instead, we have a faith problem. Fear takes hold of us when we lack faith in God. We need faith in God because we will never have a fear-free life. Until his time runs out, the enemy of our souls will continuously seek ways to destroy us, so we must constantly rely on and believe in the power of the God we serve. If your goal is to be fear free, you will almost always be disappointed. Therefore, the approach ought not to be fear avoidance, but instead, it should be fear confrontation.

CONFRONT FEAR

Fear tells us to run or go the opposite direction from the object or situation that poses a threat. Fear also tells us to stop. If you are advancing toward something and the devil manages to plant a lie in your mind, thus making you see that thing as threatening, fear can convince you to stop. It can tell you to stop trying, stop working, stop praying, stop hoping, and stop planning. Fear means you no good.

To overcome fear, you must do the very opposite of what it directs you to do. So, if it tells you to stop, then keep going. If it tells you to run away from the perceived danger, then run toward it. And if it tells you to stop working or planning, then keep working and planning. Do whatever fear tells you not to do.

In doing the opposite of what fear dictates, you will confront fear. For example, suppose you fear flying. The devil has lied to you that if you get on an airplane, the plane will crash, or you will feel like you're suffocating and can't breathe. You believe these lies, and therefore, you have never set foot on an airplane. In fact, you don't even own a passport. To confront and not run away from this perceived danger, you must get on an airplane; you must travel by air.

There are two approaches to confronting this type of fear: flooding or implosion and systematic desensitization. If flooding or implosion is used, you would go from being afraid of flying to packing your bags and traveling by air. There would be no intermediary steps to get you to travel by air. In this case you are in one go, flooded with the very stimulus that make you fearful.

In using systematic desensitization, you would gradually expose yourself to the perceived danger until you can face it. For example, you could start by looking at pictures of airplanes, look at videos or movies about airplanes, and meet people using airplanes as a means of transportation. Next you may tour an airplane. You would physically go into an airplane, not with the intent to travel, but to expose yourself to the threatening object. While touring the airplane, you could sit in the seats, buckle yourself in, look at the restroom, see what the cockpit looks like, and learn about the safety measures on the airplane. Next while touring an airplane the pilot could start the engine with you seated with the seat belt on. Next, you could sit in the airplane with the seatbelt on and the pilot could simply run the airplane down the runway without taking off. Next, you could take a short airplane trip. You could lengthen each trip you take until you become more comfortable and can take any trip you wish.

From the surface, fear of flying may look like all it does is stop you from flying, but this is not the case. Suppose you are an author, but you fear flying. Now, suppose doors are opening for you and you are asked to speak about your books in locations that require travel by air. Suppose one of your dreams is to do at least one foreign mission trip, but you are afraid of flying. Suppose you have parents or grand or great grandchildren across the world and you genuinely want to spend time with them, but you are afraid of flying. This fear will not only keep you on the ground, but it will also keep you from fulfilling your purpose and from enjoying life. Fear will steal your quality of life. Fear will suffocate your gifts until they can no longer breathe. So, what appears to be simply a fear of flying could steal more from you than you think. The same goes for all other fears that people face every day.

Another example: you are afraid of appearing in front of an audience. It is understood that public speaking or public performance is simply not some people's strength. But even so, no one should be crippled by fear when their post in ministry requires their appearance before an audience. This is a very common fear in the body of Christ. Many with a melodious voice and many who can teach and give sound admonitions from the Word of God are paralyzed by fear of speaking in front of a crowd.

Think for a moment about how many people are evading, pushing away, and running from the call of God upon their lives because of fear. Think for a moment about what that does to the person in fear and to the people who would hear them sing or deliver the Word of God. You, the fear-struck individual, will never grow in your gift because fear has inhibited you from using it, and people will never be blessed

272

by what God has put in you because you never confronted the fear.

Fear will not leave on its own. And without a miraculous intervention from God, which rarely happens, prayer and fasting alone does not counteract fear. While I totally believe in prayer and fasting, and we should pray about everything, after praying and fasting, you must face your fear. After Jesus did forty days of praying and fasting, He was ready to start His earthly ministry. Fear was not an issue for Jesus, but if it had been, He could not have carried out the commands of His Father if He stayed the whole time in prayer in the wilderness. The same goes for you. You cannot work the ministry to which you are called if you pray and fast all the time. You must exit your prayer closet and face the thing that stands between you and the call of God upon your life.

It is very unlikely that upon praying, you will suddenly feel comfortable flying or standing before an audience. But prayer will give you the grace to face the perceived threat, and through communion with the Father, the Holy Spirit will change your perspective of the situation, making you see it for what it is—not as a threat, but a gift for others through you and an opportunity to serve God. So yes, praying is good, but if you don't take the step toward the threat while praying and believing God, the fear-producing thing will only get louder and bigger.

Fear does not plan on staying for a period of time and then move on somewhere else when that time expires. Fear is a stronghold from the start. Fear does not start out as a foothold or what I call a toehold. A stronghold is a defensive structure. A stronghold sets up itself in such a way that makes it difficult to penetrate. This is why prayer is necessary, but again, you must work out the good work that God starts in you when you pray. You must add works to faith because faith without works is dead (James 2:20). You prayed and declared the Word of God over your situation, and you believe that you are delivered, but you will never really be delivered if you don't get on that airplane and visit your grandchildren or get in front of the congregation and sing that solo.

Remember, fear is the papa demon, so fear is not a derivative of some other underlying issue; instead, it is the source. There is no small fear, and there is no modest fear. Fear is fear and its intent is to block you entirely. If not dealt with, fear will not leave, but instead it will get bigger and stronger until it takes over. You cannot wait for fear to leave because that day will not come. You must take action to put it out.

You must open your mouth and speak, even when you're afraid of speaking. You must step forward even while you feel afraid of moving. You cannot wait to feel unafraid before taking that step because fear is there to stay. You must do the very thing you are afraid of doing or face the very thing you are afraid of facing.

In Joshua 1:9 (NIV), God says, "Have I not commanded you? Be strong and courageous. Do not be afraid; do not be discouraged, for the Lord your God will be with you wherever you go." That was after God told him to be strong and courageous in verses 6 and 7. It seems as if after being told twice to be courageous—verses 6 and 7—Joshua was still showing signs of fear, so in verse 9, God reiterated what He already told him, but also in a mildly scolding tone: "Have I not commanded you?" In other words, "Didn't I tell you this already, so why are you acting this way?" So, Joshua's life was not void of fear, but we see nowhere in Scripture that he abdicated his assignment from God. Instead, he not only faced his fear, but he burrowed through it and went from conquering to conquering with the nation of Israel.

CLEAR YOUR HEAD

To conquer fear, you must see things as they are and think about things as they are. Fear is a counterfeit; it makes things that are not real look real, and it makes things that don't even exist look and feel like they exist. And because fear is of your adversary, fear does not make bad look good, it makes good look bad and makes anything it can influence, even if it has some good in it, look worse than it really is.

Whatever fear tells you will be a lie. Fear will tell you that you are going to fail the examination you've been studying for over the past several months. It will tell you that you will not get the promotion, that your wedding will not go as planned, that you are going to die from the illness with which you are diagnosed, and the list can go on. The lies of the enemy will flood your mind until you believe them, and the natural follow-up to believing something is to talk in accordance with what you believe and then act accordingly. Therefore, to overcome fear, you must clear your head. You must examine how you view and talk about things, and if they are built upon anything that is false or nonexistent, you must erase them.

For example, you have been diagnosed with breast cancer and now you think you're going to die. You came to this conclusion because the devil has lied to you, and you believe him. You are consumed with thoughts about your funeral and all the women you know who have died of cancer. Cancer is indeed a life-threatening disease, but many people survive it, and you could be among them. If you don't clear your head, the voice of fear telling you that you are going to die will be louder than the voice that tells you God can heal you. If you don't guard your heart and mind, this lie could embed itself in your mind and your spirit; therefore, you must be intentional about clearing your head.

Note that the lies that fear tells lack evidence. For example, you're in a doctoral program and are about to take the comprehensive exams. You have done due diligence and have prepared the best you can for the comps, but you cannot stop thinking about failing the exams. Now you dread the embarrassment of failure, and the fear of not graduating with your classmates is overwhelming. There is absolutely no evidence that you are going to fail the exam but somehow fear was able to convince you that you're going to fail.

Because fear is crippling and you already bought the lie that you're going to fail, your mind goes blank, your palms are sweaty, and your heart is pounding when you sit down to take the exam. Despite knowing the information, you fail the exam. Fear has gotten what it wants. It stemmed your confidence. It stole growth and progression from you, and if not dealt with, this will only be the beginning.

The plan of the enemy is for you to look at things and think about things from his perspective, which is always from a place of untruth. His lies will inundate you. He wants to bombard you with his lies so that you find it difficult to think differently. But the antidote to his lies is the Word of God. God's Word is the truth. Ephesians 5:26 tells us that the Word of God sanctifies and cleanses. To clear your head, you must find a Word spoken by God the Father that is the opposite of the lie that the enemy has introduced to you.

For example, if he tells you that you are going to fail the exam, replace that lie with the truth of God's Word that says that God will not withhold any good thing from those who walk uprightly before Him (Psalm 84:1). When you read it, put your name in the verse. Make it your own. Claim the promise, believe the promise, and denounce the lie of the enemy. If he tells you that you won't get the promotion, you can be at peace because your God has assured you that He will supply all your needs according to His riches in glory (Philippians 4:19).

Since the lies of the enemy get in your head to make you believe what he has told you and therefore walk in fear, you must clear your head if you want to overcome fear, and the only way to do so is by the washing of the Word of God.

FAITH OVER FEAR

We can read and hear the Word of God all day long, but it will do us no good if we do not believe what we read and hear. The conquering agent for fear is faith in the Word of God. "In the beginning was the Word, and the Word was with God, and the Word was God" (John 1:1, KJV). This means the Word is God and God is the Word; they are inseparable, and they both existed from the beginning. Therefore, to believe the Word of God is to believe God, and to have faith in the Word of God is to have faith in God.

Faith in God is to trust that He has your life in His strong and capable hands. Faith in God is to find strength and refuge in Him, not your own capabilities. It is to know in thought and in action that He is your refuge from the assaults of the enemy. Faith in God is to have the assurance that what you have prayed for has already happened in the spirit realm and will come to fruition in the earthly realm. Therefore, if fear tells you that you are going to die from breast cancer, faith will tell you that—though you have not seen your healing in the natural— your faith in God is substance for your desired healing and the proof that it does exist. This is the mental posture of a person who has faith in God, and with this state of mind, there is no room for fear. The voice of the Holy Spirit will get louder and stronger than the voice of fear as it is being fed by faith in God.

Faith in God will make you sure of His promises and will keep your trust in Him from wavering. Having faith in God will give you stability in life. Therefore, regardless of what fear tries to tell you, you will not be like children "tossed back and forth by the waves, and blown here and there by every wind of teaching and by the cunning and craftiness of people in their deceitful scheming" (Ephesians 4:14). You will know undoubtedly that the Word of God says the opposite of whatever fear tells you.

It is much easier to not to be fearful about the future when we know that the Lord of Hosts, the all-knowing and all-powerful God, is on your side. Faith in God will give you a firm foundation on which to stand. Isaiah 26:4 (NIV) says, "Trust in the Lord forever, for the Lord, the Lord himself, is the Rock eternal." Faith will establish the everlasting Rock in your life, and this is the Rock on which you can stand so that you can tower over fear.

If you listen to fear when it exaggerates the imperfections in your life and makes things look worse than they are, you will have no peace. But if you give your burdens to the Lord, He will take care of you. Faith requires that we become like children to God. We must trust Him blindly. We must run to Him and "complain" to Him about our concerns, just like a child would do with his/her earthly father.

When I was a child, I felt safe because I had a father, and I knew my needs would be met. Well, you have a Father who is the Father of all, including your earthly father. Your earthly father may have been very good to you, but your Heavenly

Father is superior to your earthly father. This is an invitation to have peace and contentment, not worry and anxiety. Give God your concerns, and He will take care of them.

In Matthew 7, Jesus invites us to ask, seek, and know. He wants us to come to Him so that He can work through us to conquer that giant called fear. In verses 9 to 11 (NIV) He says:

> *Which of you, if your son asks for bread, will give him a stone? Or if he asks for a fish, will give him a snake? If you, then, though you are evil, know how to give good gifts to your children, how much more will your Father in heaven give good gifts to those who ask him!*

So, think about it. Your earthly father might have been good to you, but Jesus is saying that if your imperfect father was as good to you, how much more will the perfect Heavenly Father be to you? He wants you to have faith in Him, and by doing so, your faith in your well-able God will tower over fear.

The Holy Spirit will bring peace to you as you read and meditate on Scripture. When you read the Word of God, it washes your inner man and renews your mind. Said succinctly, the Word of God builds your faith.

As stated in Romans 10:17, faith only comes by hearing the Word of God, and that is to hear with our spirit or heart, not with our physical ears. When you hear the Word of God this way, you will have the faith to believe that anyone who believes in God will never be put to shame (Romans 10:11). So, no need to be afraid of shame due to failing an exam or not getting a promotion. When you have faith in the God, as the Apostle John states, you will have confidence that He hears you when you call on Him.

1 John 5:14–15 (NIV) — *This is the confidence we have in approaching God: that if we ask anything according to his will, he hears us. And if we know that he hears us—whatever we ask—we know that we have what we asked of him.*

To me, nothing else in this world can give greater peace than to know that the God of creation, the God who is more than enough hears me when I call on Him. This leaves no room for fear or unrest in my spirit. How about you?

I played the character Hopeful in Pilgrim's Progress many years ago. This allegory teaches a profound message about faith. John Bunyan, the author of Pilgrim's Progress, has two lions blocking the path to the heavenly City. The lions are ready to tear to shreds anyone who passes by. One of the characters named Christian was traveling on that path toward the City. He grew increasingly fearful, but slowly pressed on. As he got closer to the lions, he discovered that God had the lions chained, and only their growls could reach him. Christian then passed between them unharmed. Fear is your enemy, but know that God has it chained, and only its growl can reach you.

Treat Fear Like Your Enemy

Fear is not your friend; it is your enemy, and you must treat it as such. Fear has come to steal from you, to kill, and to destroy what you have. The intent of fear is to weaken your faith and sever you from God. This enemy, the devil, is not kind to you, and he is not gentle with you. These facts about this enemy should raise a level of anger toward him that makes you fight just as viciously against him as he does against you.

If he comes to kill and destroy what God has put in your life, you should be set on killing anything he tries to insert in your life. Therefore, the very appearance of fear should raise a violent, godly anger in you. The aim is to kill, not injure, so you must fight to kill.

The Bible says in 1 Peter 5:8 (AMP, emphasis added), "Be sober [well balanced and self-disciplined], be <u>alert and cautious</u> at all times. That enemy of yours, the devil, prowls around like a roaring lion [<u>fiercely hungry</u>], seeking someone to devour." When treating fear like your enemy, you must be on the alert to detect the very start of his attempts to weigh you down with fear. You must be cautious and alert enough to detect fear before it takes root in you.

Usually no one has casual conversations or entertains their enemy. Under normal circumstances people do not create an environment for their enemy to feel comfortable around them. This is what you must do to fear: Create an environment that makes it too uncomfortable for fear to go there, let alone stay there. Do not debate, argue, or bargain with fear. The minute you detect it, you must identify it as your enemy, and you must set out to destroy it or get it as far from you as possible.

An environment in which fear cannot stay, let alone thrive, is one that is saturated by the Word of God, thanksgiving and praise, and worship to God. God is your powerbase, so, "be strong in the Lord [draw your strength from Him and be empowered through your union with Him] and in the power of His [boundless] might" (Ephesians 6:10, AMP).

You must have no dealings with fear, resist it. "Resist the devil and he will flee from you" (James 4:7, KJV). But before you can resist fear, you must submit to God. So, in treating fear like your enemy, you are rejecting it, you are rising above it, and you are submitting to Jesus your Lord. This will strengthen your union with Him and in the power of His might.

The only way to submit to God is to live in obedience to His Word. If you do that, you will gain the strength you need to resist the devil. You will be fortified to push back when he tries to lie to you. You will be equipped to make it clear to him on every occasion that he is your enemy and you to him. Draw your strength from the powerbase, who is God Himself. There you will find the strength and stamina to treat fear like your enemy, and you will have the fortitude to "stand against the wiles of the devil" (Ephesians 6:11).

Look to the Lord

The Psalmist David, a man after God's own heart experienced fear. He said in Psalm 34:4 (KJV), "I sought the Lord, and he heard me, and delivered me from all my fears" David is the same one who said, "When I am afraid, I put my trust in you." (Psalm 56:3). David's approach to overcoming fear was to look to the Lord.

Abraham and others in the Bible were the same. When Abraham feared his enemies, God said, "Fear not Abraham; for I am thy shield" (Genesis 15:1). In other words, Abraham should not look on his enemies, but to God because He is his shield.

When Jacob was stunned because of disbelief, God spoke to him and said, "Do not be afraid to go down to Egypt, for I will make you into a great nation there. I will go down to Egypt with you, and I will surely bring you back again" (Genesis 46:3–4, NIV). God assured Jacob that if he depended on Him, he would have no reason to fear. In other words, look on God, not on the surrounding circumstances.

When Israel feared the future, God said to the people through Isaiah, "Fear not, for I am with you; be not dismayed, for I am your God; I will strengthen you, I will help you, I will uphold you with my righteous right hand" (Isaiah 41:10). Verse 13 (emphasis added) says, "For I, the Lord your God, hold your right hand; it is I who say to you, 'Fear not, I am the one who helps you.'" We see the same thing in Deuteronomy 31:6 (emphasis added), which says, "Be strong and courageous. Do not fear or be in dread of them, for it is the Lord your God who goes with you. He will not leave you or forsake you." For the children of Israel, the remedy for fear was to look to their God.

Fear must be a huge issue for us because, as reported by theologians, there are over 365 mentions about fear throughout the Bible. Jesus never wasted words, yet, He repeatedly said, "Fear not," "Be not afraid," and "Do not be anxious." Repetition by Jesus is not redundancy; it is emphasis. It indicates importance.

When you are overwhelmed by fear, you can find peace and calmness by looking to the Lord. You can conquer fear by making the words of the Psalmist your own: "God is our refuge and strength, a very present help in trouble. Therefore, will we not fear, though the earth be removed, and though the mountains be carried into the midst of the sea . . . The Lord of hosts is with us" (Psalm 46:1–2,11, KJV).

You must know that if you stay in the will of the Lord, your times are in His hands, and nothing can overtake you if He does not allow it. You must exercise a moment-by-moment trust in the God who will fight all your battles if you let Him do it. You must maintain an unshakable faith and belief that the God you serve has all things concerning you under control and that nothing can harm you beyond His plan.

Look to the Lord like a child looks to his father. Exchange your fears for a simple childlike trust. Robert Lehigh of Bible Helps tells this story:

> *Many years ago, a mother and her four-year-old daughter were preparing to retire for the night. The child was afraid of the dark. When the candle was blown out for the night, the little girl caught a glimpse of the moon outside the window and she said, "Mother, is the moon God's light?"*
>
> *"Yes," replied the mother, "God's light is always shining."*
>
> *The little girl said, "Will God blow out His light and go to sleep too?"*
>
> *The mother responded, "No, my child, God never goes to sleep."*
>
> *Then, out of the simplicity of a child's heart, the little girl said, "Mommy, as long as God is awake, I'm not afraid."*

Jesus did not promise that He would be with you sometimes. He promised to be with you always, even unto the end of the world (Matthew 28:20). He promised that He will never leave you or forsake you (Deuteronomy 31:6). God never slumbers or sleeps (Psalm 121:4). He promised that if you can believe that His Word is truth, you will conquer fear.

You are loved unconditionally, and 1 John 4:18 actually starts by saying so. It says, "There is no fear in love; but perfect love casts out fear." So, let the revelation of your Heavenly Father's love today silence the fears that are challenging your faith in God. You are more than a conqueror (Romans 8:37), and you can do all things through Christ who strengthens you (Philippians 4:13).

Chapter Sixteen: Seven Main Takeaways

1. We do not actually have a fear problem, instead, we have a faith problem. Fear takes hold of us when we lack faith in God.

2. To overcome fear, you must do the very opposite of what it directs you to do.

3. The conquering agent for fear is faith in the Word of God.

4. The voice of the Holy Spirit will get louder and stronger than the voice of fear as it is being fed by faith in God.

5. It is much easier to not to be fearful about the future when we know that the Lord of Hosts, the all-knowing and all-powerful God, is on your side.

6. Fear is not your friend; it is your enemy, and you must treat it as such.

7. An environment in which fear cannot stay, let alone thrive, is one that is saturated by the Word of God, thanksgiving and praise, and worship to God.

The Cure for All

*We must allow the Word of God to confront us, to disturb
our security, to undermine our complacency and to
overthrow our patterns of thought and behavior.*
—*John R.W. Stott*

I have talked about seven conditions throughout the previous chapters: distraction, doubt, discouragement, depression, frustration, failure, and fear. I have given some details about each condition and have given some recommendations on how to counteract them. One could say that the chapters covered so far have offered seven prescriptions, one for each condition. But here I want to give you one prescription with multiple ingredients that can treat all seven conditions.

Have you ever been sick or know of anyone who is sick but has multiple symptoms? Perhaps they have a headache, a sore throat, a fever, muscle or body aches, vomiting, and diarrhea. It might appear as if they have multiple illnesses concurrently, but the fact is they have one illness, possibly influenza, with multiple symptoms. Consequently, this person needs one prescription that includes specific ingredients that will address all the symptoms. There may be ingredients in the prescription that can treat only one symptom, and there could be ingredients that treat multiple symptoms. But ultimately, this one prescription will treat all symptoms.

The seven conditions discussed are symptoms of one condition that I am calling satanic attack, and the prescription is refuge in God. When we are under attack, we are in danger, and when in danger, the sensible thing to do is seek refuge. A place of refuge provides shelter from danger or distress. Our place of safety and protection from satanic attack is in God alone.

I started this discussion in chapter one with a full discourse of the relationship or the lack thereof between God and Satan. We know Satan hates God. We know he wanted to replace God in heaven and that he still seeks to replace Him. Satan has always had an insatiable appetite for worship. What he wants the most is to get the worship that is given to God, but he can never replace God.

Satan hates God and despite his ill feelings toward God, he cannot touch God. If he hates God, he will naturally hate those who love God, and if he cannot get to God, he will do all he possibly can to get to us. Satan is a created being, so God is naturally superior to him. Therefore, God is not in feud with Satan, but Stan is in feud with Him, and in Satan's mind, the matter is not settled. Therefore, we are under his attack. In John 25:18–19 (NIV), Jesus says:

> If the world hates you, keep in mind that it hated me first. If you belonged to the world, it would love you as its own. As it is, you do not belong to the world, but I have chosen you out of the world. That is why the world hates you.

Our relationship with and dependence on the Lord is the source of our life. Our lives are fruitful only because we abide in Jesus, the Vine, but abiding in Him is also the reason the world/Satan will hate us. Jesus warned and prepared His disciples that the same hatred that provoked those who rejected Him to call for His crucifixion would soon be emitted upon them. It is true that Jesus was speaking to His disciples, but all Scripture was written for our learning and admonition (Romans 15:4, 1 Timothy 3:16). Therefore, if this warning was for the disciples, it is also for all those who would follow Him then and in any time thereafter. That includes you and me.

Satanic Attack

Before I outright attribute all occasions of distraction, doubt, discouragement, depression, frustration, failure, and fear to the attack of Satan, I must direct our attention to our own character flaws or personal danger zones. Our danger zones create cracks in our spiritual and emotional domains for the enemy to pick at until they become footholds and, if not dealt with, become strongholds.

Many of our personal danger zones or character flaws seem harmless. A personal danger zone could be poor time management or lack of organization, and as harmless as these seem to be, they give room for Satan to work in our lives. But because we are unaware of this fact, we sometimes blame Satan for everything, and thus do not take responsibility for anything. The responsibility lies with you if you are disorganized and do not manage your time properly. But Satan will quickly strategize against you after collecting information on you by observing your conduct. He will waste no time in establishing himself in these areas. In this case, the satanic attack is not poor time management or lack of organization; it is what Satan makes of your personal danger zones.

Because you are already disorganized, he can easily distract you. Distraction also seems harmless, so you probably won't give it the attention it needs. But when distracted, you will not be focused enough to complete your tasks and achieve your goals, and you become frustrated and discouraged. Repeated frustrating events due to incomplete tasks then lead you to feeling like a failure. Failure then leads to doubt in your abilities. Now Satan can start lying to you. He will highlight your failures and tell you that you do not have the knowledge and skills like everyone else to do what you want to do anyway. So now he is planting fear in you. He is setting up residence in your personal danger zones, and as this cycle continues, depression sets in.

Do you see how you can unknowingly create a weak spot for Satan to slowly pick at until he establishes himself in it? These two seemingly harmless personal character flaws can give Satan an opening in which he can magnify and ultimately manifest himself. Please note that this all starts with the individual, not Satan. The devil is always going about, prowling like a roaring lion looking for its prey (1 Peter 5:8). He is always hunting for opportunities to devour you, but he cannot devour you if you are fortified and on guard.

Lions are predators and so is Satan. According to lionalert.org, lions stalk their prey and often charge when the prey is facing away and cannot see them coming. It is no different with us and Satan. Satan stalks us as his prey. He watches our every move and listens to our every word. This gives him the information he needs—when, where, and how to attack—and he surreptitiously attacks when we are going about our business not knowing that our disorganization, our procrastination, or our poor time management are providing him the grounds he needs to establish strongholds in our lives.

Another example: you are materialistic. You recklessly spend your money on things you do not need, and when you do purchase anything, you buy things that are most expensive and unaffordable. Therefore, you create unnecessary debt, which then creates unnecessary stress in your life and in your marriage. Many have made the mistake of blaming the devil for attacking their finances when it is greed and materialism that are the culprits.

Unknown to many, materialism and poor money management are personal danger zones in which the devil can establish a stronghold. The devil can use the financial problems that you create to ruin your marriage, ruin your businesses, ruin your future, and more. Also, he can use it to make you doubt God. You, the spender, are convinced that you must look the best, have the best, and so whatever you have must be the biggest, latest, and greatest. After all, you serve the King, and you must look like the King's child.

People with this mindset will even defend their misplaced beliefs with Scriptures such as Psalm 23:1 (NIV): "The Lord is my shepherd, I lack nothing," and John 14:13–14, which says, "And I will do whatever you ask in my name, so that the Father may be glorified in the Son. You may ask me for anything in my name, and I will do it." The spender will take verses like John 14:13–14 out of context, not realizing that what they ask of the Father must be in accordance with His will. So, when they ask amiss—that is to ask with wrong motives—so that they can spend on their own pleasures (James 4:3) and do not see results, they begin to doubt God. In their mind, God is not answering prayers. When they have mismanaged their money and then pray to the Father to provide for an essential need or even to fill their own lust, their faith may waver when He does not answer their prayers. It is then that the enemy moves in to establish himself.

Doubt in God can spiral into unsure commitment to God. Doubt introduces worry and anxiety, and these are derivatives of fear. So now, you are fearful about your future instead of resting in the Lord. Fear, being the papa demon, now opens you up to all the other conditions—distraction, discouragement, depression, frustration, and failure. Your lack of discipline—your own doing, not the devil's—has created the right conditions for Satan to attack you.

REFUGE IN GOD

The safest place to be is in the arms of God. Proverbs 18:10 (KJV, emphasis added) says, "The name of the Lord is a strong [fortified] tower; the righteous run to it and are safe." Whether we need to be saved from our personal danger zones or from satanic attacks, the place to find refuge is in the name of God.

We are all flawed. The Adamic nature is in all of us, so all of us have personal danger zones that can be exploited by Satan. But with the help of the Holy Spirit, we can control our personal danger zones instead of being controlled by them. God is your refuge. He is your salvation from the harm that your personal danger zones can do to you and from the attacks of Satan. He sees you in your pain and in your times of need, and He is waiting for you to run to Him for protection, comfort, and healing. He is your greatest source of comfort and a "refuge and strength, a very present help in trouble" (Psalm 46:1).

It is believed that David wrote Psalm 46. He probably wrote this Psalm after pondering the many victories he had with God's help over the many neighboring nations. Verses 6 and 7, at minimum, show us that the people of Israel did not place their hope in their military forces, and that they were not afraid of the nations. They trusted in God alone and were not fearful of their enemies. Psalm 46 is a reminder to all who call on the name of God that we serve an all-mighty, all-powerful, sovereign God who can shield us from the attacks of Satan. Despite how challenging or difficult life gets, God can deliver. His love and care for us are matchless.

There is only one way to find refuge in God and that is to trust Him. You must trust what He says now and what He has said in His Word. You must have the assurance that if you call upon God in your distress, He will hear you (Psalm 18:6). You must cast your cares upon Him (1 Peter 5:7) and you will find rest, not turmoil. Your faith must override your feelings and emotions. You must let faith do the work. So, when fear knocks on your door, you should let faith answer it. When discouragement tries to smother you, fight back with the Word. You will find refuge in God only if you are still and know that He alone is God.

You find refuge in God when you engage the Word of God in your life. That is, to apply the Word to your situations. Whatever faces you, you must find a spoken Word in the Bible that speaks the opposite of what is challenging you and meditate on it. That Word will go into the battlefield, which is your mind, and change your perspective on whatever is happening. God's Word is the only place we find security and protection because it is the only source of truth.

Sometimes I wonder why some of us who call on Jesus seek refuge elsewhere when life gets difficult. I propose that when trouble comes, be it in the natural or spiritual, we will run for refuge in the closest place. If you're out in an open field and a storm starts, you will need shelter. But there are two buildings. One is close by, and the other is farther away. Instinctively, you will run to the closest building.

So, could it be that believers in Christ run elsewhere for refuge because wherever they go is what's closest to them? If they are already close to God when the challenging times come, they will naturally run to Him for refuge. On the other hand, if they're closer to their bank accounts and stocks and bonds than they are to God, they will run to their natural resources for shelter, not God. The message here is this: We must stay close to God so that we can readily get to Him and readily run into His name, which is a place of protection from danger and trouble. Even more importantly, we should abide in His shadow. To abide is to rest or dwell or to live. So, we do not want to visit this secret place. We should make it our dwelling place. By doing so, we can experientially declare the God in whom we trust to be our refuge and fortress.

Proverbs 18:10 says that the name of the Lord is strong and that it is a place of safety for the righteous. His name embodies who He is. His name signifies all that He is. He is love, mercy, salvation, knowledge, hope, healing, deliverance, and much more. He is the lifter of your head (Psalm 3:3), so if you are discouraged or depressed, he can lift you up. You were created in Christ Jesus unto good works (Ephesians 2:10), and He said He will send rain on your land and will bless the work of your hands (Deuteronomy 28:12), so if you are losing hope because of failures and mistakes in your life, He is your place of refuge. He is not slack concerning His promises (2 Peter 3:9), and His promises are yes and amen (2 Corinthians 1:20), therefore, if Satan is attacking you with doubt, God is your refuge. If you have no peace, start meditating on His Word, love His Word, and obey His Word. You will have great peace if you love His Word, and nothing will make you stumble (Psalm 119:165).

I suggest you take a close look at His name and what it embodies, and you will find that all you need is in Him. Philippians 2:9 tells us that God exalted Jesus and gave Him a name that is above every name. Therefore, if it has a name, the name of Jesus towers over it. If the name is distraction, doubt, discouragement, depression, frustration, failure, or fear, the name of Jesus is above it. You can find shelter from anything and everything in His name, and you must know this so that when the enemy attacks, you don't look elsewhere for cover. All you need is in Jesus. There is no satanic attack or stronghold from which the name of the Lord cannot shield you.

Chapter Seventeen: Seven Main Takeaways

1. Our danger zones create cracks in our spiritual and emotional domains for the enemy to pick at until they become footholds, and if not dealt with, become strongholds.

2. Personal danger zones are character flaws, many of which are seemingly harmless.

3. The safest place to be is in the arms of God.

4. With the help of the Holy Spirit, we can control our personal danger zones, instead of us being controlled by them.

5. There is only one way to find refuge in God and that is to trust Him.

6. You find refuge in God when you engage the Word of God in your life. That is, to apply the Word to your situations. Whatever faces you, you must find a spoken Word in the Bible that speaks the opposite of what is challenging you and meditate on it.

7. If it has a name, the name of Jesus towers over it.

AUTHOR

D R. ROSEMARIE DOWNER is a dedicated follower of Christ who aspires to having the closest relationship with Christ possible. Her service in the body of Christ primarily involves teaching and preaching. She also spent well over 30 years serving in youth ministries. Other focus areas in her ministry include women and single adults. Also, she often ministers on issues that address emotional healing and well-being. She counts every opportunity to minister as an ultimate privilege from God the Father and does not take it lightly.

She is the founder and former President of BRYDGES (Building Responsible Youth by Delivering Genuine Enrichment Services), over which she functioned as the president for 15 years—2001 through 2016. BRYDGES provides enrichment services that address the emotional, educational, social, and spiritual needs of children and youths. She is a published author of six nonfiction Christian books, several parenting handbooks, a comprehensive ministry development course—*Find and Occupy Your Place*, and the *Continuum of Care Youth Ministry Development Handbook*.

Dr. Downer earned her doctorate degree in developmental psychology at the University of Maryland College Park in 1997. She served at the U.S. Department of Agriculture as a social science researcher for 20 years and as an adjunct professor at Bowie State University for 24 years. She is now retired from both positions and is doing what she dreamed of doing for years, and that is to write nonfiction books to edify the body of Christ.

The pivotal scripture verse for her ministry is 3 John 2: "Beloved, I wish above all things that thou mayest prosper and be in health, even as thy soul prospereth." Her most favorite Bible verse is Philippians 1:6: "Being confident of this very thing, that he which hath begun a good work in you will perform it until the day of Jesus Christ." Her favorite Bible character is Moses because he had the relationship with Abba Father that she so very deeply desires. Moses was able to talk to God the Father face-to-face and without riddle because of the close relationship he had with Him, and that is her desire!

OTHER BOOKS

➢ *The High Call of Forgiveness. It's a Mandate*

A divine revelation of God's perspective on forgiveness. Filled with spiritual and practical nuggets written for our inspiration, edification, and transformation.

➢ *The High Call of Forgiveness. Leader Guide*

The teacher component of the study series that accompanies the book, The High Call of Forgiveness.

➢ *The High Call of Forgiveness. Student Workbook*

The student component of the study series that accompanies the book, The High Call of Forgiveness.

➢ *The Spoken Word on Forgiveness. A 40-Day Devotional*

A 40-day daily discussion of and reflection on specific Scriptures about forgiveness.

➢ *The Self-Scarred Church. Healing for the Seven Most Damaging Self-Inflicted Wounds to the Church*

This book recommends Bible-based approaches for seven self-inflicted wounds in the church that has hindered her growth and effectives: Lack of Vision, Survival Mentality, Pharisaical Tendencies, Crab Syndrome, Poverty Mentality, Recognition Curse, and King Leadership.

➢ *Church or God? Religion or Relationship?*

This book details how we, often unknowingly, choose idols that pose as good things over God. It makes an appeal to followers of Jesus Christ to put God first. The urgent call is to love God with all our heart, soul, and might, to even love Him (the Person Jesus Christ) more than good things such as ministry.

➢ *BOS — Building on Strengths. Homeless Parents Parenting Program*

An interactive parenting curriculum designed specifically for homeless families.

➢ *Children's Psychological Well-Being as a Function of Housing Status and Process Resources in Low-Income Families*

A study of the impact of homelessness on children's self-esteem and the parent-child relationship.

➢ *Find and Occupy Your Place*

An interactive course to help students identify their spiritual gift and a place to serve in ministry.

300

➢ *The Continuum of Care Youth Ministry Handbook*

A practical guide for leaders and staff of youth ministries.

END NOTES

[1] The Truth About God. http://www.compellingtruth.org

[2] Amy Swanson. What Are All the Names of Angels in the Bible? October 28, 2020.https://www.christianity.com/wiki/angels-and-demons/what-are-all-the-names-of-angels-in-the-bible.html.

[3] Adam Gazzaley & Larry D. Resen. The Distracted Mind. Ancient Brains in a High-Tech World. The MIT Press, 2016.

[4] Nate Klemp. Harvard Psychologists Reveal the Real Reason We're All So Distracted. June 24, 2019. https://www.inc.com/nate-klemp/harvard-psychologists-reveal-real-reason-were-all-so-distracted.html.

[5] Footholds and Strongholds. The Crossing Church. October 27, 2019. https://crossingparagould.com/sermons-master/footholds-and-strongholds

[6] Satan Called a Convention. Inspirational Christian Story about Losing Focus on Jesus. https://www.heavensinspirations.com/satan-convention.html.

[7] WIKIBOOKS. Hebrew Roots/The original Foundation/Faith https://en.wikibooks.org/wiki/Hebrew_Roots/The_original_foundation/Faith#.

[8] Biblical Hermeneutics. Why does the KJV translate ὀλιγοπιστίαν as "unbelief" in Matthew 17:20? October 16, 2020. https://hermeneutics.stackexchange.com/questions/.

[9] Guinness, Os. God in the Dark. 23. Wheaton: Crossway Books, 1996.

[10] Rosemary Bardsley. God's Word for You. What Did Peter Doubt? 2020. https://www.godswordforyou.com/answers/1487-what-did-peter-doubt.html

[11] Clarence L. Haynes, Jr. 7 Warning Signs of a Carnally Minded Christian. December 23, 2020. https://www.crosswalk.com/faith/spiritual-life/warning-signs-of-a-carnally-minded-christian.html

[12] Steven Cole. Lesson 5: Overcoming Discouragement (Ezra 5:1-17). July 31, 2023. https://bible.org/seriespage/lesson-5-overcoming-discouragement-ezra-51-17.

[13] Jon Bloom. Lord, Deliver Me from Distraction. December 6, 2016. https://www.desiringgod.org/articles/lord-deliver-me-from-distraction.

[14] Grant Richison. 1 Peter 5:7. February 1, 1998.
https://versebyversecommentary.com/1998/02/01/1-peter-57/

[15] Daniel K. Hall-Flavin, M.D. Clinical Depression: What Does That Mean?
May 13, 2017. https://www.mayoclinic.org/diseases-
conditions/depression/expert-answers/clinical-depression/faq-20057770.

[16] Anamika Sahu, Preeti Gupta, & Biswadip Chatterjee. Depression is More
Than Just Sadness: A Case of Excessive Anger and Its Management in
Depression. Indian Journal of Psychological Medicine. 2014 Jan-Mar;
36(1): 77-79. doi: 10.4103/0253-7176.127259. PMCID:
PMC3959025PMID: 24701016.
https://www.ncbi.nlm.nih.gov/pmc/articles/PMC3959025/

[17] The Diagnostic and Statistic Manual of Mental Disorders, 5th edition (DSM-
5)

[18] Valencia Higuera. Medically reviewed by Bethany Juby, PsyD. Situational
Depression or Clinical Depression. Medical News Today. July 28, 2022.
https://www.medicalnewstoday.com/articles/314698.

[19] Kathyrn Greene-McCreight. Darkness Is My Only Companion: A Christian
Response to Mental Illness. Brazos Press, 2006, p. 88; submitted by Lee
Eclov to PreachingToday.com.

[20] Online Etymology Dictionary. https://www.etymonline.com/word/despair

[21] Got Questions. Your Questions. Biblical Answers. What does the Bible say
about compassion? https://www.gotquestions.org/Bible-compassion.html

[22] Got Questions. Your Questions. Biblical Answers. How can we "rest in the
Lord" (Psalm 37:7)? https://www.gotquestions.org/rest-in-the-Lord.html

[23] Oxford Rotale. Nine Famous People Who Failed Spectacularly Before They
Found Success. https://www.oxford-royale.com/articles/9-famous-people-
failed-spectacularly-before-success/

[24] Eudie Pak. Walt Disney's Rocky Road to Success. June 17, 2020.
https://www.biography.com/movies-tv/walt-disney-failures

[25] Eudie Pak. Walt Disney's Rocky Road to Success. June 17, 2020.
https://www.biography.com/movies-tv/walt-disney-failures

[26] Stephen Dowling. Failure Is the Best Medicine. BBC Future. March 13, 2013.
https://www.bbc.com/future/article/20130312-failure-is-the-best-medicine#

[27] The Strive Team. The Steven Spielberg Success Story. Strive Stories. https://thestrive.co/steven-spielberg-success-story/

[28] The Writers College Times. J K Rowling: From Failure To Unimagined Success. https://www.writerscollegeblog.com/j-k-rowling-from-failure-to-unimagined-success

[29] Paula Thompson, Ed.D. What is failure and how can we make the most of it? August 18, 2021. https://www.betterup.com/blog/what-is-failure

[30] Ralph Heath. Celebrating Failure: The Power of Taking Risks, Making Mistakes, and Thinking Big. 2009

[31] Warren Bennis. Leaders: The Strategies for Taking Charge. 2007

[32] Escape Games. The Three Types of Fear. October 8, 2019. https://escapegames.ca/three-types-of-fear/

www.ingramcontent.com/pod-product-compliance
Lightning Source LLC
Chambersburg PA
CBHW060900120626
46553CB00001B/157